The Big Book of

soft toys

by MABS TYLER

photographs by Gina Harris
line illustrations by John Kingsford

McGRAW-HILL BOOK COMPANY
New York   St. Louis   San Francisco   Toronto

To Angela

Contents

Introduction

SINCE BEFORE recorded memory the making of toys has been among the most satisfying of domestic accomplishments.

The most popular of all toys, from then until now, has been the one which was right for the child for whom it was designed.

THE BIG BOOK OF SOFT TOYS offers a range of toys which, while not demanding a skill beyond that of the average aunt, mother or grandmother, contains something which will please most children.

Many of the toys, in fact, are simple enough in design for quite young children to make for themselves. And these simple shapes can be turned into something more decorative and elaborate by colourful embroidery.

Before starting to make any of the toys it is important to read the General Hints given below.

Acknowledgements

Many thanks must be given to friends and students for practical help with drawings, sewing and checking, and to all who gave encouragement and showed interest in the book's progress.

General Hints

READ ALL INSTRUCTIONS FULLY BEFORE STARTING TO MAKE A TOY.

Patterns when cut from thin cardboard (templates) are easier to trace round, and they last longer.

Mark on each template (a) the number of pieces to be cut from it, (b) any directions for sewing.

Keep all the templates for each toy fastened together. Place the biggest templates on the fabric first.

Cut out all the necessary pieces for the toy before starting to sew it.

Keep all the pieces for the toy together in a bag.

Embroider only simple designs on any small parts.

When sewing the parts together check that all decorated sides will be on the outside of the toy, e.g. balls, dice.

Be careful to pair right and left sides especially when embroidering, e.g. animal sides, wings.

Leave openings for stuffing in the least noticeable places.

Use stuffing in small soft pieces to make a smooth toy.

Do not overfill slither toys, or they may be too heavy to play with easily.

Have no hanging pieces, loose decoration or long embroidery stitches on toys designed to be much handled.

When sewing knits or other similar 'stretchy' fabric, use a longer stitch, preferably a backstitch, to give elasticity.

Tack fur and fur fabric and long-piled fabric on the wrong side with small stitches, leaving the stitches in for added strength.

Grid System

The pattern for each toy is overlaid by a blue grid. Each square on this grid represents one inch. To transfer the pattern, draw a grid of 1-inch squares. On this grid mark with dots where the lines of the drawing cross the lines of the blue grid. Join up the dots to get your pattern at full size.

There are two sizes of grid used in the book: ¼-inch and ½-inch. Each is the equivalent of an inch on the final pattern, so that the quarter-inch grid has to be enlarged four times, and the half-inch grid enlarged twice. You can, of course, make the toys larger than their intended size by drawing out your own grid of, say, 1½- or 2-inch squares.

(Continued on Page 6)

Right: Jemima Jane, a lovely Victorian Miss. Instructions for making her are given on Page 173.

Using felt

No allowance need be made for turnings because felt does not fray.

There is no 'right' or 'wrong' side.

Use a very sharply pointed pencil for tracing; never use ball point pens or felt-tip pens.

Place pattern and fabric on a hard surface to give a clearer outline.

Use a white pencil or tailor's chalk on dark colours.

Keep the traced side as the wrong side when sewing the toy.

When cutting two matching pieces from a template, e.g. two sides of an animal, reverse the template or pattern when tracing the second piece so that the pencil marks on both pieces will be on the inside of the finished toy.

Cut inside the pencil lines to avoid grubby seams.

Always pin and tack close to the edge to avoid dirty marks.

When leaving work unfinished, stick a needle under finished embroidery, or on the edge.

Mark the positions of features, etc., with tacking threads, *not* pencil.

To transfer a design for embroidering, trace the design on to thin paper, place it in position on the felt and work small running stitches in a contrasting colour through both paper and felt, afterwards tearing away the paper. The running stitches can be pulled out when the embroidery is finished.

Do not pull embroidery stitches too tight or the felt will pucker.

Sewing can be done on the right side.

Using fabric

Trace round the template on to the wrong side of the fabric and cut ½ in. outside the line to allow for turnings.

When cutting two matching pieces from a template, e.g. two sides of an animal, reverse the template for the second piece so that the wrong side of the material will be on the inside of the toy.

Sew or stitch on the pencil line.

After sewing trim off the surplus seam allowance.

Snip v's out of all curves.

Snip into all corners as close to the stitching as possible to keep seams flat.

Use fabric with a firm close weave. Loosely woven fabric, unless it is lined, will not keep in the stuffing.

Tack the pieces together outside the stitching line.

Practise sewing doll's features on paper or fabric cut to the same size as the doll's face before drawing or embroidering on to the toy.

Useful things to have

Sharp cutting out scissors.

Scissors for cutting paper and card.

Small, very sharply pointed scissors.

A selection of needles.

Wire nippers.

Stuffing sticks – a blunted pencil, blunted wooden skewer, blunted orange stick, blunted cocktail pick.

Very sharp pencils, black and white, or white tailor's chalk.

Felt-tip pens – black, red, brown, blue.

Transparent thread.

Tape measure.

Ruler.

A pair of compasses.

Masking tape.

Colourless upholstery adhesive.

Thin cardboard.

Tracing paper.

Piece box containing remnants and scraps of various fabrics, lace, fur, fur fabric, old nylon stockings, suede or kid gloves, Christmas ribbons and cords, sequins, beads, foam rubber, pipe cleaners.

Terms

Gingham – closely woven thin cotton material generally in a variety of checked and striped patterns.

Courtelle – fluffy-pile man-made jersey fabric, used for dressing gowns.

Vilene – man-made compressed fibre, used for interlining; in various thicknesses, does not fray.

Fusible Vilene can be ironed on to fabrics as a backing, so preventing any fraying.

Wadding – compressed cotton fibres enclosed in a very thin skin to make a flat padding.

Tarlatan – stiffened loosely woven cotton material used to make stiff ballet tutus.

Calico – firmly woven strong cotton material, white or unbleached (sheeting).

Crash – coarsely woven unbleached linen, very strong.

Cambric – finely woven soft cotton material used for handkerchiefs.

Poplin – firmly woven cotton material with smooth semi-shiny surface.

Kapok – fluffy loose fibres, used for stuffing.

Ricrac braid – decorative braid in which threads are pulled tighter on one side giving it a wavy line.

Velcro – a type of fastener comprising two pieces, one with hooks and the other with loops, which hold firmly when pressed together.

Masking tape – an adhesive strong paper tape.

Dowel rod – thin hard round wooden rod.

Felt-tip pens – marker pens with an ink reservoir, thin fibre tips for fine work and thick felt tips for broader outlines.

Pipe cleaner chenille – a continuous length (up to ten feet) of thin pliable wire encased in a fluffy thick covering.

Dolly pegs – old-fashioned wooden clothes pegs cut in one piece with a round knob and two legs.

Lurex thread – a fine metal thread in gold, silver and colours.

Stitches

Running stitch

can be used for seaming together two pieces of thin or medium thicknesses of fabric or, with added variations, as a decorative stitch. Work from left to right putting the needle in and out in one motion and keeping the spaces the same size as the stitches.

Variations on running stitch

Whipped. Thread through each running stitch in the same direction to give a corded effect.

Double whipped. Work two rows of threading, the second one in the opposite direction from the first one.

Threaded. Thread up through one stitch and down through the next one.

Double threaded. Two rows of threading are worked, the second one in the opposite direction to the first.

Block running. Rows of running stitches are worked with stitches exactly above each other. These can be threaded and double threaded, whipped and double whipped. A check design is obtained if rows of three stitches are worked with the second rows of blocks in the spaces underneath the first row and so on.

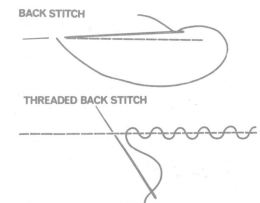

BACK STITCH

THREADED BACK STITCH

Back stitch. Work one running stitch. Insert the needle into the same hole, bringing it out a stitch's length to the left. Continue, working back into each previous stitch, completely filling the space. Back stitch can be threaded and double threaded, whipped and double whipped.

Chain stitch. Bring the thread out on the right side of the work and hold it under the left thumb. Put the needle back into the same hole, bringing it out again over the held thread. Do not pull the thread too tight. This stitch can be whipped and threaded.

DOUBLE RUNNING

CHAIN

Double running. Work a second row of running stitches on top of the first row so that the second row of stitches fill in the spaces in between the stitches of the first row. This can be used as an alternative to backstitch.

WHIPPED CHAIN – can also be threaded

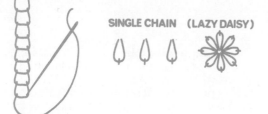

OPEN CHAIN

SINGLE CHAIN (LAZY DAISY)

Open chain stitch. This is formed in the same way as chain stitch, but the needle is inserted to the right of the first stitch and slanted to the left, to come out under the first stitch. Keep the loop loose enough to take the second stitch.

Fly stitch. This too is a form of open chain stitch. Hold the the thread under the left thumb and insert the needle to the right of the first stitch, bringing it out lower down in the middle of the two stitches and over the loop. Insert the needle under the loop to hold it, bringing it out to the left under the first stitch. This stitch can be done horizontally, vertically and singly as a filling stitch.

Snail trail or coral stitch. Hold thread horizontally under left thumb. Take a slanting stitch to the left through the material and including the held thread. Gently pull up to form a knot, and repeat the process.

Buttonhole stitch. Work from left to right. Hold the thread to the right under the left thumb. Insert the needle about ⅛ in. above the hole bringing it out close to the hole and over the held thread. Pull the thread to hold the loop and hold it under the thumb again. Insert the needle in line and to the right of the last stitch bringing it out under the insertion point in line with the first stitch and over the held thread. The stitches should be at right angles to the row of loops.

Pointed buttonhole. As for buttonhole, but three buttonhole stitches are made into each hole; in the first one the needle slants down to the left, the second stitch is vertical and in the third the needle slants down to the right.

Stem stitch. Work from left to right. It is similar to backstitch in reverse, the needle brought out half way along the last stitch and touching it, giving a corded effect.

Couching. A cord or several threads are held in position by working vertical stitches over them, close to each side of the threads.

Herring bone. Worked on two parallel lines from left to right. Bring the thread out on the top line. Take a stitch from right to left on the bottom line so that the thread slopes down to the right. Take the next stitch in the top line so that the thread slopes up to the right, crossing the previous thread.

Cross stitch. Worked on two lines. Work a row of stitches sloping from left to right between the two lines. A second row worked in the opposite direction using the same holes crosses over the first row of threads.

Joining stitches

Oversewing. Work from right to left. Hold the two edges of the material together and insert the needle at right angles from back to front through both thicknesses. Continue so, keeping the spaces even, so that the stitches will slant evenly.

Crossed oversewing is obtained by working a second row from left to right, using the same holes.

Double locking oversewing. Work as for oversewing, but taking two stitches into each hole, so that the slanting stitch and the straight stitch from the same hole give a zigzag effect.

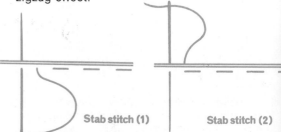

Stab stitch (1)   Stab stitch (2)

Stab stitch. This is used when joining two thick fabrics such as felt, so that one piece is not stretched more than the other as it would be if running stitch were used. The effect is like running stitch. Insert the needle at right angles to the edges of material from front to back and then from back to front.

Fishbone stitch. This stitch makes a flat seam join, not ridged as in oversewing. Place the two pieces of material with the edges butting on each other and touching. Work from right to left and take a stitch from back to front first in one piece and then in the other.

Ladder stitch. This is another flat seam join. Lay the two pieces of material with edges butting against each other. Take a small stitch parallel to the edges first in one piece and then in the other. Pull the thread firmly but not tight enough to pucker the material.

Laced buttonhole. Work buttonhole stitch on the edges of both pieces of material. Lay the two buttonholed edges butting on each other. Lace the edges together by sewing through the loops on each edge.

CHAPTER ONE

Soft toy balls

The soft balls dealt with here are made from two basic shapes, but there are many other possibilities giving great scope for experiment and invention. All sizes of ball can be made from each of the shapes, according to the size of template used; the basic oval segment can be short and fat, or long and thin; the shape of the segment adapted by moving the position of the widest part from the centre and closer to one end of it, as in Humpty Dumpty. Other soft balls can be very attractive made from wool, wound round card rings and tied and cut for a fluffy ball, or knitted or crocheted and then filled with stuffing.

An embroidered ball in six segments

You will need :

A piece of felt measuring approximately 7 in by 14 in ; some embroidery silks for a decorated ball as in the picture ; matching cotton for joining the pieces ; a small piece of thin cardboard to make a template ; kapok or similar for stuffing.

Make the template

On the thin card make a cross (Fig. 1) by drawing a line 6 in. long with a second line 2 in. long at right angles across the centre of it. Draw curved lines from one end of the long line to the other, touching each end of the short line to give the shape of the template from which each segment is cut (Fig. 2).

Cut out your felt

Trace round the template on the felt with a very sharp pencil six times and cut the pieces (Fig. 3), keeping the traced sides as the wrong side so that any pencil marks will not show. Any embroidery to be done on the sections should be done on the separate pieces before joining them together (Fig. 4). Choose fairly simple designs. Keep the stitches firm but not too tight or the felt may pucker.

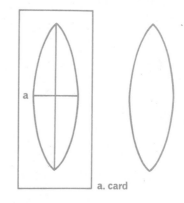

a. card

Fig. 1

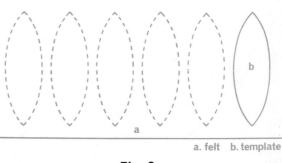

a. felt   b. template

Fig. 3

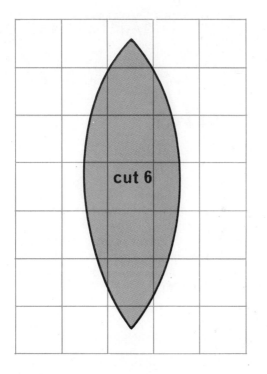

Fig. 2

Fig. 4

Make up

Pin two pieces together with the right sides outside, pinning close to the edges to avoid pin marks showing, and oversew the two edges with matching cotton (Fig. 5). Join the other pieces on in the same way, leaving the last two sides open. Fill it with small pieces of kapok or chosen stuffing until it is firm and smooth and then sew up the opening.

A ball with embroidered edges

A variation on this embroidered ball can be made by embroidering the edges of each segment with blanket or buttonhole stitch and then joining the sections by lacing together the embroidery, doing this firmly so that no big spaces are left or the stuffing will be pushed out.

A ball in four segments

Smaller balls can be made from four segments. They are, in fact, stronger because more segments mean more seams and this necessarily weakens the ball. Similarly, larger balls are a better shape if more segments are used.

Fig. 5

Find out the size

To determine the size of segments (Fig. 6) : for a 3 in. ball in four segments, multiply the length by two to get an approximate circumference and divide by the number of segments ;

e.g. : $3 \times 2 \div 4 = 1\frac{1}{2}$ in.

so each segment will measure 3 in. by 1 ½ in.
   Or for a larger playball measuring 12 in. in eight segments,

$12 \times 2 \div 8 = 3$ in.

so each segment will measure 12 in. by 3 in. The curves on each side of the template must be smooth and each side must match.

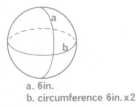

a. 6in.
b. circumference 6in.×2

Fig. 6

A bouncing ball on elastic

A 4 in. or 5 in. ball would be large enough for this kind of ball. If it is bigger it will be too heavy to play with easily or the elastic will snap.

You will need :

Felt for a light ball ; or plastic material ; or imitation leather ; or fluffy man-made fibre ; or cotton material such as gingham ; kapok and a length of round elastic.

If you are using the latter materials they must be sewn on the wrong side and the balls turned out before they are filled with stuffing. Cotton or fraying materials must have turnings allowed for, so after tracing the shape on the wrong side of the material, cut the pieces outside the pencil line (Fig. 7), and stitch, either machine or firm backstitch (Fig. 8), on the pencil line.

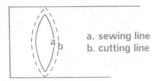

a. sewing line
b. cutting line

Fig. 7

back stitch

Fig. 8

Sew the knotted end of a length of elastic very firmly inside the ball before completing the stuffing and sewing up. If the joins of the pointed ends of the segments are not strong enough, cut a circle or flower motif and sew on at each end, threading the elastic through it at one end (Fig. 9).

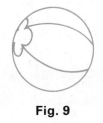

Fig. 9

A giant playball

Although more sewing is involved, the actual making and handling is easy, because of its size. The pictured one is not really a 'giant', but is 12 in. long, so that each segment measures 12 in. by 3 in. in the middle at its widest part, tapering to a point at each end. A rainbow ball can be made by using a different colour of felt or material for each section.

Join the sections together with firm over-sewing, leaving open half of the last seam. Fill quite firmly with stuffing and sew up the opening. Again a neat finish is obtained by sewing a circle over the joins of the pointed ends.

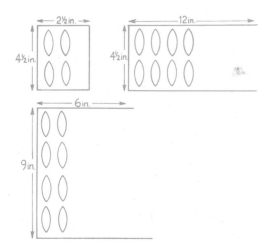

Fig. 10

Small balls for counting

You will need:

Small pieces of felt; stuffing; matching cotton; a length of fine cord; a strip of balsa wood; and five small cup hooks.

Any number of balls can be made, and in any colours, but it will probably be helpful to the young 'counter' if one colour is used for each group of balls.

The amount of felt needed will vary according to the number of balls involved. For one ball a piece 4½ in. by 2½ in. will make a 2 in. ball in four segments. The size will increase for each group, the final one of

five balls (20 segments) needing to be 4½ in. by 12-in. or 9 in. by 6 in. (Fig. 10). The pictured ones are in five distinctive colours of 2 in. balls strung from hooks in a balsa wood strip. They could also be strung from a frame on a base so that they would stand up (Fig. 11).

Making up

To avoid losing any of the small segments, cut only enough at one time to complete the balls for each group. Join the pieces on the right sides with oversewing, leaving the last sides open.

Make a large knot at the end of a length of fine cord — silver cord of the kind used for tying Christmas parcels was used here — and wrap a ball of kapok round the knot. Push some kapok into the felt ball and on top of that place the ball of stuffing containing the knot, with the end of cord through the opening at the pointed end of the segments (Fig. 12). Push in more filling to make it firm, and sew up the opening. Make a loop in the end of the cord (Fig. 13). This is number one.

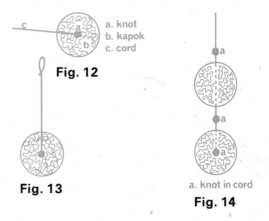

a. knot
b. kapok
c. cord

Fig. 12

Fig. 13

a. knot in cord

Fig. 14

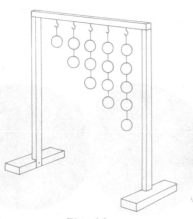

Fig. 11

For number two have a slightly longer piece of cord and make the first ball on it as just described. Join up the pieces for the second ball, leaving the last two sides open. Make a knot in the cord, close to the first ball and large enough to keep the balls apart (Fig. 14). Put a little filling in the ball, lay the cord in the ball so that the knot is close to the outside edge. Cover the cord closely with more filling to make a firm ball, and sew up the opening.

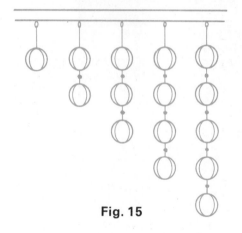

Fig. 15

Fig. 16

Make up the rest of the groups in the same way. Tie loops in the ends of the cords so that the top balls in each section are level when hanging.

Cut a length from a piece of balsa wood, or dowel rod, screw in small cup or curtain hooks and fasten the cords to them (Fig. 15).

Small balls for a baby's carriage

Brightly coloured soft felt balls are a quick and easy present to make for stringing along the front of a baby's carriage.

> *You will need :*
> Pieces of felt in five or six bright colours ; kapok for stuffing ; matching cotton ; a template of the shape of each segment.

Each ball has four segments in it and these can be all the same colour or each segment a different colour for little rainbow balls.

Make a template

To make a template for a 3 in. ball, draw a line 3 in. long and across the centre of it, at right angles, draw a line 1½ in. long. From each end of the long line draw a curve touching each end of the short line, and cut out segment shape from thin cardboard.

Work on the felt

Trace round the template on the felt and cut out four shapes for each ball.

Embroider the pieces before joining them together. Join them on the right side with matching cotton, leaving the last two sides open.

Ease the kapok in smoothly in small pieces, pressing it gently into the seams to make a good round shape. Sew up the opening.

Finish off

Cut two small circles or flower shapes (Fig. 16), punch a hole in the centre of them and sew at each side over the joined points. Complete the rest of the balls in the same way.

Thread round elastic into a bodkin and thread each ball through the punched holes in the ends.

Smaller felt balls

Similar small balls of 2 in. length will need a larger number to stretch across the pram. Templates for these would measure 1 in. across the middle.

14

A ball from twelve pentagon-shaped pieces

You will need :

Felt in one colour, or two colours or many colours; stuffing; embroidery silks; a piece of thin cardboard for a template; a design for embroidery; a protractor or a ruler with angles marked on it.

The ball can have an embroidered motif in the centre of each pentagon, or can be embroidered round all the edges which are laced together firmly and then stuffed.

Make the template

The half size template for the ball is given here (Fig. 17), but making a different sized one is quite simple. Take the protractor or ruler. Draw a line 2 in. long on the card. Place the 90° line on the protractor at the left side end of the line and mark with a dot the 72° angle on the left (Fig. 18). Join the left side end of the line to the dot and make this second line 2 in. long. Repeat this, always working from the left side of the line, to the left, making each new line 2 in. long and you will eventually have your pentagon shape. Trace round the pentagon on to the felt (Fig. 19) and cut out twelve shapes.

Embroidery

Always use a very finely pointed pencil for drawing on felt. Do the embroidery now before joining the sections. Designs should be simple because the shapes are quite small (Fig. 20). Do not use a pencil to mark the design but draw it on thin paper, pin it on to the felt and sew the design on to the felt through the paper with small running stitches (Fig. 21). Tear away the paper. The embroidery will cover most of the stitches, or they can be pulled out later.

Make up the ball in two halves. Oversew five of the pieces (Fig. 22), to the sixth, one on each edge making a flower shape, and sewing on the right side. Sew the edges of the five pieces to each other making a bowl shape (Fig. 23). Repeat this with the other six pieces. The two bowl shapes are sewn together to make the ball, the points of one fitting into the 'v's on the other. Oversew them together leaving the last two sides open. Push in the stuffing gently, easing it into the seams for a good shape. When the ball is firm, sew up the opening.

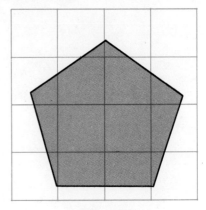

Fig. 17

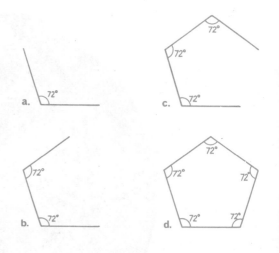

Fig. 18

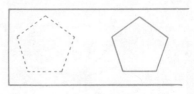

Fig. 19

Fig. 20

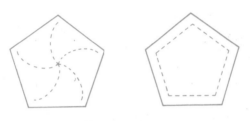

Fig. 21

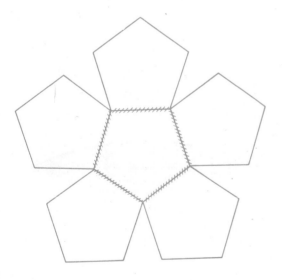

Fig. 22

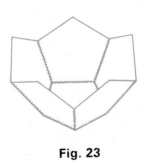

Fig. 23

A cat-faced ball

You will need :

The same materials as for the 6 in. ball ; plus two pointed ear shapes ; some scraps of green felt for eyes and some bright green embroidery silk.

Making up

Make up the ball following the directions for the six segment ball. Cut four ovals pointed at each end, in green felt (Fig. 24a) and sew two of them on each side of the ball, slanting in towards the centre, with a thick black vertical line embroidered across the centres (Fig. 25). Sew straight lines for whiskers on each side of the centre of the face, underneath the eyes. Sew an ear (Fig. 24b) very firmly over the eyes on each side of the ball.

The cat face ball can also be mounted on a piece of dowel rod. Pad the top of the dowel with a wad of stuffing (Fig. 27), if necessary tie it round and round with cotton or string, and insert it into the ball before filling it, so that the pointed ends of the join fit around it. Pad it securely with more stuffing to keep it in place.

Make a rattle

Any of the balls, except the very small ones, can be made into rattles by putting a few dried peas or tiny stones into a small tin box (Fig. 26), wrapping the box firmly in a ball of stuffing and inserting it in the middle of the ball with more stuffing wedged round it.

A rugby-shaped ball

You will need :

A piece of felt 10½ in. by 13 in. ; some stuffing and matching cotton.

The template

The card template for this is long and thin, measuring 10 in. by 2 in. in the middle at the widest part, so that the finished ball will be 12 in. all round the middle (Fig. 28). Cut out six pieces by tracing round the template and make it up from the directions for the 6 in. ball.

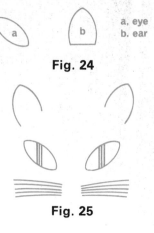

a, eye
b. ear

Fig. 24

Fig. 25

a. tin with dried peas
b. stuffing

Fig. 26

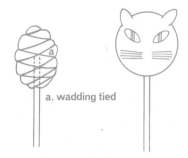

a. wadding tied

Fig. 27

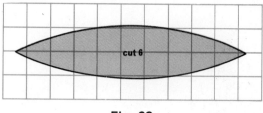

cut 6

Fig. 28

A Humpty Dumpty

The template for him is based on that for the 6 in. ball but the cross line giving the width is placed three-quarters of the way down instead of across the middle, making the fattest part in the lower half of the shape (Fig. 32).

Embroider

Make it up as for the 6 in. ball. If it is to be used as a ball, then embroider features and hair and any additions of clothing to keep the ball outline smooth with no free loose pieces to hinder throwing and catching it.

For a toy

If it is to be played with as a toy, then limbs and clothes can be added like any other doll.

Cut rectangles of felt for arms and legs, joining them down the long sides and one short end. Use only a little stuffing so that the limbs are flexible, or bind together pipe cleaners to match the lengths of felt and sew the felt round them (Fig. 29). Attach them at shoulders and hips, and they can then be bent to the required shape.

A sleeveless jacket of the same colour as the felt arms can be sewn on to him (Fig. 30).

Cut a round white collar with a big red bow to finish it off.

Four little shoe shapes (Fig. 31) in black felt can be sewn together in pairs, lightly stuffed and sewn on to the ends of the legs.

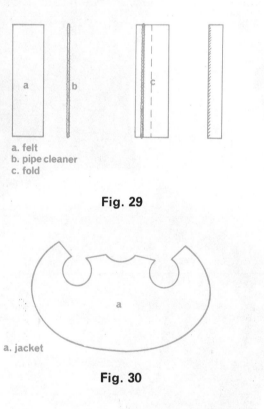

a. felt
b. pipe cleaner
c. fold

Fig. 29

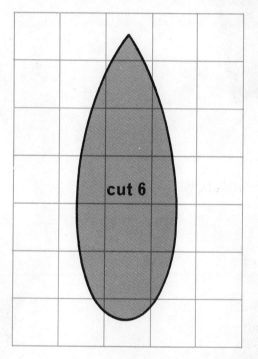

cut 6

Fig. 32

a. jacket

Fig. 30

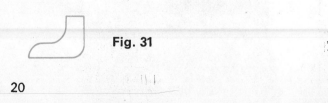

Fig. 31

CHAPTER TWO

Dice, bricks and tiles

Many games have been invented for using dice. They are popular with young children as an aid for learning to count, for sorting, or for recognising numbers and groups of objects. Big soft dice are easy to handle in play and made in bright colours are attractive too. Felt is easy to work with because it does not fray,

Traditional dice

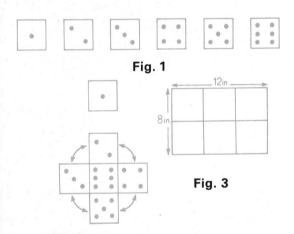

Fig. 1

Fig. 2

Fig. 3

You will need :

Kapok or similar stuffing ; embroidery silks ; matching cotton ; felt or fabric in the main colour for the dice itself and a contrasting colour or colours for the spots.

This one is in dark blue felt with yellow spots and is a 3 in. cube.

Cut six 3 in. squares from the blue felt and 21 spots from the contrasting piece. (Draw round a 2 pence piece). Dice are designed in a traditional pattern and numbers must always be in the same sequence so that 1

but other fabrics can be used successfully provided that turnings are allowed for when cutting out the shapes. Sizes shown here are 3 in. and 4 in. but they can of course be made to any desired size by altering the measurements of the squares. Very small dice are difficult to embroider.

is opposite to 6, 2 opposite to 5, and 3 opposite to 4. Sew the spots on to their squares in a traditional pattern as shown in (Fig. 1).

Now lay the squares in their right order. Sew one side of squares 2, 3, 4, 5 to square 6 forming a cross. Make it into a box shape by sewing up the sides (Fig. 2), making sure that all the spots are on the outside. Sew two sides of remaining square 1 to the open end of the box.

Push the stuffing gently but firmly into corners and seams to keep it a good shape. Sew up the remaining two sides.

A picture cube

This soft cube with a different little picture on each side is very simple to make, and the colours you choose for the actual cube and the pictures appliquèd on it turn it into a very gay toy for a small child.

You will need :

A piece of felt 8 in. by 12 in. ; some small pieces of felt in bright colours ; some thin cardboard to make templates ; and stuffing and embroidery silks.

Embroidered pictures

Cut the large piece of felt into six squares measuring 4 in. (Fig. 3). Each square must be embroidered before any sewing up is done. The six pictures in the drawing are a teapot, some balloons, a Christmas tree, a

Fig. 4

Fig. 5　　　　**Fig. 6**

Fig. 7

a. sail
b. boat

Fig. 8

Fig. 9

Fig. 10

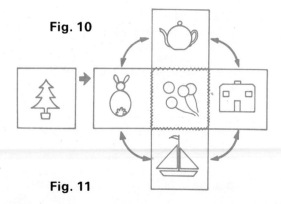

Fig. 11

sailing ship, a rabbit and a house. Any silhouette which is not too fussy can be used, a cat, dog, bird, flower, aeroplane, or car (Fig. 4). The pictures are easy to trace on to the felt if they are cut out from thin cardboard.

The balloons
The balloons are four circles traced round a 10p piece, sewn on to the square with very small stitches and their strings embroidered in running stitch (Fig. 5).

The house
This is a square of purple felt with the top corners snipped off to make the roof, and a small square on top for a chimney. An oblong of green for the door and two yellow windows complete it, the whole sewn on to the square with matching cotton (Fig. 6).

The sailing ship
This can be cut from a single square of felt by cutting it as shown (Fig. 7), but it is more interesting if different colours are used. Sew the boat shape near the bottom edge of the square. From the middle of it embroider a mast in black chain or stem stitch and arrange the sails one each side of it.

The Christmas tree
Cut this out of green felt freely without a pattern because the sides do not have to match (Fig. 8).

The yellow felt rabbit
Draw this from two circles, the smaller one for the head overlapping on to the larger body one (Fig. 9). Add the ears and trace on to the felt. The fluffy tail is made from white silky wool sewn over and over in loops which are cut and trimmed. Embroider the whiskers in yellow cotton.

The teapot
is a circle with a piece cut off at the bottom to make it straight, and a handle, spout and knob added. Cut it out in one piece and sew on (Fig. 10).

Assembly of the cube
When all the squares are embroidered sew four of them round one with all the right sides on top. Make a box by sewing the sides together, keeping the right sides outside (Fig. 11). Sew on the remaining piece like a lid, leaving two sides unsewn. Push

small pieces of kapok gently into the corners and seams using a blunt pencil. Sew up the remaining two sides, pushing in any extra stuffing as you go.

An alphabet cube

The pictured cube has green letters on a yellow cube and is 3 in. square, the letters being 1½ in. (Fig. 12). Choose colours which contrast well so that they stand out boldly. Sew each letter into the middle of a square and arrange the squares in any order. When sewing up be careful to keep the right sides outside. Finish off like the dice.

A number cube

This one in bright orange felt with dark brown numbers is a 4 in. cube.

You will need:
A piece of felt 8 in. by 12 in.; or each square could be a different colour; contrasting felt; matching cottons.

Cut out six 4 in. squares. If fabric is used it should be very firm in weave and each square should measure 5 in. (Fig. 13), allowing ½ in. each side for turnings.
The figures are 2 in. long (Fig. 14). Use a good contrast for them. Sew a figure in the middle of each square and finish off the cube like the dice.

Solid bricks

Bricks in different sizes and colours are another favourite toy with young children, and are quite simple to make.

You will need:
For a 4 in. brick a thick piece of card measuring 12 in. by 16 in. and six squares of felt each measuring 4⅛ in. square; some matching cotton.
The extra ⅛ in. on the felt allows both for the thickness of the card and for the sewing up; some masking tape.

Mark the card in 4 in. squares (Fig. 15) and cut away the shaded parts. Score across the dotted lines with a sharp penknife and bend the squares carefully away from the cuts (Fig. 16). Form it into a cube and stick masking tape along all the edges to seal and strengthen them.

Fig. 12

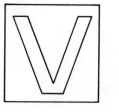

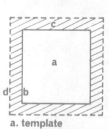

Fig. 13

a. template
b. sewing line
c. fabric wrong side
d. cutting line

Fig. 14

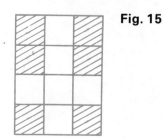

Fig. 15

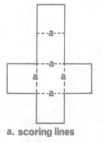

a. scoring lines

Fig. 16

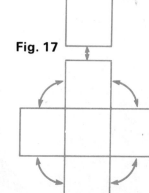

cut away all shaded parts

Fig. 17

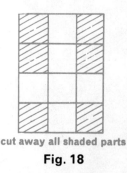

cut away all shaded parts

Fig. 18

25

Sew four felt squares round one square making a cross (Fig. 17), and sew their sides together to make a box. Sew on one side of the remaining square to make a lid. Slide the card cube into the felt box and sew down the three remaining sides.

Make a set of bricks by cutting the squares ½ in. smaller for each brick. The process of making is the same for any size brick. Very gay bricks can be made by using different-coloured felts for each side.

The shaped card for the brick can be used as a template on the felt to cut out the felt shape in one piece instead of separate squares (Fig. 18). This gives a box with less joins. Care must be taken to allow a margin all round the traced shape to allow for the thickness of the card.

An oblong brick

For an oblong brick measuring 6 in. by 3 in. by 1½ in.

You will need :

A piece of card 9 in. square ; a ·9½ in. square of felt ; some masking tape ; matching sewing cotton.

Mark the card and cut away the shaded portions (Fig. 19). The card can be used as a template for cutting the felt shape, leaving a margin of about ⅛ in. all round the shape for sewing up and the thickness of the card.

Oversew the four pairs of short sides together to form a box shape with a lid.

Score along the dotted lines on the card (Fig. 20) and carefully bend the sides away from the cuts. Form into a brick and bind every side with masking tape. Slide the brick into the felt box and sew down the lid.

As an alternative, a more tailored, neater brick is obtained by cutting separate pieces of felt for top, base and sides.

For this you will need to cut pieces of felt :

Two pieces 6⅛ in. by 3⅛ in. for the top and the base,
Two pieces 6⅛ in. by 1⅝ in. for the long sides,
Two pieces 3⅛ in. by 1⅝ in. for the short sides.

Join a long side piece to the long sides on the base, and similarly the short sides. The rest of the making up is the same.

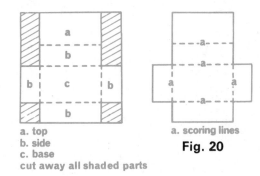

a. top
b. side
c. base
cut away all shaded parts

Fig. 19

a. scoring lines

Fig. 20

A pillar

This one in blue felt measures 6 in. by 1 in. by 1 in.

You will need :

A piece of felt 4½ in. by 8½ in. ; a piece of thick card 4 in. by 8 in. ; masking tape ; matching cotton.

Draw the shape on the card (Fig. 21) and cut away the shaded parts. Use the card as a template for tracing the shape on to the felt, allowing ⅛ in. for thickness of the card (Fig. 22). If you wish to make it up in separate pieces, you will need four pieces 6⅛ in. by 1⅛ in. and 2 pieces 1⅛ in. square. Make it up in the same way as the oblong brick.

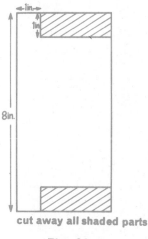

cut away all shaded parts

Fig. 21

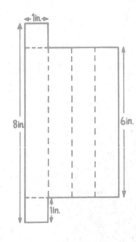

Fig. 22

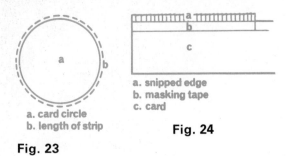

a. card circle
b. length of strip

Fig. 23

a. snipped edge
b. masking tape
c. card

Fig. 24

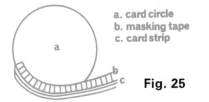

a. card circle
b. masking tape
c. card strip

Fig. 25

A drum shape

The shape is made up from two circles and a long strip long enough to go right round the circles (Fig. 23). Different sizes can be made by varying the size of the circles and the width of the strip.

You will need :
Card, not too thick ; felt ; masking tape ; matching cotton.

Use the cards as templates to trace the felt shapes, cutting them ⅛ in. bigger all round.
Oversew one edge of the felt strip to the felt circle and join the ends of the strip. Stick masking tape all along one long edge of the card strip, using half the width of the tape, leaving the other half width free. Snip this free width into a fringe taking the cuts up to the edge of the the card (Fig. 24). Place the edge of the circle to the edge of the strip and stick the fringed masking tape on to it, bending the long card as you go to follow the curve of the circle (Fig. 25). Repeat this with the second card circle. Slide this drum into the felt shape and sew the remaining felt circle on top.

A cylinder

This is the same design as the drum, the circles being smaller and the long strip wider. The making up is the same. Long pillars are made with 1 in. diameter circles and 6 in. wide strips, to match the square pillars already described.

A pyramid

To make one in pink felt on a 3 in. square base,

You will need :
A piece of card 9 in. square ; felt 9½ in. square ; masking tape ; cotton matching the felt.

Mark the card into 3 in. squares and mark the centre of each side of the square. Join these centre points to each corner of the middle 3 in. square (Fig. 26). Cut away the shaded parts.
Trace your felt shape from this template allowing the extra ⅛ in. all round (Fig. 27). Score along the sides of the centre card square and bend the triangular shapes away from the cuts, so forming a pyramid. Bind all the edges with masking tape.
Oversew the sides of three of the felt triangles, slide the card pyramid inside and sew up the remaining triangle.

A solid triangle

This shape is easier to handle if both card shape and felt can be cut out in one piece, (Fig. 28).

You will need :
Thin card about 16 in. by 7 in. ; felt ¼ in. larger ; masking tape ; matching sewing cotton.

Draw an inch wide strip across the middle of the length of card ; mark a 6 in. line in the middle. Draw a right-angled triangle on this base on both sides of the strip (Fig. 29). Trace from this template on to the felt,

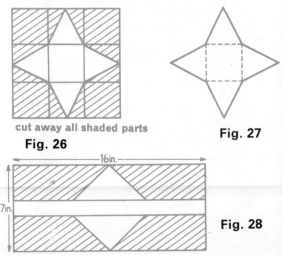

cut away all shaded parts
Fig. 26

Fig. 27

Fig. 28

cut away all shaded parts

allowing an extra ⅛ in. all round. Score the sides of the base of the card rectangle, bending carefully away from the cuts. Bind all the edges together with masking tape.

Sew one strip at one side of the triangle to both sides of the triangle, slide in the card shape, and sew the second strip to the other sides of the triangle.

Varous sizes can be made in this shape by altering the measurements of the triangle.

A square arch
You will need :

Felt ; card ; masking tape ; sewing cotton. The pictured arch measures 4 in. by 2 in. by 1 in. The size of felt needed is 14¼ in. by 5¼ in. and the card 14 in. by 5 in.

Draw a cross in the middle of the card with the upright 4 in. wide and the horizontal cross piece 1 in. wide (Fig. 30). Cut away the shaded parts as shown. Draw a rectangle at each end of the upright measuring 2 in. by 1 in. Cut away these rectangles (Fig. 31).

Use this card as a template to cut the felt shape, allowing ⅛ in. extra all round. A smaller piece of felt measuring 5¼ in. by 6½ in. can be used for the felt shape if the long side strips are sewn on separately (Fig. 32).

From this piece of felt cut two strips measuring 5¼ in. by 1 in. leaving a rectangle 5¼ in. by 4¼ in.

Cut the arch shape from this piece and sew on a long strip at each side as shown, to make the required shape. Score all the dotted lines on the card and bend the sections away from the cuts thus forming the arch. Bind all the edges with masking tape.

To make the felt cover
Sew one long side of the 1 in. strips of felt to one half of the arch so that the joining up of the ends of the strips comes in the centre of the under side of the arch. Slide in the card shape and sew the other side of the strip to the other side of the arch, taking care to match up the corners with the first side.

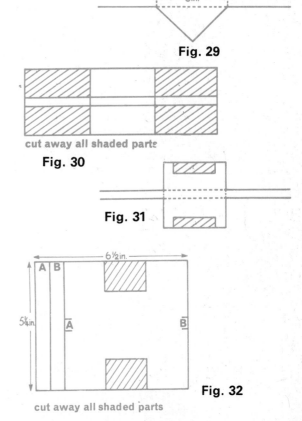

Fig. 29

cut away all shaded parts

Fig. 30

Fig. 31

cut away all shaded parts

Fig. 32

A semi-circular arch
You will need :

Card ; felt, about 8 in. by 6½ in. ; masking tape ; cotton.

On the card draw a semi-circle on a 5 in. diameter and a second one inside on a 3 in. diameter (Fig. 33). Cut round both arcs. Trace round this arch for the second side and extend the ends for an inch each side (Fig. 34). Cut two strips of card 8 in. by 1 in. and 4 in. by 1 in. Use these cards as templates to cut the felt shapes allowing ⅛ in. extra (Fig. 35).

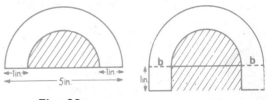

Fig. 33

b. scoring line

Fig. 34

To make up the card arch, score across the dotted lines at the base of the larger arch and bend them away from the cuts until they are at right angles to the arch. Stick masking tape along one side of the long strip using half the width of tape, snip the edges of the other half width of tape and stick it on to the outer curve of the arch, bending the card gently to fit the curve. If each cut piece of masking tape is pressed down in turn, it will help to bend the strip into place.

Repeat this with the shorter strip on the shorter curve on the same arch. Join on the second side of the arch in the same way and then bind with tape the edges of the base of the arch.

Mark 1 in. from each end of the long strip of felt and pin the centre part to the outer curve of a semi-circular piece.

Oversew the edges, and sew the remaining inch each side along the edge of the base.

Repeat this with the shorter strip on the same arch, again sewing the remaining inch each side to the base. Sew the smaller curve of the second arch on to the strip. Slide the card arch inside the felt and sew up the long curve.

Many sizes can be made but very small ones are difficult to sew on the inner curve.

Hollow bricks

There are six of these in bright coloured felt, the largest one 5 in. and the smallest 1¼ in., each one ¾ in. smaller. Each brick needs five squares of card and ten squares of felt. Sizes of felt needed to cut these squares for each size are:

25⅝ in. by 10¼ in. for the largest,
21⅞ in. by 8¾ in.,
18⅛ in. by 7¼ in.,
14⅜ in. by 5¾ in.,
10⅝ in. by 4¼ in.,
6⅞ in. by 2¾ in.
Cards needed are
Five 5 in. squares
Five 4¼ in.,
Five 3½ in.,
Five 2¾ in.,
Five 2 in.
Five 1¼ in.

It is wise to cut the largest squares first.

Beginning with the largest brick, cut ten pieces of felt in squares measuring 5⅛ in. Join them together in two's by oversewing the edges on three sides, keeping the pencil marked edges inside. Slide a card inside the

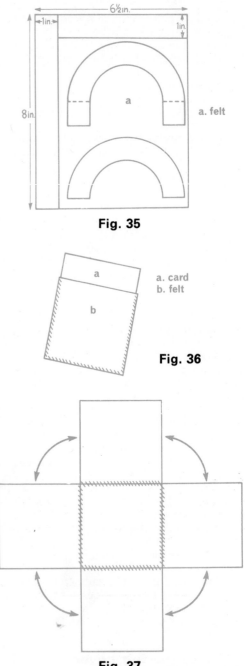

Fig. 35

Fig. 36

a. card
b. felt

Fig. 37

felt pocket and oversew remaining edges (Fig. 36). When all five squares are sewn, sew four squares round one square. Form into a box by sewing together the sides of these four squares (Fig. 37). Repeat this with each of the other five bricks.

32

Mosaic tiles

Mosaic tiles of many shapes can be arranged in hundreds of different patterns and designs, both simple and intricate. These have provided a fascinating pastime for many years; perhaps since the Italians began hundreds of years ago with small squares of coloured stone and glass to beautify ceilings, walls and floors in houses and temples. Those in Ravenna are still glorious today.

The shapes here are easy to handle, being felt or material covered card, and will make an endless number of designs, especially if they are planned on one unit or multiples of one unit. For instance, a number of 3 in. squares can be cut into halves and quarters, and thirds, in several ways, or can be used with 6 in. squares and still fit into quite intricate patterns. Squares of different sizes will not fit together so satisfactorily.

You will need :

Fairly thick card ; felt ; sewing cotton.

Cut ten 3 in. squares of card. Leave five of them as squares and cut the others (Fig. 38). Using a square as a template, trace and cut out two squares of felt measuring 3⅛ in. to allow for the thickness of the card. Place the two felts together and oversew round three sides. Slide the card into the felt pocket and oversew the remaining edges. Repeat this with the other squares and then with the other shapes.

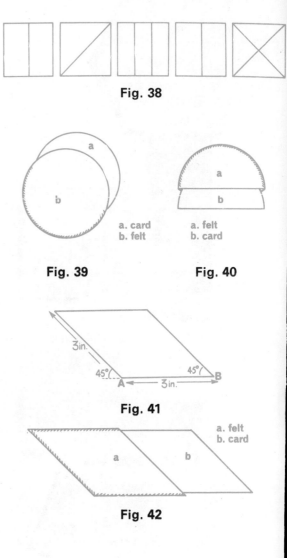

Fig. 38

a. card
b. felt

a. felt
b. card

Fig. 39

Fig. 40

Fig. 41

a. felt
b. card

Fig. 42

Circular tiles

Draw four circles of 3 in. diameter. Cut one circle in half and another one in quarters. Cut two felt shapes ⅛ in. larger for each of the shapes.

Sew the felt circles together half-way round, slide in the card and sew up the opening (Fig. 39). For the semi-circles, join the curved sides and slide in the cards (Fig. 40) ; join any two sides in the quarter circles first, slide in the cards and sew up the opening.

Diamond shapes

Cut diamond shapes by using a protractor or the angle section on a ruler. Draw a line 3 in. long (AB in Fig. 41). Place the ruler along the line with the 90° line on it at A and mark with a dot where the 45° line points to the left. Join A to the dot and make the line 3 in. long. Repeat this at B. Join up the ends of the line to make the diamond shape. Cover this with felt in the same way (Fig. 42).

34

Plan the letters or numbers in a rectangle 5 in. by 4 in. making the lines or curves of the letter 1 in. wide (Fig. 46). Make templates, trace round these shapes on to the felt and cut them out. Place the pieces together with right sides outside and oversew.

Oversewing must be planned, because in many cases stuffing must be done at the same time.

Letter 'D' — sew the inner curves first, then stuff as you sew the outer edges.

Letter 'R' — sew inner curve and inner edge of uprights. Oversew outer edge stuffing as you go.

Letter 'P' — similar to D.

Letter 'E' — similar to R.

Letter 'A' — sew inner triangle and inner edges of legs. Sew outer edges, filling with stuffing.

Figure 6 — sew inner edges. Sew outer edges starting at the top and stuff in small sections round the curve.

Figure 8 — sew the two inner edges. Sew the outer edges in very small sections and stuff. Be careful not to pull the stitches when stuffing.

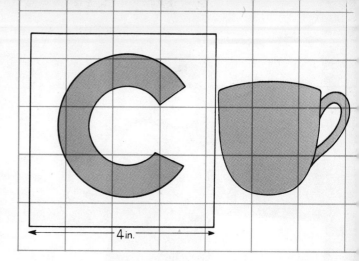

Fig. 43

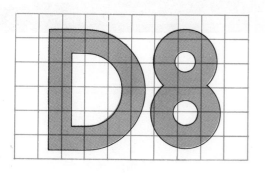

Fig. 45

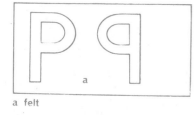

a felt

Fig. 46

Fig. 44

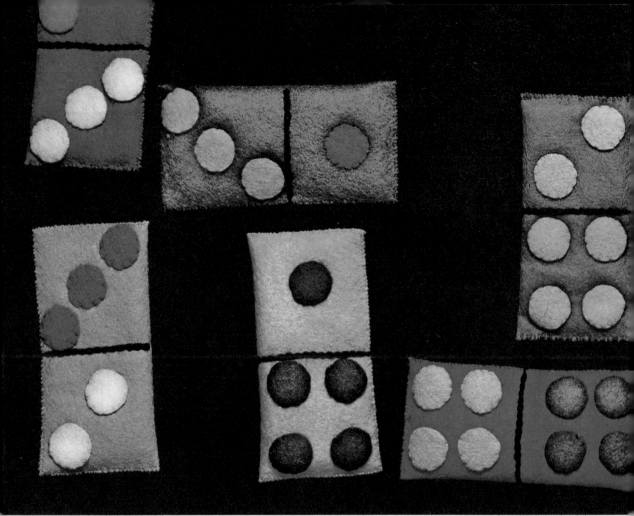

Dominoes

In many-coloured felts instead of the traditional black and white, a full set of these dominoes will still provide a game. Each of these measures 4 in. by 2 in. with spots traced round a small button.

You will need :

To make a full set — 28 squares of felt measuring 4 in.; enough contrasting felt to make 168 spots; also either 28 pieces of card measuring slightly less than 4 in. by 2 in. to stiffen the felt; or 4 in. by 2 in. rectangles of foam rubber or interlining to make a softer domino. The pictured ones have foam rubber inserts.

Fold the square of felt in half and across the centre of one half, work a line of chain stitch or stem stitch in black embroidery silk (Fig. 47). Place the spots in position on

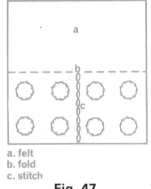

a. felt
b. fold
c. stitch

Fig. 47

each side of the line and sew them in place with matching cotton. Fold the squares in half with right sides outside and oversew the two short sides. Slide in the card or interlining and oversew the remaining edge.

38

CHAPTER THREE

Puppets

Puppets can be very simple or very elaborate, with all the stages in between. They progress from the early experimental ones made by young children for immediate use with bare essentials and their own imagination to clothe the puppet as princess or clown, witch or dragon. These are made from homely materials, easily obtained, such as cardboard picnic plates, cheese boxes, margarine cartons, cream and yogurt cartons, or cardboard tubes. Some of them can be mounted on sticks for easy handling.

Others demand more skill in their making, involving cutting out from a pattern, sewing them and adding details of clothing and decoration to determine their character. Again, more sophisticated ones are made of craft materials like clay, wood, wire, papier-mâché and potter's plaster, using new techniques with new tools — carving, moulding, sculpting.

Most children enjoy using puppets and often the shy, withdrawn child will become talkative and quite eloquent when it is *his* puppet who is seen and heard while he himself is safely out of sight and quite anonymous behind his screen.

Glove puppets – basic shapes

Two basic shapes are used here which can be adapted in many ways to give a great variety of characters. Most of the animals can be made — as well as fabulous creatures and monsters, space people, everyday policemen, soldiers, sailors, nursery rhyme and story characters, people from history and people from other lands. Both shapes are glove puppets, one with a mouth and the other with arms.

Puppets with a mouth

Any materials can be used, but an allowance for seams and a hem must be added to the pattern if the material is likely to fray. Felt or Vilene are some of the easiest ones to use because they do not fray when they are cut.

The template

The template shape is an oblong with one rounded end. Individual ones can be made by drawing round your hand placed flat on a piece of card with thumb close to the fingers, from the wrist on one side, round the fingers to the other side of the wrist (Fig. 1a). Leave an extra allowance all round to allow for the thickness of your hand and extra again

when cutting out the fabric to allow for movement of the fingers when using the puppet. It should look like (Fig. 1b).

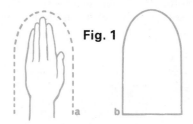

Fig. 1

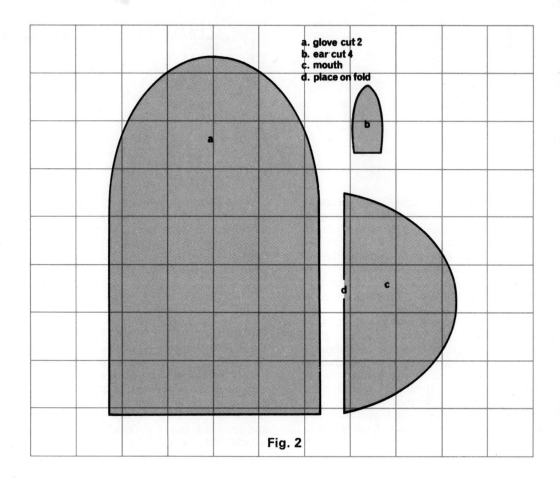

a. glove cut 2
b. ear cut 4
c. mouth
d. place on fold

a

b

d   c

Fig. 2

A rabbit

This rabbit is just a head with a mouth, which is worked with one hand. Your thumb fits into the lower half of the mouth and fingers into the upper half. You can make dozens of different 'faces' by opening and closing your fingers and thumb, and by clenching them and twisting them so that the rabbit seems to be talking and laughing. This one is made from fluffy white man-made fibre, the kind which is often used to make warm dressing gowns.

You will need :

A hand's length of fluffy man-made fibre measuring from just below your wrist to your finger tips and the width to go right round the thickest part of your hand (Fig. 2). (Allow an inch or so extra on the width to give room for movement and an extra 2 in. on the length to use for the long ears) ; a piece of pinky orange felt for the inside of the mouth ; some strands of black and pink embroidery silk ; a little narrow ribbon bow, and a pattern.

Cut out the felt

Lay your template on the material and cut two pieces, remembering to allow the little extra for movement. The ears template is shaped like a pointed arch and its length should be a little more than half the width of your hand. Cut four pieces from the pattern (Fig. 3).

Make another template for the mouth by drawing round the top of the hand template from where it begins to curve. Place this on the folded pink felt, with the straight edge of

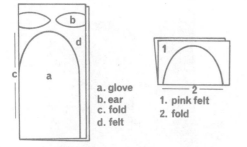

a. glove
b. ear
c. fold
d. felt

Fig. 3

1. pink felt
2. fold

Fig. 4

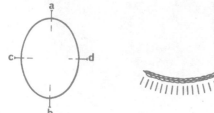

Fig. 5

Fig. 6

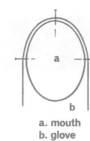

a. mouth
b. glove

Fig. 7

Fig. 8

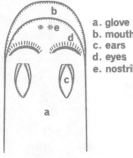

a. glove
b. mouth
c. ears
d. eyes
e. nostrils

Fig. 9

the template on the fold (Fig. 4). Cut it out. Mark the fold at each end with a pin. Fold it in half the other way and mark each end with a pin so that it is in quarters (Fig. 5).

Features

Embroider the features on to one piece of man-made fibre being careful to make them look towards the curve. Fold the piece in half lengthwise to find the middle of the curve. Embroider a nostril each side of this point by working four little straight stitches close together in pink silk. For the closed eyes draw two curves in pencil and work a line of chain stitch in black embroidery silk, and underneath it a line of straight stitches for eyelashes (Fig. 6).

Place two ear pieces together with right sides outside and oversew the two edges closely together, leaving the straight edge which is the bottom of the ear. Fold the two corners to the centre of the straight edge and stitch down (Fig. 7). Repeat for the second ear. Sew them in place just above the eyes, with the fold facing forward. Sew them down across the front, and then bend them forward and sew across the back. This double stitching will help to make them stand up.

Now pin point 'a' on the pink felt to the centre of the face curve, between the two nostrils, and pin 'c' and 'd' to either side. Sew this half of the mouth to the face with tiny stitches. Find the centre of the back glove piece and to it pin point 'b' on the mouth and similarly 'c' and 'd', and stitch this in place (Figs. 5 and 8). Close the mouth so that the upper and lower parts fit over each other and oversew the glove seams from points 'e' and 'd' to the wrist (Fig. 9). Sew the little ribbon bow between the ears and your puppet is ready.

A lamb

This can also be made in fluffy white man-made fibre or in white felt. A little less material is needed because it has no ears included in the pattern. Make it up in the same way as the rabbit.

A frog

For this simple type of puppet use bright grass green felt with an orange inner mouth. Cut large circles in white interlining material or white felt for the eyes with large sequin centres (Fig. 10), or circles of card covered with fine glittering metal-thread material, fastened down with long straight stitches in black above and below the circles. Make up as the rabbit.

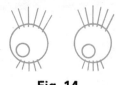

Fig. 14

Fig. 15

a. sequin
b. white felt

Fig. 10

A lion

The lion is made in orange felt with a scarlet mouth, some tawny coloured wool for a mane and scraps of black felt for features. Cut a small oval shape in black felt for a nose (Fig. 11) and sew it on in the centre of the rounded end about an inch away from the edge. Embroider the mouth in black embroidery silk. For the eyes cut two ovals pointed at each end in white or pale yellow felt, sew a circle of black felt in the middle of each (Fig. 12) and sew them above the nose at an angle, slanting towards the nose, with three or four straight stitches above them for brows. Sew loops of wool closely together all round the top and sides of the face for his mane (Fig. 13). Finish the making up in the same way as the rabbit.

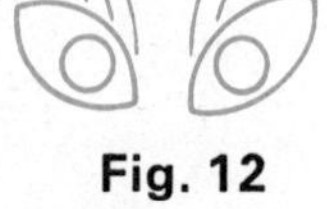

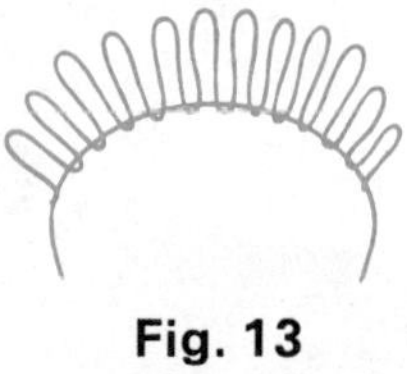

A schoolgirl

You will need :

Natural coloured or flesh felt for the head ; a pink or red felt mouth ; scraps of blue and white felt for her eyes ; brown or blonde wool for her hair ; some ribbon for bows.

Two small straight stitch spots are sewn for her nose each side of the centre of the curve. The eyes are exaggerated in size to give a rather comical looking face. Cut two large circles in white felt with two smaller circles in blue placed to one side and near the bottom of them to give her a sideways glance (Fig. 14). Fasten them to the face with large stitches at the top and bottom for eyelashes. Cut about 20 strands of wool 8 in. long. Lay them across the head above the eyes and sew them down the centre with back stitch to simulate a parting. Catch them down at each side of the face and sew on a ribbon bow at each side (Fig. 15). The strands of wool can be cut longer than 8 in. if liked and the ends braided instead. Make up as for the rabbit.

Fig. 11   **Fig. 12**   **Fig. 13**

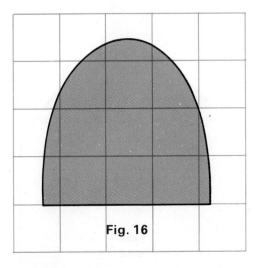

Fig. 16

A duck

You will need :

Yellow felt for the head ; red felt for the mouth : bright orange felt for the beak ; white and black felt pieces for the eyes.

The template for the beak is a smaller version of the puppet template (Fig. 16).

Cut four pieces of orange felt for the beak. Join them together in pairs oversewing round the curved edge (Fig. 17).

Cut out two circles of white felt with black circles in the centre for eyes and sew them in position.

Place the straight edge of the beak under the curved end of the face piece and sew down round the curved end with small invisible stitches which are taken through only one thickness of the beak.

Match the position of the other beak on the other half of the puppet and sew on similarly. Finish the making up as for the rabbit.

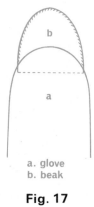

a. glove
b. beak

Fig. 17

The chick

This is similar to the duck in most respects except that the beak is pointed at the end (Fig. 18). The stages for making it are the same as for the duck.

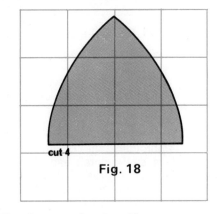

cut 4

Fig. 18

The brown/polar bear

You will need :

Brown or fawn felt for a brown bear ; white fluffy man-made fibre or white felt for a little polar bear ; black and white felt ; black embroidery silk.

Cut four pieces from the ear template (Fig. 19) and join them in two's for each ear by oversewing the curved edges together. Cut a small shield shape in black felt for a nose and sew it in place and embroider the mouth underneath it in black embroidery silk. Sew two small circles in white felt with black felt centres on for eyes.

Cut slightly larger black felt circles for the polar bear and omit the white circles.

Fold the corners of the ears to the centre and sew on the face with ladder stitch (Fig. 20), taking a stitch in the ear and a stitch in the face, sewing all round both at front and back ; this will make the ears stand up. Making up is the same as for the rabbit.

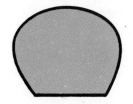

Fig. 19
(actual size)

Fig. 20

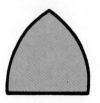

Fig. 21 (actual size)

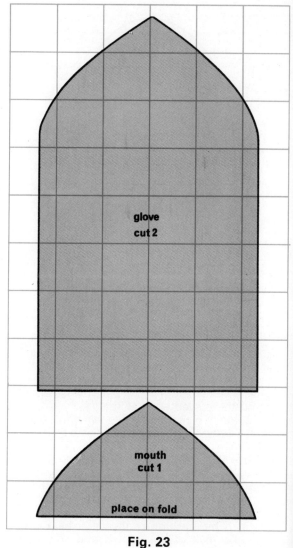

glove
cut 2

mouth
cut 1

place on fold

Fig. 23

The cat

This is made in black or grey or ginger coloured felt. Two pointed ears similar in shape but smaller than those on the rabbit, are added (Fig. 21), a nose like the bear's, and green embroidery silk or fine metal thread whiskers embroidered each side of it (Fig. 22). A pair of green felt oval eyes slanted in to the nose and fastened down with an upright stitch like a bar in black silk, finishes the features.

Cut four pieces of felt for the ears. Oversew the curved edges of two pieces together for each ear, fold the corners in to the centre and sew on to the face on both sides of the ear with ladder stitch. Make up the remainder as for the rabbit.

Fig. 22

The snake

You will need :

A slightly different shape of template, the rounded end becomes more pointed (Fig. 23) rather like a large size rabbit's ear, the mouthpiece also having this shape ; some sequins ; fine metal thread ; a 3 in. length of pipe cleaner.

Cut two circles of black felt and embroider all round with straight stitches of fine red metal thread and sew them on fairly close together.

Sew a band of red and green and gold sequins down the middle of the head, between the eyes, and spreading out into three or four lines at the mouth.

Bind the pipe cleaner closely with fine bright blue metal thread, bend it into a V and sew it to the underside of the race piece as fangs. Make up like the rabbit.

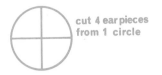

cut 4 ear pieces
from 1 circle

Fig. 24

The elephant

You will need :

Dark grey felt for the body with a
scarlet felt mouth ; a 3½ in. circle
of grey felt cut into four will make
the ears (Fig. 24) ; a 4 in. strip
of grey felt 1¾ in. wide and
narrowing off at one end for the
trunk (Fig. 25) ; a pipe cleaner
twisted into a 4 in. length to stiffen
the trunk.

Sew on two black circles for the eyes. Oversew two ear pieces all round for each ear
and sew on by its corner above and to the
side of the eyes. Oversew together the
curved sides of the trunk, insert the pipe
cleaner and pad softly with very small pieces
of kapok. Sew on to the curve of the face
with ladder stitch to make it stand away
from the face. Complete the making like the
rabbit.

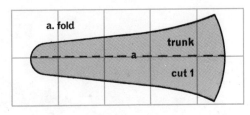

a. fold

trunk

a

cut 1

Fig. 25

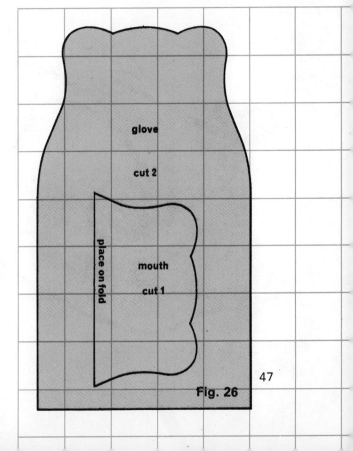

glove

cut 2

place on fold

mouth

cut 1

47

Fig. 26

A dragon

You will need:

Bright green, orange, red felt;
sequins; embroidery silk.

The rounded end of the template has again
been altered to show a shaped snout with
protuberant nostrils (Fig. 26), and the inner
mouth will naturally take the same outline.
The mouth is lined with a bright orange
felt — the dragon itself being in bright
green — with a long forked red tongue
(Fig. 27) fastened at the fold at the back of
the mouth and hanging out at the side.

The eyes are cut from bright orange felt
with a large sequin or a ring of smaller
sequins in the centre, sewn on at an angle
slanting towards the nose. A line of chain
stitch from the inner corners of them, curves
down and round each nostril. Sew a sequin
in the nostril with a ring of chain stitch
surrounding it (Fig. 28).

A strip of red felt with one edge serrated
is sewn down the back. Make up like the
rabbit.

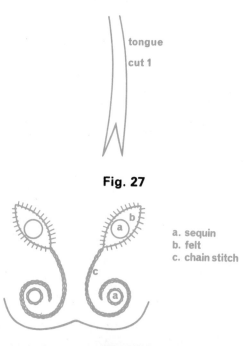

tongue
cut 1

Fig. 27

a. sequin
b. felt
c. chain stitch

Fig. 28

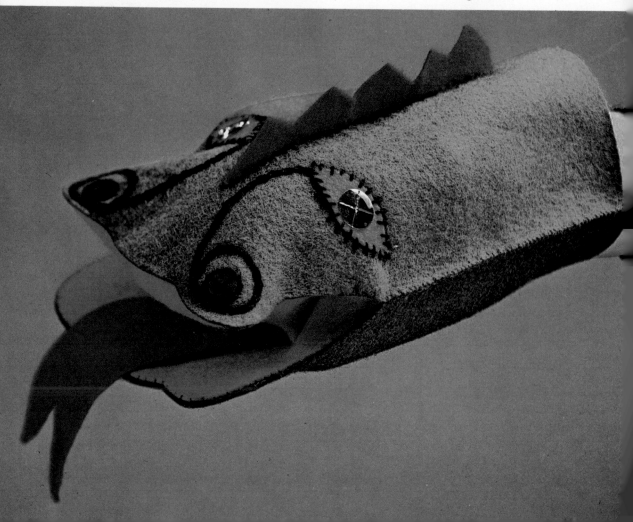

Puppets with arms

The same basic shape of template is used for all the puppets, with simple details added to make the different characters. When adding clothing remember that the front view is important, particularly in a puppet performance before an audience, and this should be kept in mind when 'dressing' the puppet.

When separate faces are added, as in Red Riding Hood, they can be sewn on top of the puppet base, giving extra strength to the head.

When backs of heads are added plus a hat, as in the guardsman, it is better to cut away the under parts of face and back of head or the finished puppet may be top-heavy and badly balanced for small hands to manipulate.

Usually the thumb and small finger are inserted in the puppet's hands and the other three fingers in the head. The facial expression of these puppets cannot be altered by moving the fingers as in the previous puppets.

Smaller children may find a puppet on a stick easier to handle and these puppets can be adapted quite easily to fit on to a piece of dowel rod.

A lion

You will need :

A piece of tawny or orange coloured felt about 10 in. by 14 in. ; some scraps of brown felt for features ; black embroidery silk ; matching cotton ; some tawny or light brown wool for the mane ; and a template (Fig. 29).

Trace the puppet pattern on to a piece of thin card and cut it out. Trace round it on to the piece of felt using a very sharply-pointed soft pencil, and cut out two shapes. Keep the pencil marked side as the wrong side, but if possible, when cutting the shapes, cut just inside the pencil lines, otherwise the finished seam may look grubby.

On one of the pieces arrange the features. Cut a thin oval shape for the nose and sew it on in the middle of the face. Embroider two curving lines from the base of the nose towards the sides of the face. For the eyes, cut out two ovals pointed at each end, and sew them on at an angle, slanting in to-

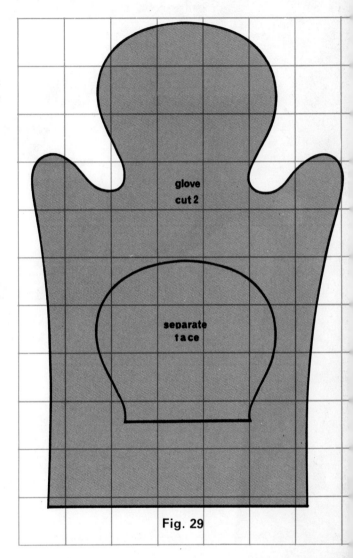

glove
cut 2

separate
face

Fig. 29

Fig. 30

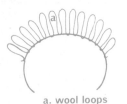

a. wool loops

Fig. 31

wards the nose (Fig. 30). Embroider some long straight stitches along the top edges.

Around the edge, and across the bottom of the face, in a circle work a row of loops close together for the mane, using the wool (Fig. 31).

Place the two puppet pieces together with right sides outside and pin them (on the edge of the felt to avoid pin marks) matching the top of the head, hands and bottom edges and oversew them together with matching cotton. Your lion is ready.

A bear

You will need :

Fawn or brown felt; some scraps of dark brown or black felt; a strand of black embroidery silk; matching cotton.

Cut two round-topped ears in thin card (Fig. 32) and tape them to the head of the puppet template (Fig. 33). Place the template on the felt and trace one outline, then turn the template over and trace the second piece in reverse. It is a good plan always to reverse the template when cutting two pieces which are to be joined, then any variation in the outline of the template on either side will not matter, and in the case of the bear, the ears will match when placed together.

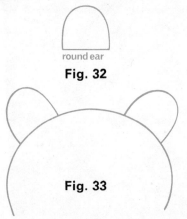

round ear

Fig. 32

Fig. 33

Features

From the dark felt cut out two rather small round eyes, a shield-shaped nose and two palm pieces. Sew the nose in the middle of the face, and embroider two curving lines from the bottom of it for a mouth. Sew on the eyes and embroider three or four slanting stitches above them pointing towards the ears. Sew the palm pieces on to the hands (Fig. 34). Finish sewing it together as for the lion.

Fig. 34

A cat

You will need :

Black felt; scraps of green felt for eyes; a strip of bright colour for a collar; some fine green metal thread; black cotton and a template.

Before tracing the shape, stick two pointed ears on to the basic template (Fig. 35). Cut out two shapes from the felt, reversing the template for the second piece.

Mark the centre of the face and on each side of it embroider some long stitches in fine green metal thread, for whiskers. Cut two ovals pointed at each end for eyes and sew on at an angle slanting towards the centre (Fig. 36). Embroider a black bar of stitches vertically across the middle of each eye. Sew a strip of coloured felt across the front of the neck, and finish off with a little bow. Oversew the edges together.

pointed ear

Fig. 35

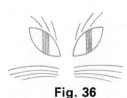

Fig. 36

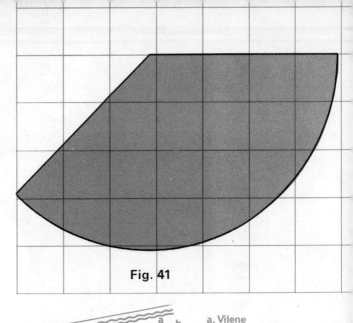

Fig. 41

The clown

He has a white face superimposed on the basic shape, made in pale blue felt.

You will need :

Blue felt; white felt for the face and hat; some scraps of red felt for nose and mouth, a strand of black embroidery silk; a length of Vilene (bonded interlining) for a neck ruff; some red wool for pom-poms; and your template.

Cut two blue felt shapes from your template and cut one head shape in white felt (Fig. 37).
 On this white felt face sew the features. Cut a small circle of red felt, gather it up round the edge, place a hard ball of stuffing in the centre of it and draw up the edges to form a ball (Fig. 38). Sew this in the middle of the face for a nose. Cut a strip of red felt 2 in. by ½ in. for the mouth, cut it in a crescent shape (Fig. 39) and sew it under the nose. The eyes are embroidered with black embroidery silk; two triangles both pointing the same way with an embroidered

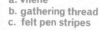

a. Vilene
b. gathering thread
c. felt pen stripes

Fig. 42

spot in the corner of the acute angle (Fig. 40). Over the whole eye embroider a cross in chain stitch. Sew the completed face on to the matching glove piece.
 Make five pom-poms in the red wool; winding the wool about 20 times around two fingers, tie a strand of wool tightly round them and trim the ends evenly into a ball shape. Sew three pom-poms down the front of the dress, keeping two for the hat.
 Pin the two glove pieces together right sides outside and oversew the edges.
 Cut a 4 in. circle in white felt, and out of it cut a segment, about ⅜ of it (Fig. 41). Fold over the straight edges until the circular edge fits round the head at an angle, and sew them down.
 Sew two pom-poms down the front opposite to the joined edges and sew it in place on the head tilting it slightly to one side and being careful not to take any stitches right through all the layers of felt.
 Down each long side of the strip of Vilene (bonded interlining) draw red and blue lines with felt-tip pens. Run a gathering thread through the centre and gather it up to fit the neck (Fig. 42). Secure it on the shoulders with a few stitches.

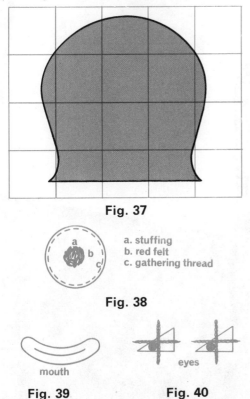

Fig. 37

a. stuffing
b. red felt
c. gathering thread

Fig. 38

mouth

eyes

Fig. 39   **Fig. 40**

A pirate

He has both face and back of head imposed on the basic shape.

You will need :

The main glove is cut from crimson felt ; the face from reddish brown felt ; back of head, beard, eyepatch from black felt ; his scarf and pistols from golden yellow felt ; cut the skull and crossbones from a scrap of white felt.

Cut two shapes in red felt from the template. Cut out from the top part of the template both face and head.

Decorate the face first. Cut a shallow crescent in red felt for his mouth and sew it in place on the brown face. Cut a similar crescent in black and sew on above the mouth for a moustache. An oval in white with a black circle sewn in its centre is his one good eye and a black semi-circular patch in black felt covers his bad one (Fig. 43). His beard is a triangular shape in black felt, the top edge cut into a slight curve and the point of the triangle cut into a fringe (Fig. 44) and then sewn on, by the curve, round the mouth and sides of the face.

Pin the completed face on to the matching glove piece and pin the black head shape on to the other piece.

Four thicknesses of felt plus the hat will make the head too heavy to manipulate, so the head shapes on the actual glove pieces can be cut off. Before cutting them away, sew both head and face shape to the glove along the neck edges with small firm matching stitches. Now cut away the glove head shapes leaving about ¼ in. Sew this edge down firmly, if possible keeping the stitches from showing on the right side.

Cut a narrow strip of black felt for a belt and cut out two pistol shapes in the yellow felt (Fig. 45). Pin the pistol shapes on the front of the glove at waist level and pin the belt on over them. Sew them all to the glove.

Place both gloves together with right sides outside and oversew all round with matching cotton.

Cut two strips of yellow felt slightly wider at one end, tie the wider ends into a knot and pin on to the neck over the join with the knot under the chin. Sew the two ends to each side of the neck.

Cut two hat shapes from the template (Fig. 46), in black felt, and a skull and crossbones in white felt (Fig. 47). Sew the motif in the centre of one hat shape and sew the two shapes together leaving the bottom edges open. Fit the hat on to the head and sew on along the face and back of the head. Sew up the rest of the brim each side of the face.

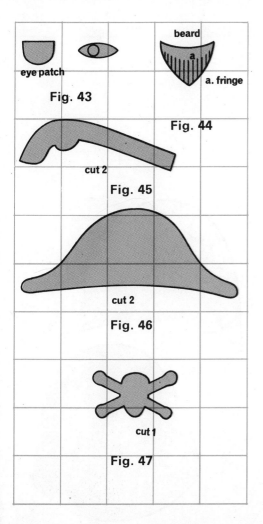

eye patch

Fig. 43

beard

a. fringe

Fig. 44

cut 2

Fig. 45

cut 2

Fig. 46

cut 1

Fig. 47

Santa Claus

You will need :

As well as red felt for the two glove shapes, an extra strip of red felt for the hood ; a piece of flesh-coloured felt for the face ; some strips of white felt or flannel to trim the hood and coat ; some white fluffy wool for hair and whiskers.

The features

Cut two shapes in red felt from the template. Cut the face shape from the top part of the template. Sew the features on to the face ; a crescent of red for a smiling mouth, two semi-circles in white with small circles of black sewn into matching corners (or he will be cross-eyed). Sew these in place, keeping them in the bottom half of the face. Cut five or six strands of silky white wool and sew them in the centre above the mouth for a moustache. Sew loops of the white wool all round the face and chin for hair and whiskers. Sew a ¾ in. wide strip of white all down the front of the glove.

Sew the two glove pieces together with right sides outside.

The hood

Cut a strip of red felt 9 in. by 2¾ in. Sew a ½ in. strip of white all along one long edge. Fold the red strip in half and oversew the edges to make a hood. Fit it round the face so that the front corners fold round on the front of the glove on each side to frame the face. Sew the two front corners to the glove, leaving the back of the hood free.

An English policeman

You will need :

Royal blue felt ; flesh-coloured felt for the face ; brown felt for the back of the head and moustache ; black felt for his helmet ; red felt for his mouth ; silver metal thread ; three small silver beads.

Cut out two puppet shapes in royal blue felt, one face shape in flesh or natural colour and one in brown.

The features

Work on the face first. Cut a crescent shape in red and sew in place for a mouth and above it a moustache in black or brown felt. Two pointed end ovals with blue circles set in them for eyes.

Sew the face piece in place over the royal blue face and cut off the blue one. Repeat this with the back of the head, and sew down at the back also.

Sew three small siver buttons or beads down the front of the tunic.

Cut a strip of blue ⅜ in. wide and long enough to stretch across the front of the neck for a collar. Embroider a small motif in fine silver metal thread (Fig. 48) each side of the centre and sew the band in place over he join of face and tunic.

Sew the two glove pieces together on the right side.

Cut two pieces in black felt from the helmet template (Fig. 49). In the centre of one embroider in silver metal thread, a motif similar to, but larger than, the ones on the collar. Oversew the two curved sides of the helmet, fit in place on the head and sew down on the back and front of the head, being careful not to take the stitches through both thicknesses.

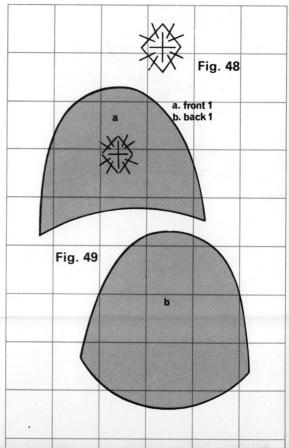

Fig. 48

a. front 1
b. back 1

Fig. 49

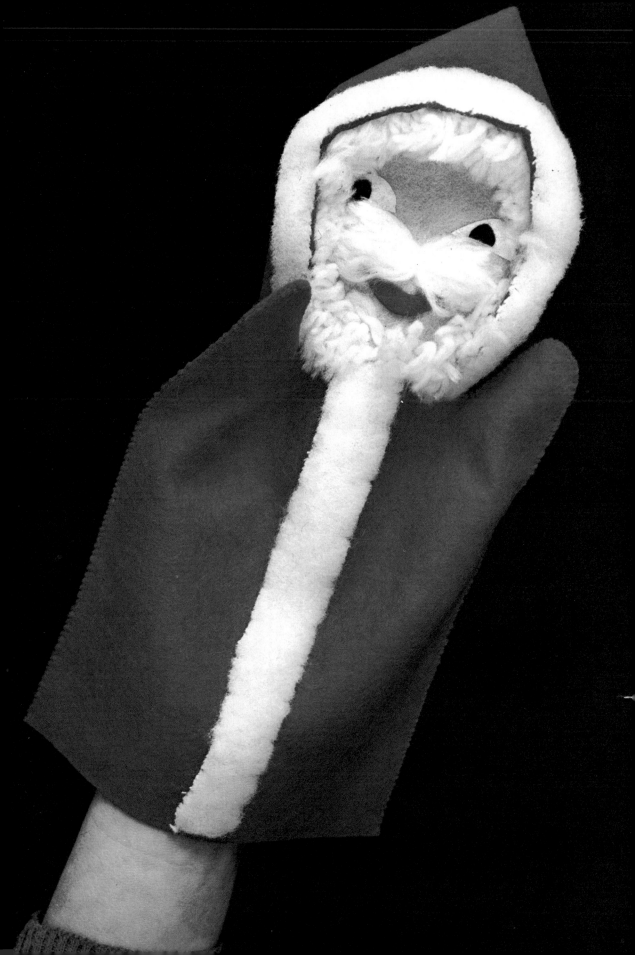

An English guardsman

The guardsman glove is cut out in two colours for each piece.

You will need :

Royal blue felt for the lower half for his trousers and scarlet felt for the top for his jacket; natural or flesh colour felt for the head and face; black felt for his bearskin and belt; some gold sequins; a little gold metal thread.

The blue and the red felt each need to measure 13 in. by 3½ in. Place the long edge of blue over the red and tack them together (Fig. 50). Lay the template on this so that the bottom edge is level with the edge of the blue felt and the neck is on the edge of the red felt. Cut out two shapes reversing the template for the second piece.

Place the head part of the template on the flesh-coloured felt allowing the felt to over-lap on to the red for joining and cut out two head shapes.

The features

Sew the features on to one of the flesh-coloured pieces and then sew the two head pieces together on the right side.

The uniform

Sew the red and blue felt together on both right and wrong sides for strength. Keep stitches from showing through on the right side. On one of the pieces (the front) sew five or six gold sequins in a row for buttons, and embroider a motif in gold thread each side of the centre of the neck.

Trim the neck part of the head pieces to slip inside the red collar and sew it in place with tiny stitches. Sew both pieces together on the right side.

The belt

Cut a strip of black felt about ⅜ in. wide and long enough to go right round the waist of the glove to hide the join of the red and blue felt. Embroider a buckle shape in gold thread in the centre front of the belt and sew it in place.

The helmet

Cut two helmet pieces in black felt and oversew the two rounded edges (Fig. 51). Place in position on the head just over the eyes in front and sew on round the head not allowing the stitches to go through two thicknesses.

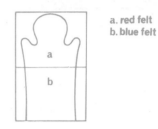

a. red felt
b. blue felt

Fig. 50

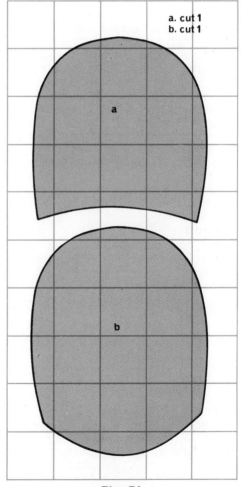

a. cut 1
b. cut 1

Fig. 51

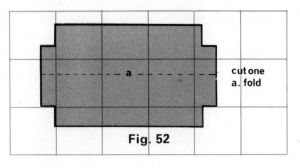

a
cut one
a. fold

Fig. 52

The features

The eyes are green circles on white; her mouth is a down-turned crescent in red. Pin the face piece to one of the glove pieces and sew them together on the right side.. Tease out some grey wool and sew it raggedly on each side of the face.

The hat

Cut about ⅜ of a 4 in. circle for a hat. Sew together the straight edges, place in position straight over the eyes and sew to the face and head not letting stitches go through.

An English sailor

You will need :

Royal blue felt; black felt; white felt; a piece of flesh colour felt for his face.

Cut out two glove shapes in blue, one head shape in flesh colour and one in black felt. Cut two triangular-shaped pieces in white felt for the front of his collar and a rectangle for the back, curve one side of the rectangle and sew on to the neck of one glove piece. Sew the two triangles on the front piece with the wide ends on the shoulders and the narrow ends meeting at the waist. Finish off with a twist of black felt. Make up the glove in the same way as for the policeman. Cut a narrow curved piece of white felt long enough to fit along the front of the neck over the join and sew it in place.

The cap

Cut out the cap shape in black felt and fold it in half lengthwise (Fig. 52). Oversew the two short edges. Across the front sew a narrow strip of white Vilene or felt. Fit it on to the head with a slight slant and sew it in place.

A witch

She is a useful puppet because there is one in nearly every fairy story which can be made into a puppet play.

You will need :

Some black felt; some brownish red for her face; some scraps for features; some grey wool for hair.

Cut out two shapes in black and one face shape in the brown felt.

Red Riding Hood — four story puppets

There are four characters in this story, Red Riding Hood the heroine, her grandmother, the wicked wolf and her father, the wood-cutter.

Red Riding Hood

You will need :

Pale blue felt for her dress; flesh-coloured felt for her face; red and white felt for her cloak and hood and brown wool for her hair.

Make up the glove, sewing in the face with the glove seams. Cut about eight strands of brown wool 10 in. or 11 in. long and sew the middle of them to the top of the head. Embroider a few vertical stitches on the forehead for a fringe. Catch the strands of wool each side of the face and braid the ends.

The hood

The hood is made in the same way as that for Father Christmas.

The cloak

The cloak is a rectangle 5½ in. by 4½ in., the shorter side being sewn on to the back of the hood. Cut two little collar shapes in white Vilene or felt and sew on at the neck to hide the join.

Grannie

You will need:

Purple felt for the dress; grey felt for her face; white wool for hair; lace for her cap.

Make her up just like Red Riding Hood. Round her face sew loops of white wool for hair, twist the wool two or three times round

Grannie's hair

Fig. 53

a finger, hold the loops close to the face and sew in place (Fig. 53). Repeat this, sewing each set of loops as close as possible to the preceding ones. Sew a gathered lace or ribbon frill round her neck and a wider piece of lace over her head for a cap or bonnet.

The wolf

You will need :
Very dark brown, orange, black, red and white felt.

The wolf's eyes are orange with black centres, sewn on at an angle slanting it to the centre of the face.

The snout is sewn on in two parts, an upper and a lower so that it juts from the face with its red tongue hanging out at one side.

The mouth

The red lining to the mouth is cut in shape like a pointed ear (Fig. 54) with the sides curving from a straight base to a point. The white interlining and the brown outer cover are similar in shape to the red but curve from a much wider base (Fig. 55).

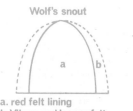

Wolf's snout

a. red felt lining
b. Vilene and brown felt

Fig. 54

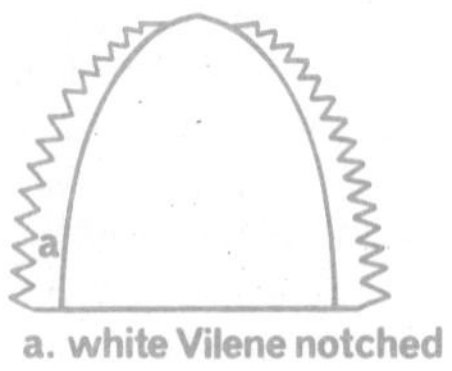

a. white Vilene notched

Fig. 55

a. brown felt
b. face
c. red lining

Fig. 56

Cut two brown pieces, two red pieces and two white interlining pieces. Sew the red piece on to the white interlining in the middle so that an edge of white stands out all round the curved sides of the red. Cut the protruding white edge into notches, for teeth (Fig. 55). Place the brown felt shape on top of the white so that its curved edges are sewn on to those of the red felt. Because the straight edge of the brown piece is longer than the straight edge of the red it will be like an arch over the red (Fig. 56). Sew it with ladder stitch on to the face following the curve of the brown felt (Fig. 54).

The tongue

Make up the other part of the mouth to match but before sewing it on to the face, cut a long tongue shape in red felt and sew the narrower end of it on to the straight edge of the red felt (the back of the throat) so that it hangs out to one side. Sew the part on to the face so that the two red linings are set close together and the two brown edges form a circle.

Ears

The ears are curved leaf shapes — cut four of them and sew two outer curves of each together for each ear. Cut the other edges into feather-shaped notches. Pin them in place on the head and sew them in with the seam as you sew the two glove pieces together.

The woodcutter father of Red Riding Hood

You will need :
Dark green felt ; flesh-coloured felt ; brown felt ; red felt ; white felt.

Cut the glove in dark green felt with the face in flesh colour and the back of the head in brown felt. He has a curved crescent of red for a mouth with a moustache in brown felt above it. Two brown circles on white pointed ovals are his eyes. His beard is a triangle of brown felt with one curving side and the pointed end cut into a fringe and sewn on under the mouth (Fig. 57). All these features are sewn on to the flesh-coloured face.

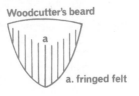

Woodcutter's beard

a

a. fringed felt

Fig. 57

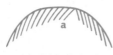

a

a. straight stitches

Fig. 58

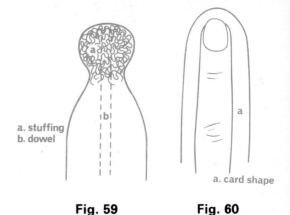

a. stuffing
b. dowel

a

a. card shape

Fig. 59   **Fig. 60**

Sew the face piece on to one glove and the brown head on to the other at the neck edge afterwards cutting away the green head from the glove. Sew the glove pieces together. Hair is made by sewing slanting stitches on the top edge of the face (Fig. 58).

A cat puppet on a stick

You will need :

Black felt; a scrap of green felt for eyes; some fine green metal thread for whiskers; a little stuffing; a piece of dowel rod of the required length.

The cat is cut from the basic pattern with pointed ears added but with the arms omitted and sloping shoulders instead. Make up as for the cat puppet. Pad the top of the dowel rod with a little wadding and tie it securely (Fig. 59). Push it up into the head with more stuffing all round it to keep it in place.

Many more characters can be made from these puppet templates, and characters from any traditional or original stories or rhymes will turn them into realistic plays.

Finger puppets

These are very small characters and because of this must be kept very simple and not in the least fussy. All kinds of small pieces of felt can be used because the back and front need not necessarily be the same colour. They are just big enough to fit over a finger for half its length, to the middle knuckle.

The template for them is easily made by placing a finger flat on a piece of card and drawing round it leaving a ¼ in. margin of extra width all round (Fig. 60). (If the longest finger is used you will be sure that the finished puppet will fit any other finger). Use this template to trace round on the felt and cut out two pieces for each puppet.

The girl

You will need :

Pale pink felt; some yellow silk or floss or wool for hair; pink embroidery silk; blue embroidery silk; some beads.

Cut two pieces in pink felt. Sew the mouth first — one long and one short stitch each side of the centre in pink embroidery silk (Fig. 61). The eyes are two open ended single chain stitches with blue spots in the corners and straight stitch eyelashes (Fig. 62). Sew some straight stitches in yellow down the forehead for a fringe (Fig. 63). Cut short lengths of yellow silk and sew in the middle on top of the head and bring the ends down each side of the face.

For a necklace start off with sewing cotton at one side of the neck, thread on sufficient beads to make a short loop and fasten off at the other side.

Sew the two felt pieces together on the right side.

Fig. 61   **Fig. 62**

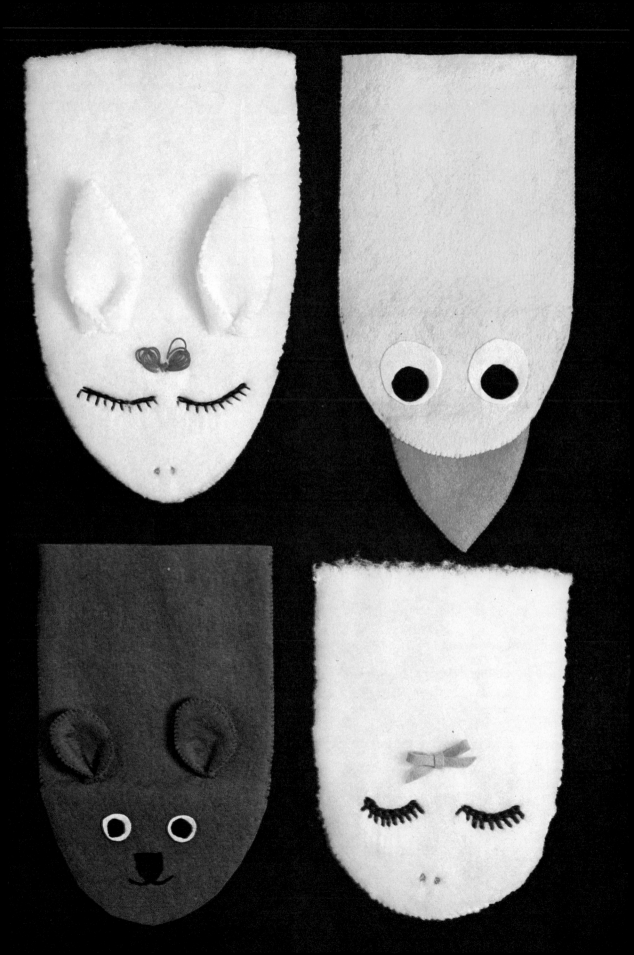

Fig. 63

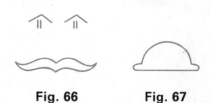

Fig. 66   **Fig. 67**

A lion

You will need :

Orange, beige felt ; tawny wool ; embroidery silk.

Cut two pieces in orange felt. A thin oval in beige or brown felt is sewn down the middle of the face for a nose and the mouth is two curved lines embroidered in stem stitch from the bottom of the nose. Eyes are two single chain stitches slanting in to the nose with a centre spot. Sew loops of tawny wool all round the face for a mane and sew the two felt pieces together (Fig. 64).

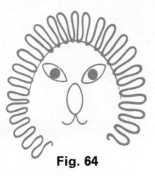

Fig. 64

A man

You will need :

Pink, black, red and white felt ; embroidery silk.

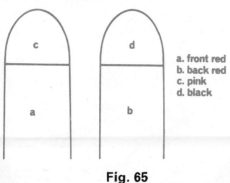

a. front red
b. back red
c. pink
d. black

Fig. 65

The front and back are treated differently. The curved end is cut in pink for the face and black for the back of the head (Fig. 65) and both joined on to red felt to make each piece the right size. Embroider the mouth as you did for the girl. The eyes are two small straight stitches with two straight stitches over them at an angle (Fig. 66). The moustache can be cut in black felt and sewn on in the middle leaving the ends free, or it can be embroidered.

Sew the two pieces together matching the felts. Cut a small collar in white and sew on over the join. The hat is in black felt sewn on across the head (Fig. 67).

A rabbit

This can be made in white felt or man-made fibre. The ears are lined with pink felt. Cut two shapes in white. Cut two white ears and two pink ears. Embroider a round pink spot for a nose with three or four whiskers each side. Sew together one pink felt piece and one white piece for each ear. Fold the corners in to the middle and sew on to the face piece with the pink sides forward. Sew the back and front together on the right sides (Fig. 68).

Fig. 68

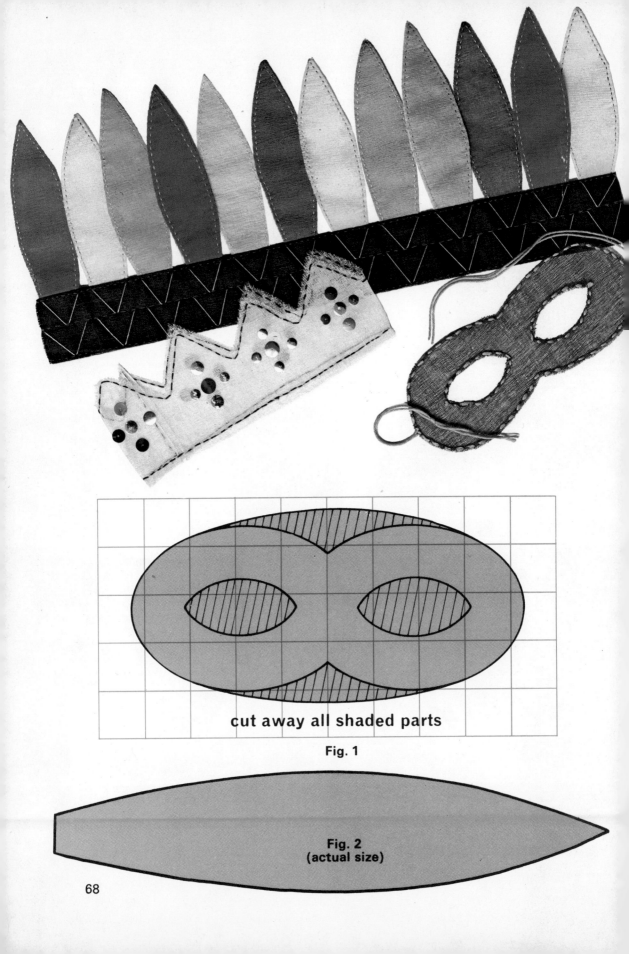

cut away all shaded parts

Fig. 1

Fig. 2
(actual size)

68

CHAPTER FOUR

Masks and head-dresses

Masks for all sorts of games and simple dramatisation, where elaborate costumes for dressing up are not practicable, can be made from Vilene or Tarlatan. Vilene in black and white is made in different thicknesses, and the white can very easily be painted or crayoned. Tarlatan comes in many lovely bright colours, as well as black and white, and is best used for masks and head-dresses in two or more thicknesses.

A highwayman's mask

This can be made in either material. Cut a pattern from an oval shape which stretches from ear to ear and is wide enough to cover the top half of the face to the tip of the nose, about 8 in. by 4 in. Cut it into a shallow 'v' above and below the nose. Fold it in half and mark the position of the eyes. Cut out two ovals pointed at each end. Place this pattern on the Tarlatan layers and cut it out (Fig. 1). With double embroidery silk in a contrasting colour, stitch the layers together with running stitch round the outside edges, and round the eye edges. Fasten strands of silk at each side to tie at the back of the head or sew on elastic to hold it firmly on the head.

A Red Indian head-dress

You will need :

A piece of Tarlatan for a band, and several smaller pieces in different colours; and some embroidery silks.

Cut a piece of coloured Tarlatan 8 in. wide and long enough to fit round your head and to overlap a little. Draw a leaf or feather shape about 6 in. long (Fig. 2) and cut out about 12 in double Tarlatan in several colours.

Fasten the layers of each feather shape together with running stitch. Fold the long piece of Tarlatan in half and arrange the feathers along one edge. Fold the strip in half again to cover the end of the feathers so that they are enclosed in the band (Fig. 3). Sew them in place with running stitch and work some simple designs on the band. Sew a piece of Velcro at each end of the band and it can then be made to fit your head comfortably.

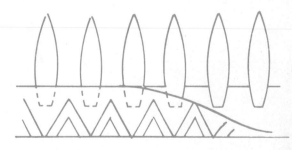

Fig. 3

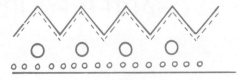

Fig. 4

Fig. 5

A simple crown

Make this a double strip of Tarlatan. Cut one edge into points or leaf shapes and fasten the double layers together with running stitch. Sequins and fine metal thread can be used to decorate it. Sew on Velcro at each end to fasten it.

The points are shown in Fig. 4, the leaf shapes in Fig. 5.

A pirate's hat

You will need :

Black Tarlatan and a little white Vilene or felt.

Draw the shape of the hat on paper then cut this out to use as a pattern.

Cut out:

the hat in double Tarlatan for back and front (Fig. 6).

the skull and crossbones (Fig. 7) for the front in white Vilene and stick on the front with a clear adhesive.

Sew the two hat pieces together with running stitch as indicated in Fig. 6 but leave a big enough opening to fit your head.

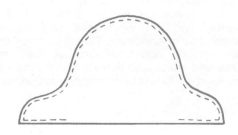

Fig. 6

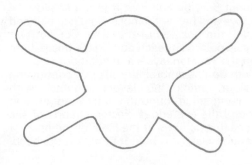

**Fig. 7
(actual size)**

A cat mask

You will need :

Vilene ; five black pipe cleaners ;
green sequins ; and elastic.

On paper draw a circle big enough to cover
your face. Shape the bottom into a pointed
chin by cutting the circle away at each side.
Add pointed ears at the top (Fig. 8). Pin
this shape on to the black Vilene and cut it
out.

Coil up one of the pipe cleaners and stick
it in the centre of the face with a clear
adhesive. Fold the pipe cleaners in half and
stick down the folded ends each side of
the nose for whiskers (Fig. 9).

Cut two oval eye·shapes slanting in to
the nose. Place a piece of green Tarlatan
behind the face and mark the outline of the
eyes lightly with pencil. Stick a ring of green
sequins in each eye shape with clear
adhesive (Fig 10), then stick the Tarlatan in
position behind the face so that the sequinn-
ed eyes fill the eyeholes in the mask (Fig. 11).
Sew an end of thin elastic each side of the
mask to fit round the head.

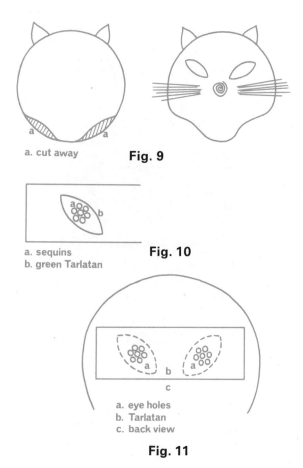

a. cut away   **Fig. 9**

a. sequins   **Fig. 10**
b. green Tarlatan

a. eye holes
b. Tarlatan
c. back view

Fig. 11

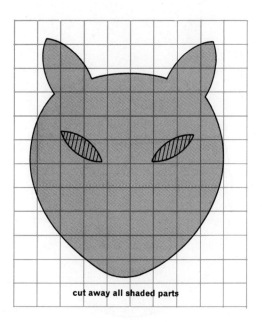

cut away all shaded parts

Fig. 8

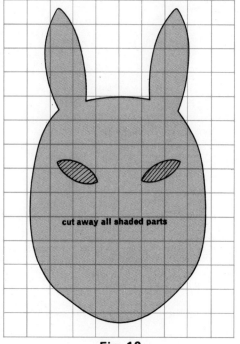

Fig. 12

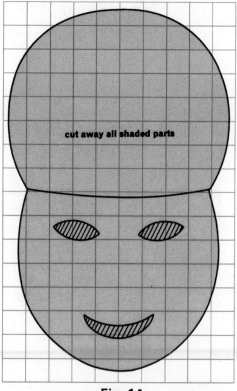

a. pink felt
b. single chain stitch

Fig. 13

An English guardsman mask

You will need :

Black and white Vilene ; pink Tarlatan.

Cut out:

the shape of face and bearskin hat in one piece of white Vilene (Fig. 14).

a separate bearskin shape in black Vilene using the top part of the pattern as a guide.

ovals for the eyes and a crescent-shaped mouth.

a face shape in pink Tarlatan.

the moustache (Fig. 15) and crescent-shaped eyebrows in black Vilene.

Stick these in place with a clear adhesive. The mouth and red cheeks can be cut out of a scrap of red Tarlatan and stuck on, or can be drawn in with a red felt-tip pen.

A white rabbit mask

For the rabbit you will need :

White Vilene ; some scraps of pink felt.

Cut out:

the face from an oval shape in double white Vilene, slightly pointed at the chin and with two long ears added at the top (Fig. 12).

nose shape in pink felt and sew it on in the centre of the face.

the oval shaped eyes above the nose and slanting inwards.

Stick a rectangle of pink Tarlatan behind the eye holes with clear adhesive. With pink embroidery silk work a mouth shape as in Fig. 13 and some straight stitches each side for whiskers. Sew an end of elastic each side at the back to fit the head.

Fig. 14

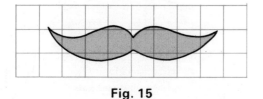

Fig. 15

Over the whole white Vilene face, place the pink Tarlatan face and stick it down round the edge.

Place the black Vilene bearskin in position and stick it down round the edge. Sew on an elastic at the sides to fit round the head.

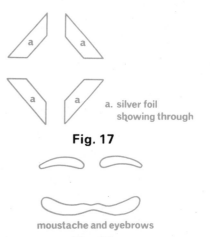

a. silver foil showing through

Fig. 17

moustache and eyebrows

Fig. 18

shape on the helmet with a white pencil and cut through all the layers of Tarlatan with a sharp penknife on a hard surface. Paste a square of silver paper behind the cut-out motif so that it shines through on the right side (Fig. 17).

Cut the eye holes — rounded ovals — and a crescent-shaped mouth. Cut round the outline of the nose.

Curly moustache and eyebrow crescents are cut from black Vilene or similar material, and stuck in place with clear adhesive (Fig. 18).

Cheeks and mouth can be coloured with a red felt-tip pen. Cover the face with the pink Tarlatan face and stick it in place round the edge.

Fit the helmet in place and oversew it round the edge and across the head with matching cotton. Sew elastic at the sides to fit round the back of the head.

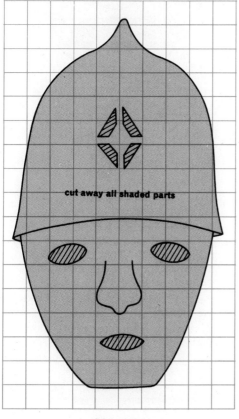

cut away all shaded parts

Fig. 16

An English policeman mask

You will need :

Thick white Vilene; royal blue Tarlatan; pink Tarlatan.

Cut out the face and helmet in one piece in white Vilene. The helmet is six layers of royal blue Tarlatan cut to shape from the top part of the pattern (Fig. 16). Draw the motif

73

A pirate mask

You will need :

Thick white Vilene; black
Vilene; a felt-tip pen.

Again the hat and face are cut out in one
piece in white Vilene. If the Vilene is not very
thick, cut it in double thickness (Fig. 19).

Cut out:
the hat shape in black Vilene,
using the hat shape on the pattern
as a guide.

ovals for the eyes.

jagged edge eyebrows.

a curved mouth.

the centre of the earring.

Cut round the outline of the nose.
  Colour the face brownish-pink with felt-
tip pens, and draw in the mouth in red and
the eyebrows and beard in black.
  Cut a crescent-shaped moustache in
black Vilene and stick it in place. Cut a ring
in gold paper to fit the earring and stick it
over the Vilene ring.
  Place the hat in position and oversew all
round the edges and across the forehead
(see Figs. 6 and 7 earlier).
  Draw the skull and crossbones in white
pencil and cut through black and white
layers all together. Sew on a narrow elastic
to fit the heads.

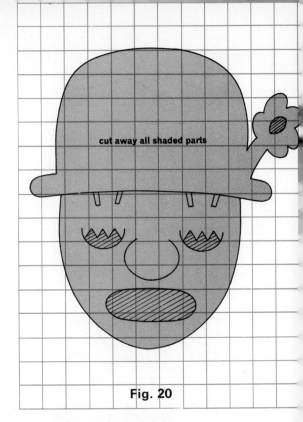

cut away all shaded parts

Fig. 20

A clown mask

You will need :

Thick white Vilene; red and yellow
Tarlatan; coloured felt-tip pens.

Cut out:
the hat and face and flower in one
piece in white Vilene, in double
thickness if the Vilene is not thick
enough (Fig. 20).

the hat shape in four layers of red
Tarlatan.

the flower in four layers of yellow
Tarlatan.

The nose and eyes are big circles.

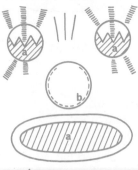

a. cut away
b. cut

Fig. 21

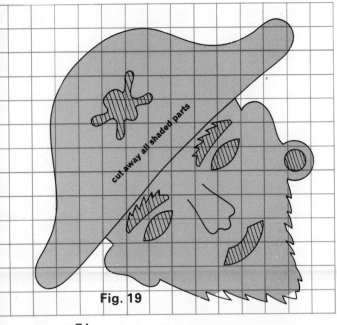

cut away all shaded parts

Fig. 19

a. Tarlatan
b. pipe cleaner

Fig. 22

Cut round the bottom half of the eyes and cut the piece out in points for eyelashes (Fig. 21).

Colour the nose red with a felt-tip pen and cut round it leaving a small piece at the top as a hinge.

Cut out the oval mouth and colour all round it with a red felt-tip pen.

Draw face decorations on eyes and cheeks and forehead with felt-tip pens.

Sew a pipe cleaner on the flower stem, place over it the yellow Tarlatan shape and oversew all round the edges (Fig. 22).

Place the hat in position and sew round the edges and over the forehead. Sew on a narrow elastic to fit the head.

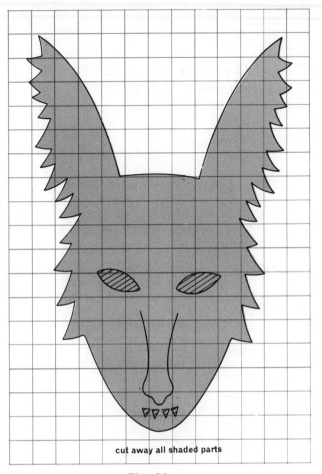

cut away all shaded parts

Fig. 23

A wolf mask

You will need :

Thick white Vilene; brown and black felt-tip pens.

Cut out:

the whole shape, face and ears, in white Vilene, double thickness if necessary (Fig. 23)

the eyes and the mouth curve with jagged teeth at the bottom.

Cut all round the outline of the snout.

Colour all over with black and brown felt-pens to simulate fur.

Sew on elastic to fit. To make the ears stand up the top half of the head and ears can be reinforced with an extra piece of Vilene cut to shape and stuck on at the back.

Masks for a play — a princess, a witch and a frog prince

The princess

You will need :

White Vilene ; gold paper ; felt-tip pens.

Cut out:

the face and crown in one piece in thick white Vilene (Fig. 24)

two rounded ovals for eyes and a curved mouth.

Cut round the outline of the nose.

Colour the face faintly pink with a pink felt-tip pen, and colour the mouth and cheeks with a red one. Draw in the eyebrows, lashes and hair with a black felt-tip pen.

Trace a gold paper crown from the template and stick it on over the Vilene one. Sew on elastic.

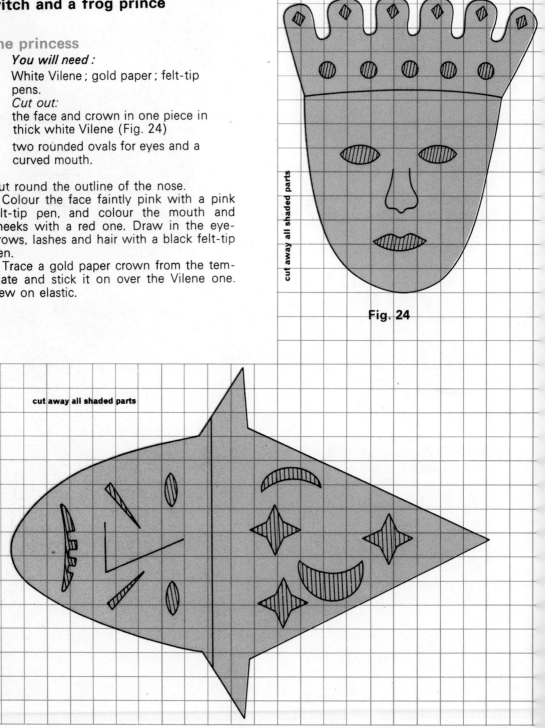

cut away all shaded parts

Fig. 24

cut away all shaded parts

Fig. 25

76

Fig. 26

The witch

You will need :

Thick white Vilene ; black Vilene ; silver paper, a little red and green foil ; some felt-tip pens.

Cut out:

the face and hat in white Vilene (Fig. 25) and a separate hat in black Vilene.

the crescents and stars from the black Vilene hat (Fig. 26) ; stick silver paper behind the black Vilene, to shine through the front.

Cut small slit-like ovals for the eyes and over them stick big triangles in red foil with an oval of green foil in the middle. When it is dry, turn it over and cut the eye shapes through the foil.

Cut down one side and along the base of a pointed nose and cut out a turned down crescent for a mouth.

Colour the face brownish-red with felt-tip pens, colour the mouth red and draw the

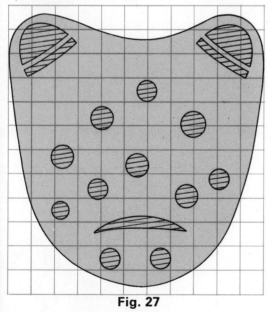

Fig. 27

eyebrows and bad temper lines and whiskery chin in black. Fit the black hat on to the shape and either stick or sew it down round the edges. Sew on narrow elastic.

The frog prince

You will need :

White Vilene ; green Tarlatan ; red and green foil.

Cut out:

the shape in thick white Vilene and in double green Tarlatan (Fig. 27).

the big curved crescent for the mouth, and the spots, cutting out two in convenient places for seeing through.

Stick red foil behind the two frog eyes at the top of the head, and green foil behind some of the spots, but *not* the peep holes. Cover the front with the green Tarlatan face shapes and oversew round the edges. Sew on elastic to fit.

CHAPTER FIVE

Toys from shapes

circles, ovals and rectangles

If you doodle when you are thinking, you will know how the doodles take all kinds of fantastic and imaginative shapes. Some of the toys here are like that because they can be evolved from many different shapes — circles, squares, ovals — placed together in various ways, to achieve a shape, or something recognisable.

A cat from circles

You will need :

Felt; embroidery silks; kapok; cotton for sewing; ribbon; card.

Draw a 6 in. circle for the body with a 4 in. circle above it and overlapping it to form a head and neck.

On the smaller circle draw two triangles with curved sides for ears, and extend the curve at the base of the large circle to make a curled tail (Fig. 1). This shape when cut out will be your template.

Trace round it twice, reversing the template the second time to keep the pencil marks all on the one side (Fig. 2).

Oversew the two pieces together leaving an opening at the base. Fill it smoothly with small pieces of kapok, pushing it gently into the corners of ears and tail, not too hard — it should be flat rather than fat.

Sew up the opening.

Cut a shield shape in black felt for a nose, and sew in position.

Embroider two curves for the mouth in stem or chain stitch and straight stitches in

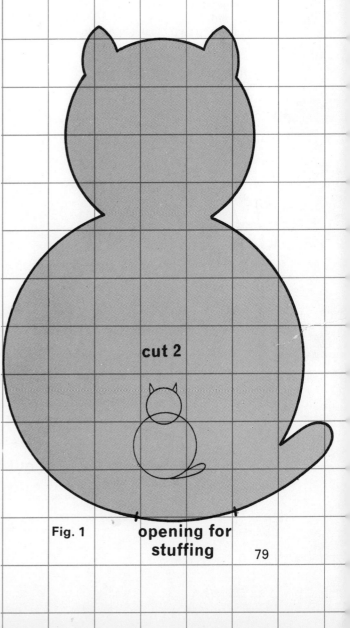

cut 2

Fig. 1

opening for stuffing

79

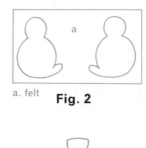

a. felt **Fig. 2**

Fig. 3

black silk for whiskers (Fig. 3).

Cut two ovals with pointed ends from green felt and two black centres for them for eyes, and sew them in position on the face, slanting in towards the nose. Tie a bright ribbon or felt bow round its neck.

A little blue bird

You will need :

Blue felt ; pink felt for the wings ; scraps of orange and white felt for the eyes, beak and feet ; thin card ; embroidery silks ; sewing cotton : kapok.

Draw a 6 in. circle on the card, and add a triangle to it at one side to form a pointed tail (Fig. 4). Draw a gusset shape pointed at each end and 2 in. wide in the middle and long enough to stretch from under the beak to the tail. In a triangle 3½ in. by 1½ in. draw the wing shape, and the feet in a diamond 1½ in. by 1 in. (Fig. 5). The beak is a curved triangle.

Cut two body pieces and one gusset in blue felt, two wing shapes in pink, four feet, two beaks and two eyes in orange, two slightly larger black circles and two much larger white circles also for the eyes.

Embroider the wings in a feather design,

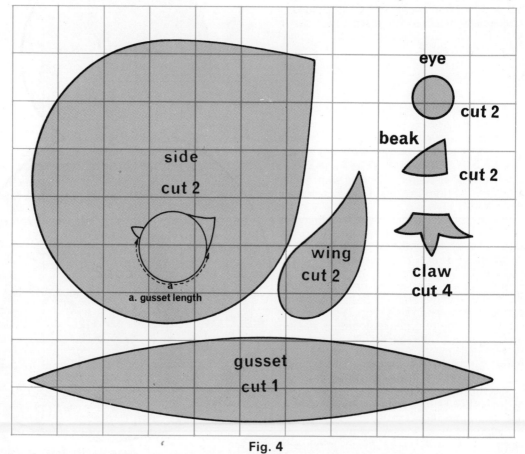

eye

cut 2

beak

cut 2

side

cut 2

a. gusset length

wing
cut 2

claw
cut 4

gusset
cut 1

Fig. 4

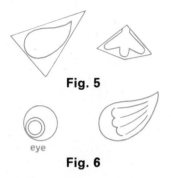

Fig. 5

eye

Fig. 6

pairing them for left and right (Fig. 6).

Sew two shapes together for each foot and sew the two beak shapes together.

Place a black circle under an orange one so that it shows a rim of black and sew both of them near to one edge of a white circle. Sew them together (Fig. 6).

Sew wings, eyes and feet in position on each side piece matching the positions of each one.

Sew the gusset to one side piece, starting at the tail. Pin it to the second side at matching points and sew it, leaving an opening at the tail for the filling. Pin the beak in position where the gusset joins the side, and sew it. Oversew the top edges of the bird.

Fill it smoothly, not too hard, with small pieces of kapok. Sew up the opening.

A rabbit from ovals

You will need :

Felt ; kapok ; card ; sewing cotton.

Draw a large and a small oval overlapping at the ends. Add a smaller oval at the opposite end of the large oval for a tail, add two long oval ears, and an oval front paw (Fig. 7).

Cut out this shape in the card and trace round it on to the piece of felt.

Cut two shapes in felt, reversing the template for the second one, pin them together with the pencilled sides inside and sew them together, leaving an opening in the base.

Push small pieces of kapok carefully into ears and tail and front paw. Stuff the head, then the rest of the body. Sew up the opening. Sew a small black circle on a white oval, and sew in position for the eyes. Work a nose and mouth in single chain stitch (Fig. 8) and three or four straight stitches each side for whiskers.

nose

eye

a

a. single chain stitch

Fig. 8

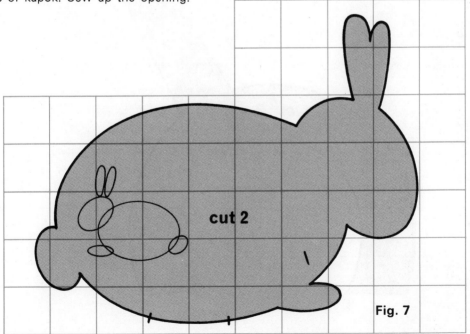

cut 2

Fig. 7

A giraffe

He is made from a circle, a rectangle and a triangle (Fig. 9).

You will need :

A piece of blue felt; scraps of orange felt for ears; black felt for the mane and tail; some kapok; orange embroidery silk; cotton; thin card.

Draw a 6 in. circle and a 3½ in. circle inside it from the same centre. Draw a line across the circle 1½ in. from the edge.

Cut off this piece and cut out the centre circle (Fig. 10). This shape is for the giraffe's legs and body.

From the point X on the circle (Fig. 10a) draw a rectangle 5 in. long and 1 in. wide. Draw a triangle at the top of this neck for a head (Fig. 10b). Round off the corners at

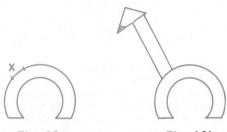

a. cut away

Fig. 10

Fig. 10a   **Fig. 10b**

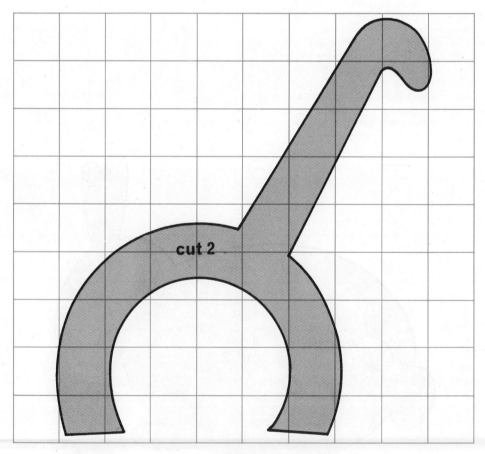

cut 2

Fig. 9

the top of the head and the mouth. This figure forms the template.

Cut out two pieces in blue felt. Cut a narrow strip of black felt for a mane and two triangular pieces for a tail. Cut two small rectangles of black for horns and two ears in orange felt.

Pin the mane on to one side-piece from the top of the head to halfway down the neck. Pin the two tail pieces in position. Pin two body pieces together.

Oversew together the inner edges of the circle. Sew the base and the outer edge of the front leg as far as the neck. Lightly fill the front leg with kapok. Oversew the front edges of the neck and over the head. Stuff the head.

Continue sewing down the back of the neck, sewing in the mane at the same time and filling with kapok as you work. Sew the body and the back leg, sewing in the tail as well, still filling with kapok.

Roll up two small rectangles of felt and stitch them to form horns. Sew them in place on top of the head with ladder stitch, taking a stitch first in the head, then in the horn. Fold the bases of the ears in half and sew them in place slightly below and behind the horns.

Embroider the eyes and mouth and snip the outer edge of the mane to form a fringe.

A snake from cylinders

The snake's head and tail are cone-shaped and each segment is a cylinder. For this one (Fig. 11) with six segments, head and tail.

You will need :
A piece of felt 12½ in. by 15¼ in. and two circles 1¾ in. diameter; (The head is 4 in. long, pointed at one end and a 1¾ in. circle at the other. The tail is 6 in. long, shaped like the head) some bright embroidery silks ; some kapok ; matching cotton for sewing ; sequins or scraps of felt for eyes and tongue ; tinsel cord for threading.

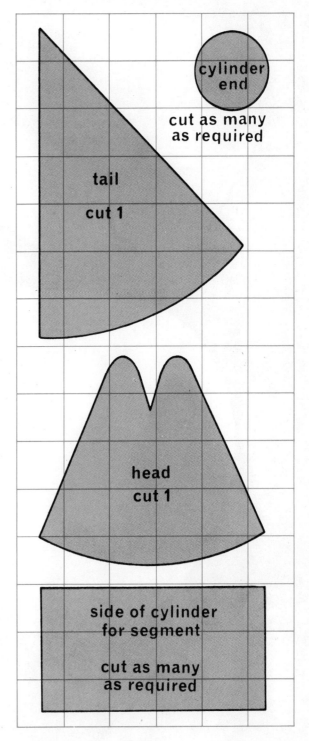

Fig. 11

fly stitch

Fig. 12

a. head
b. knot inside

Fig. 13

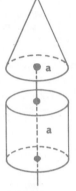

a. inside

Fig. 14

Sew the eyes and tongue in position on the head and embroider a design in fly stitch down the back (Fig. 12), in the middle, Oversew the side seams.

Make a small hole in the centre of the circle, thread in the cord and knot it securely (Fig. 13). Push kapok gently into the pointed end of the head.

Pin on the circle and oversew the edges, pushing in any extra stuffing if needed.

Embroider a fly stitch design down the centre of the cylinder piece and sew the side seam.

Thread an end of cord through one circle and knot it securely to hold it in place. Thread the end through the felt tube, and sew a circle on to it. Make a second knot to come just inside the tube, stuff round the cord, thread the cord through the second circle and sew the circle on to complete the cylinder. The knots inside each end of the cylinder will hold it in place on the cord (Fig. 14). Continue in the same way with each remaining cylinder.

For the tail, embroider a fly stitch design down length on one side, and sew up side seam, knot the cord inside the circle, thread the cord right through the tail and make a knot outside. Stuff tail and sew on circle. Cut a short length of cord, knot it at each end and sew it in the tail so that the three ends form an extension of the felt tail.

Embroider a fly stitch design over each side seam of the cylinders and of the head and tail.

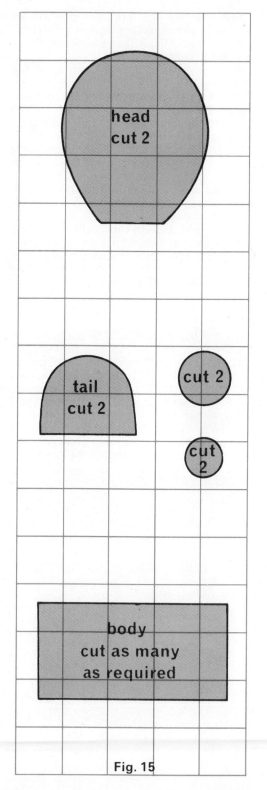

head
cut 2

tail
cut 2

cut 2

cut
2

body
cut as many
as required

Fig. 15

A caterpillar

He is made of rectangles which are folded to form squares, in bright shades of orange, yellow and green felt. His head is an oval, straight edged at one end, and the tail is an extended semi-circle. He is in twelve segments, but you can make him longer or shorter as you wish (Fig. 15)

You will need :

Ten rectangles of felt measuring 4 in. by 2 in. ; two semi-circles on a 2 in. diameter, and extended to measure 2 in. from the outside edge of the curve to the diameter (Fig. 16) ; two ovals measuring 4 in. by 3 in. ; for the eyes, two large black circles, two white ones half the size and two yellow ones slightly smaller than the white ones ; and a ¾ in. wide strip of black felt 24 in. long (this could be in pieces joined with the joins hidden in the segments) ; kapok for stuffing ; embroidery silks. (Alternatively, to use up smaller pieces of felt, you could have twenty squares sewn together in two's to make the ten segments.)

Cut a piece off the ends of the head ovals to make a straight edge. Sew them together round the curved edges, push in some stuffing, not too much, keeping it flat rather than round.

Sew the straight ends together enclosing one end of the black strip. Fold a rectangle in half and oversew the two short sides together. Fold it so that the seam is in the middle at the back and thread it on to the black strip. Oversew the edges enclosing the black strip as well, leaving about ⅛ in. to ¼ in. between it and the head (Fig. 17). Push in some stuffing and sew up the second side, again sewing in the black strip.

Continue like this with the rest of the rectangles, taking care to keep all the seams on the same side. Sew together the curved sides of the tail pieces and, after stuffing, sew the black strip in with the straight sides of it. There should be the same width of strip left between each segment.

Place a yellow circle on a white oval, slightly to one side and sew both on to a black circle to one side of it (Fig. 18). Sew them in position on the head.

a. semi circle 2in. diameter
b. extension

Fig. 16

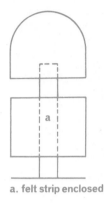

a. felt strip enclosed

Fig. 17

eye

Fig. 18

Embroider a line of contrasting fly stitch down the centre of the head, a line pointing to each eye and curls of chain stitch in front. Embroider each segment in a different design in contrasting embroidery silks.

1. A square of chain stitch with a chain stitch flower in each corner.

2. A diagonal of chain stitch with a line each side of it and single chain stitches at the sides.

3. A plaid design in stem stitch, chain and herringbone stitch.

4. A circle of fly stitch.

5. Parallel lines of fly stitch.

6. A diamond of threaded running stitch with the centre of four fly stitches.

7. Diagonal cross of chain stitch with single chain stitches on the ends and in the centre.

8. Curved square of chain stitch with a single chain stitch centre.

9. Diagonal cross of fly stitch, worked from each corner.

10. Parallel lines of fly stitch.

Tail — three lines of chain stitch spraying out from the straight edges with single chain stitches at the ends and down the sides.

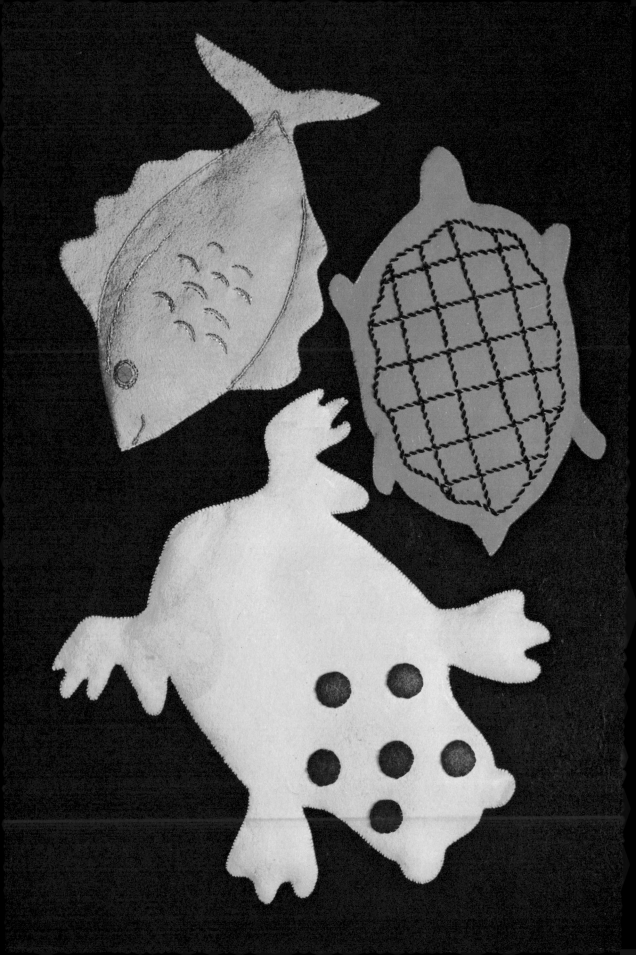

CHAPTER SIX

Two-piece toys

These toys are made from two pieces of material, two shapes sewn together and filled either with soft stuffing like kapok or foam chippings for a soft cuddly toy, or partly filled with rice or lentils for a slithery toy which can be used for throwing like a ball — it is much easier to catch because it is not a hard shape — or for sliding across a shiny surface.

Any fairly solid-looking round or square shape is suitable. The slither toy, whether it is a round fat bird, a sitting cat, a duck, frog, fish, or tortoise, should be unfussy with no hanging bits and pieces and only soft embroidery.

A slither tortoise

You will need :
A piece of felt about 12 in. by 9 in. to make a toy 8 in. long, or two pieces in different colours for top and bottom (choose a fairly dark colour for the underside or any strong cotton material) ; a card template ; embroidery silks ; sewing cotton ; rice or lentils.

Draw an oval of the size you want your tortoise to be and add a blunt head, a pointed tail and four short legs (Fig. 1).

Trace round this on to the felt or material. If you choose felt, cut round the pencil line, but if cotton material is used cut round ½ in. outside the line to allow for turnings.

Draw a wavy line all round just inside the edge of the piece. This will be the top of the tortoise (Fig. 2). Criss-cross inside it with wavy lines to indicate the pattern on the shell. Embroider on the lines and round the edge in stem stitch or whipped running stitch.

Place the pieces together with the right sides outside and pin them together at the head, tail and legs. Oversew the edges with

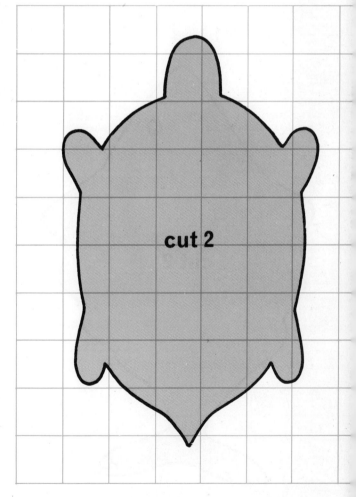

cut 2

Fig. 1

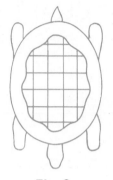

Fig. 2

matching cotton leaving the tail end open.

Pour in spoonfuls of rice until it is about a third or less full — if you have made a large size then pour in less than this proportion or the finished toy will be much too heavy. Sew up the opening.

If you are using material, embroider the top piece on the side which is not pencilled, taking care to keep the pattern inside the allowance for turnings. Pin the two pieces together at head, tail and legs with right side inside. Machine or backstitch all round the pencil line, leaving the tail end open. Trim off some of the turning allowance, cut out little v's on the curves to allow the seams to lie flat and not pucker. Turn it inside out and press the seams flat.

Pour in the filling, turn in the seam allowance at the tail end opening and sew together either with ladder stitch or oversewing.

The slither fish

You will need :

A piece of felt 12 in. by 9½ in. to make a 9 in. fish, or two pieces of different colour each measuring 6 in. by 9½ in. ; some rice or lentils for filling ; some embroidery silks ; matching sewing cotton.

Trace round the template (Fig. 3) on the felt and cut out two pieces. If using material be careful to leave about ½ in. allowance for turnings. This will not be easy to sew at the tail because of the narrow base, so use felt if possible.

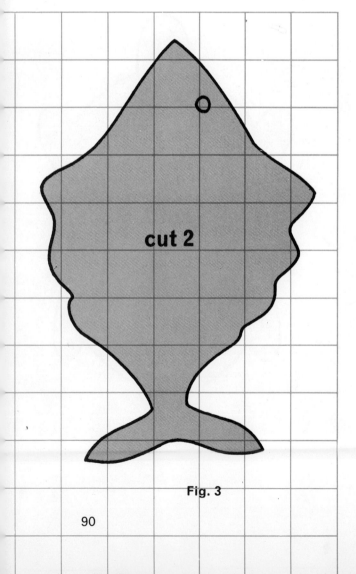

cut 2

Fig. 3

scales

eye

Fig. 4   **Fig. 5**

On the piece for the top embroider little crescents in chain stitch to resemble scales and a wavy line all round from the head, along the base of the fins and the base of the tail (Fig. 4). Sew on a circle of white felt, or embroider a big eye (Fig. 5). Pin the two sides together with right sides outside and pin at the mouth, fins and tail. Oversew the edges all round leaving the tail end open for stuffing Pour in rice or chosen filling, not more than a third full and oversew the tail edges. Sew right through the base of the tail so that no rice can get into it.

A slither frog

You will need:

A piece of felt 10½ in. by 19 in. to make a 10 in. frog, or two pieces 10½ in. by 9½ in. ; rice for filling ; embroidery silks.

Cut out two pieces from the template (Fig. 6) and embroider one piece for the top with big eyes, or sew on circles of felt, and some coloured spots on his back. Oversew all round on the right sides leaving the tail open. Sew across the base of each leg to prevent the filling getting in because the weight of it can weaken the felt across the narrow base and in the toes. Fill to much less than a third and sew up the opening.

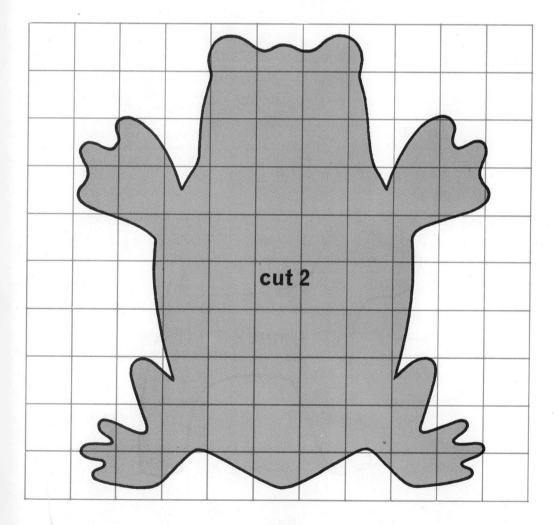

cut 2

Fig. 6

Softly stuffed two-piece toys

As these are flat toys they should not have too much stuffing because the stitches will pull tight and the seams will pucker and maybe split. Any fairly simple shape makes a satisfactory toy.

start stitching

Fig. 8

The dog

You will need :

Felt; stuffing; embroidery silks; sewing cotton.

Cut out two pieces from your pattern or template drawing, reversing the template to trace the second side so that all pencil markings will be on the wrong side, and embroider an eye on each piece. Template Fig. 7.

Pin the pieces together with right sides outside, at nose, ears, tail and feet. Oversew the edges starting at the inner edge of the front leg and sewing round it (Fig. 8), and on over the head to the back of the neck. Stop here and stuff the head and front leg with small pieces of stuffing, pushing it gently into the corners and seams of the foot and head. Continue sewing over the back and the back leg. Sew half of the inner leg seam and then stuff the back foot. Sew the rest of the leg, stuff it and stuff the body. Sew up the under body seam. Be very careful not to stuff too hard.

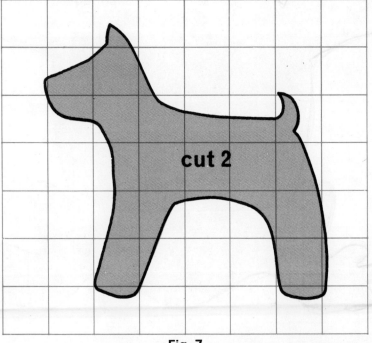

cut 2

Fig. 7

A sitting cat

The template is in one piece with ears and tail included, similar to the cat drawn from circles in Chapter Five. This one has a more natural shape.

You will need :

A piece of felt 10½ in. by 12 in. to make a 10 in. cat; small piece of green felt for eyes; some stuffing; some embroidery silks; matching cotton.

Cut out two shapes from the template and pin the pieces together, matching ears, neck, and tail (Fig. 9).

Oversew the edges beginning at the base of the tail; stuff the tail when it is sewn and then continue sewing until the head is finished. Stuff the head and continue sewing, leaving the bottom edge open. Stuff the cat's body keeping it smooth and soft. Sew up the opening.

Embroider green eyes or sew on ovals of green felt, slanting slightly inwards, a black nose and whiskers. Tie a bow round her neck.

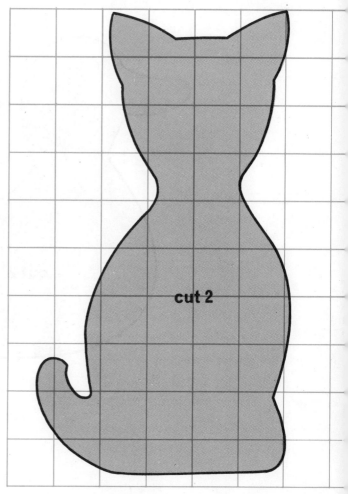

cut 2

Fig. 9

93

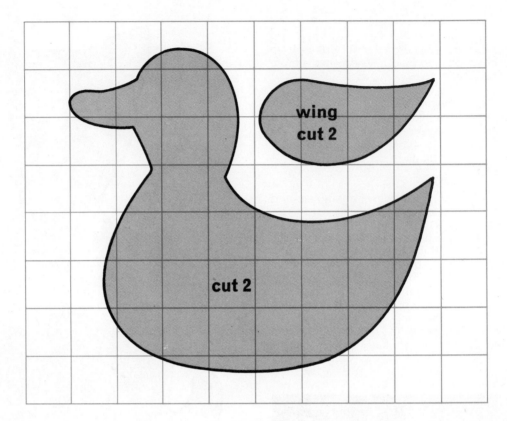

Fig. 10

The duck

You will need :

A piece of orange felt measuring
8½ in. by 14 in. ; a small
contrasting piece for a wing ; tiny
piece of black felt for eyes ; some
stuffing ; embroidery silks ; orange
cotton.

Fig. 11

The beak is cut in one with the body, but
it can be cut separately if wished, in a
contrasting colour. Cut two body pieces
and two wings (Fig. 10).

Embroider the wings in a feather design in
stem stitch or whipped running stitch,
pairing them for left and right sides (Fig. 11).
Sew them in place with invisible stitches.
Embroider a big round eye with a black

centre, or sew on circles of felt.

Pin the two duck pieces together, matching
head and tail and oversew, starting at the
tail, over the back and head and beak. Fill
the beak and head with small pieces of
stuffing. Continue sewing and stuffing,
leaving an opening in the under seam,
until the remainder of the body is filled and
sew up the opening.

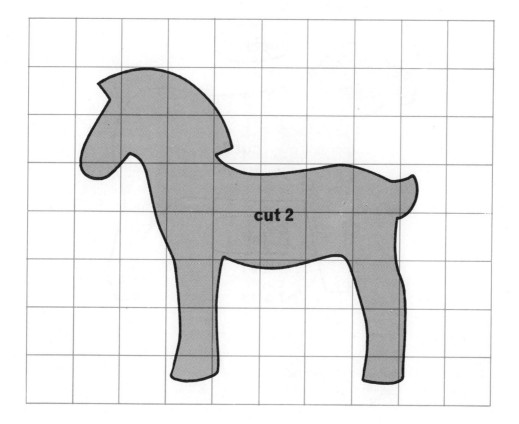

Fig. 12

The little horse

The pattern is cut in one with the mane and tail included but they can be cut separately in contrasting colour and sewn in with the seams (Fig. 12).

You will need:

A piece of felt measuring 8½ in. by 14 in.; some stuffing; matching cotton; a strand of black embroidery silk.

Cut two pieces and pin them together matching legs and head, and oversew starting at the inner seam of the front leg and stopping at the front edge of the mane. Stab stitch along the base of the mane leaving the two edges free. Stop at the back of the neck. Stuff the front leg and head. Continue sewing along the back to the tail. Stab stitch along the base of the tail leaving the two edges free. Sew the back leg and half way up the inner seam and stuff the foot. Finish sewing the rest of the inner leg seam and complete the leg stuffing. Stuff the rest of the body and sew up the under body seam.

Embroider oval eyes slanting towards the nose, and the mouth. Cut the edges of the mane and tail into a fringe.

Strips of felt for a harness, and a saddle cloth in contrasting colour can be added if wished.

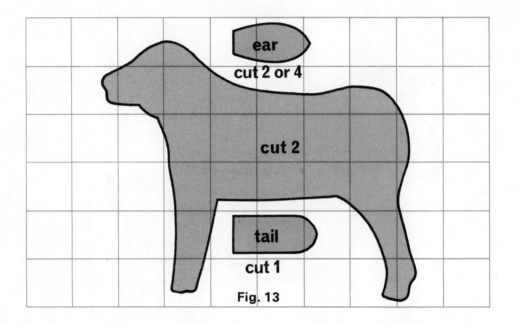

Fig. 13

A lamb

The pattern is of the head and body in one with separate ears and tail. This one is made from fluffy white man-made fibre, but any colour felt can be used (Fig. 13).

You will need :

A piece of man-made fibre 7½ in. by 11 in. ; some stuffing ; embroidery silk ; sewing cotton.

Trace round the template on to the wrong side of the man-made fibre, pressing down firmly on the edges of the template to keep it in place. (Man-made fibre is a stretchy material and not firm like felt so it will move under the template unless held fast and a bad shape will result). Remember to reverse the template to trace the second side.

Cut a rectangle for a tail and two pointed ears.

Sew seams on the wrong side for man-made fibre. Pin the shapes together with the right sides inside and matching feet and head, and tack the edges. Oversew the edges firmly, using a locking stitch by putting the needle twice into the same hole. Start sewing from the inner seam of the front leg, round chest, head, back and back leg, fastening off at the top of the inner back leg seam. Turn it inside out and gently press the seams as flat as possible. Stuff the head, legs and then the rest of the

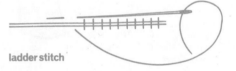

ladder stitch

Fig. 14

a. single chain stitches

Fig. 15

body. Sew up the opening with ladder stitch (Fig. 14), which is done by taking a stitch first in one side and then in the other and pulling the thread taut.

Fold the rectangle for the tail with the two edges together on the under side and sew them together, curving in the end.

Embroider yellow spots for the eyes with a ring of black back stitch round them and a nose and mouth in single chain stitches as in Fig. 15. Fold the two corners of the ears to the centre and sew them on the head near the top, with ladder stitch, so that they stand away from the head.

If the lamb is made in felt it can of course be seamed on the right side.

A pet white mouse

You will need :

A small piece of white felt measuring 4 in. by 5 in. ; a strand each of pink and of white embroidery silk ; some stuffing ; some white cotton.

Fig. 17

Cut out two pieces reversing the pattern for the second one, and two ears (Fig. 16).

Make a cord for the tail with the white embroidery silk — fold it in half and tie the ends. Pin one end down securely. Insert a pencil in the other loop and twist it until a firm hard cord is obtained. Put the two ends together and the remainder will twist into a cord. Tie a knot in the end at the required length of the tail.

Sew the pieces together on the right side, starting to sew at the under edge of the front foot and over the head, stopping at the back of the neck. Stuff the front leg with very small pieces of stuffing, pushing it into place with a blunted orange stick, or cocktail pick. Stuff the head. Pin the tail in place with the knotted end inside. Sew the back, sewing in the tail with the seam, and round the back leg. Stuff the back leg with small pieces and then the rest of the body. Sew up the opening.

Embroider eyes and nose in close straight stitches in pink silk. Fold the corners of the ears to the middle (Fig. 17) and sew in place on the head so that they point along the back. Whiskers can be sewn in with fine white nylon thread.

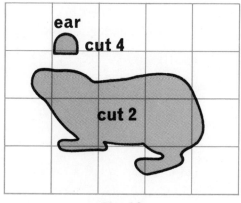

ear

cut 4

cut 2

Fig. 16

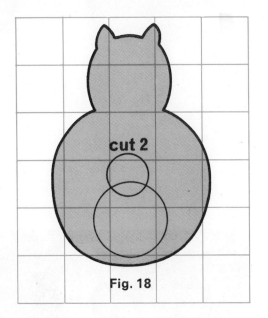

cut 2

Fig. 18

Cats on elastic
(for a baby's carriage)

Any of the previous toys cut to a smaller size can be threaded on a cord or elastic to amuse a baby as they jig about when strung across in front of him.

You will need :

A small piece of different patterned gingham for each cat; some bonded interlining for lining; kapok for stuffing; one or two pipe cleaners; a piece of round elastic.

Make a template for cutting out the cats by drawing a circle 4 in. in diameter, and over-lapping the top of it a circle 2 in. in diameter (Fig. 18). Draw two ears on top of the smaller circle. The lining should be cut ½ in. smaller all round (Fig. 19).

For each cat cut out two shapes in gingham and two in interlining. Place the interlining shape in the centre of the gingham so that an even edge is left all round. Snip small v's out of the gingham edge so that the turning will lie flat (Fig. 20).

Tack the gingham edge over the inter-lining. Repeat this with all the cat shapes. Place two pieces together with the right sides outside and sew all round the head and ears. Ease some kapok into the head in small pieces to make a rather flat finish. Continue to sew round the body leaving an

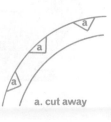

a. Vilene
b. gingham

a. cut away

Fig. 19   **Fig. 20**

opening. Stuff the body through this opening.

Cut off a piece of pipe cleaner about 2 in. long and sew a strip of gingham round it for a tail. Sew this firmly to the back of the cat, curl it round to the front and sew in place.

Embroider eyes, nose and whiskers.

When all the cats are finished thread the elastic through the necks from side to side and they are ready to be put in place.

The cats can be made rounder by lining a ½ in. wide strip of gingham with interlining and sewing each side of the cat to it, being careful to match everything up. Fusible interlining also can be ironed on to the gingham cats and then no allowance need be made for turnings.

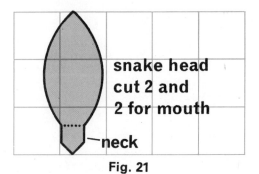

snake head
cut 2 and
2 for mouth
neck

Fig. 21

A wired snake

You will need :

A long thin piece of green felt — this one measures 24 in. from head to tail and is just over ½ in. wide in the middle of the body (the head is cut separately) ; a small piece of orange or red felt for a mouth ; two pieces of pipe cleaner chenille measuring 24 in. and 3 in. or these same lengths could be made from pipe cleaners twisted together ; about three yd. of thin gold cord (the kind used for Christmas parcels) ; matching sewing cotton.

Cut two pieces of green felt 22 in. long and ½ in. wide tapering to ⅛ in. at the tail, two diamond-shaped pieces for the head and two similar diamond shapes in red felt for the inside mouth.

Oversew two of the long edges together finishing at the tail. Sew along the second side enclosing the long length of pipe cleaner as you go. Two inches will be left projecting from the neck. Cut off the neck from the inner mouth pieces leaving about ⅛ in. of it (Fig. 22). Sew a red and a green piece together enclosing the projecting end of pipe cleaner as the second side is sewn (Fig. 23). Sew it on to the neck of the body piece, sewing the straight cut edge of the red mouth on to the straight edge of the neck of the body piece and the pointed

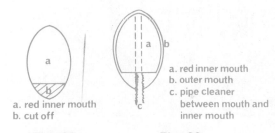

a. red inner mouth
b. cut off

a. red inner mouth
b. outer mouth
c. pipe cleaner
    between mouth and
    inner mouth

Fig. 22   Fig. 23

arrow shape of the end of the green diamond down the back. Sew the other green and red pieces together enclosing the short length of pipe cleaner when sewing the second side of it and sew it to the second side of the body in the same way, tucking the remainder of the pipe cleaner into the body.

Sew a twisted piece of gold cord to the back of the throat for a tongue. Sew the sides of the head together at the neck for about ½ in. Sew the gold cord all down the back in a diamond pattern. It can be made to seem to slither along by bending the wire, or coiled round with its head poised and alert.

A set of wired lengths

These can be twisted and bent and curved into dozens of different shapes and designs, both singly and several together.

You will need :
Many different coloured pieces of felt about ⅝ in. wide and in lengths from 3 in. or 4 in. to 24 in. or 30 in. or more if you wish, (several lengths can be joined together to make rainbow lengths) ; pipe cleaner chenille cut in lengths ; or pipe cleaners twisted together to give the required length.

Bend back the sharp ends of the wire to avoid them sticking through the felt. Cut the strip of felt about ⅛ in. longer than the pipe cleaner. Fold the felt in half down its length and oversew the edges enclosing the pipe cleaner as you go. Oversew the ends securely.

The picture shown has been made from wire lengths mounted on coarse cloth-covered board.

CHAPTER SEVEN

Toys with gussets

The flat two-piece toys described in Chapter Six can be made rounder and more solid by inserting gussets. These can be

(a) the straight strip kind with the body pieces sewn on each edge of it, or

(b) curved ones with pointed ends, inserted in the back or underneath, or both, or

(c) cut to shape to form under parts to legs so that the toy animal will sit or lie down or stand or walk.

If you make your own patterns or templates you can either draw or trace a side view of the animal in any position and add the appropriate gusset to it. The simplest one is (a) the straight strip gusset.

A dog

The dog shape has been simplified and the template (Fig, 1) includes ear and tail in one with the body.

You will need :

Felt; kapok or other soft stuffing ; embroidery silks ; matching cotton.

Cut out two side pieces from your template, in felt, and cut a straight strip ⅝ in. wide and long enough to go right round the edge of the felt body shape. If the strip has to be cut in sections, make the necessary joins at specific points, under the feet, at the top of the inner leg seams, or under the body, under the chin, or on top of the ear or tail. Joins will be less noticeable in any of these places than in the middle of the back or on the nose.

Pin one edge of the strip all round one edge of the dog shape, being careful to pin exactly at corners like feet, tail, ear, and nose. Pin close to the edges to avoid showing pin marks.

Oversew all round the edges.

Pin the second side to the strip matching points at head, ear, tail, feet exactly with the first side, or the finished toy will be twisted.

Start sewing from the inner front leg seam over the head to the back of the neck. Stuff the front leg and head carefully, pushing stuffing into the corners and seams. Continue sewing along the back and the back leg. Fill the back leg and the rest of the body with stuffing and sew up the opening.

Embroider the eyes, nose and mouth with black embroidery silk and make a collar from a narrow strip of contrasting felt.

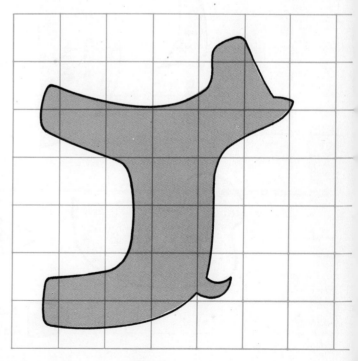

Fig. 1

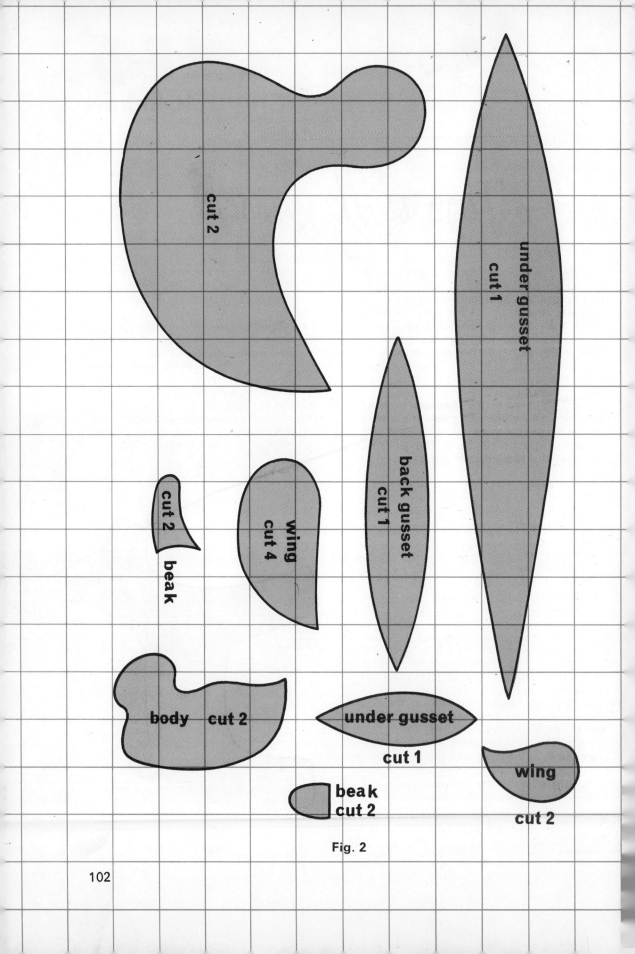

cut 2

under gusset
cut 1

back gusset
cut 1

cut 2   beak

wing
cut 4

body   cut 2

under gusset

cut 1

beak
cut 2

wing

cut 2

Fig. 2

102

A duck and ducklings

You will need for the duck:

A piece of yellow felt 10 in. by 15 in.; a small piece of orange felt for a beak; some sequins; embroidery silks; kapok or similar for stuffing; matching cotton.

The template

The shape is fairly simple and it is easy to make your own template (Fig. 2). Draw or trace a side view of the duck and make a template of it in thin card. Cut another for the beak and the wing. It has a curved gusset in the back and a longer curved one underneath. Measure along the curve of the back from the back of the neck to the tail (Fig. 3). Draw the gusset this length, tapering to a point at each end and about 1¼ in. to 1½ in. wide in the middle. For the under gusset, measure from the tail along the under body curve to just below the beak, and draw the under gusset this length, the same shape as the upper one, but 2 in. wide in the middle (Fig. 3).

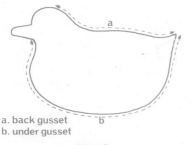

a. back gusset
b. under gusset

Fig. 3

Fig. 4

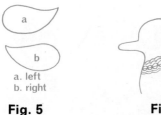

a. left
b. right

Fig. 5   **Fig. 6**

Cut out

Place the templates on the felt, starting with the under gusset which will take the full 15 in. length. Cut one under gusset, one upper gusset, two bodies, four wings from yellow felt and two beaks from the orange felt (Fig. 4).

Embroider

Embroider two of the wing shapes for left and right sides (Fig. 5), both lower body curves and tail and one half of the under gusset. Sew a ring of sequins round an embroidered spot for an eye.

The beak

Oversew the curved edges of the beak, pad it with a very little kapok, keeping it flat, and sew in position on one side of the head.

Make up

Sew both body pieces to the top gusset, placing it, and starting to sew each time from the tail. Sew one side of the under gusset to the body. Oversew the head from the top gusset to the under gusset. Pin the second side to the under gusset starting at the tail and finishing exactly under the beak. Start sewing from the beak down the neck. Stuff the head smoothly with small pieces of kapok, pushing it in gently to the seams to keep a good shape. Continue oversewing and stuffing as you go, using small pieces and keeping it free from lumps.

Sew a plain wing to an embroidered one, leaving an opening for stuffing. Ease in a little stuffing in small pieces keeping it flat. Sew up the opening and sew the wing in position with tiny invisible stitches taken about ⅛ in. below the edge of the oversewing so that the edge of the wing stands out a little from the body. Repeat with the second wing.

Tie a thread round the neck to mark the collar. Sew a ring of sequins on top of the thread and embroider one or two rows of coloured whipped or threaded running stitch above and below it (Fig. 6).

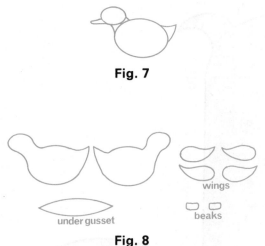

Fig. 7

wings

under gusset

beaks

Fig. 8

The ducklings

For each of them you will need:

Yellow felt 4 in. by 6 in.; orange felt; beads; embroidery silks; cotton.

They are made from a similar type of template as the duck, but not so elaborate in finish. Draw two ovals, touching one another, one for the body about 3 in. long and a smaller one touching it for the head (Fig. 7). Draw two curving lines joining them for a neck, and add a small pointed tail. This will be the body template. Draw a small curved beak and a wing (Fig. 8). The under gusset — there is no top gusset — stretches from near the chest to the tail. Draw one this length, about ¾ in. to 1 in. wide in the middle and tapering to a point at each end.

Cut out three or four ducks to follow the mother duck, but cut out all the parts for one duckling at a time making sure that it is complete. Cut two body shapes, four wings, and one under gusset from yellow felt, and two beak shapes from orange felt.

Sew a few small beads on the front part of each body piece, and embroider two of the wing pieces. Sew on a sequin or a ring of beads for an eye.

Sew a plain wing and an embroidered one together leaving a small opening. Ease in small pieces of stuffing, enough to pad it a little. Sew up the opening and sew it in position on the side piece with small invisible stitches. Repeat with the second wing.

Sew the curved sides of the beak together, ease in a little stuffing and sew it in place on one of the side pieces.

Place the two body pieces together and oversew the edges from the tail to under the beak. Sew one side of the under gusset to the body. Pin the gusset to the second side, matching it exactly with the first side. Start sewing from under the beak, down the neck and front of the body. Fill the head with small pieces of stuffing, and continue sewing, stuffing the rest of the body as you sew.

A hen and chicks

These can be made in the same way. The hen's beak is smaller and she would have a scalloped red comb on top of her head (Fig. 9)—cut in two pieces, the scalloped edges oversewn and the whole then sewn in with the head seam. Two red wattles, one each side of the beak, hanging down below it each side of the neck, could be cut single or double in red felt. The chicks resemble the ducks but with much smaller pointed beaks.

Fig. 9

105

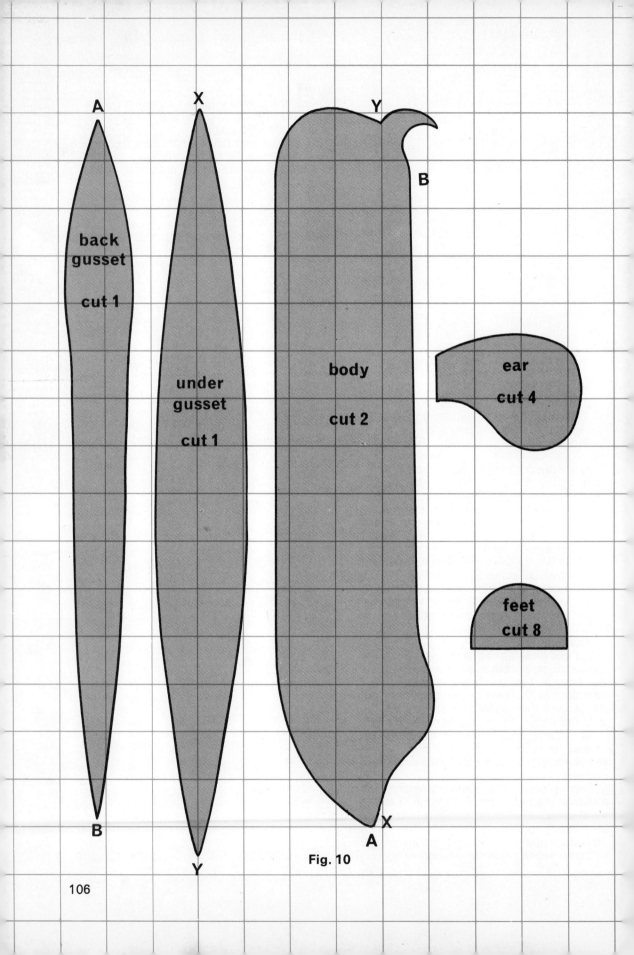

A

X

Y

back
gusset

cut 1

B

under
gusset

cut 1

body

cut 2

ear
cut 4

feet
cut 8

B

Y

A X

Fig. 10

106

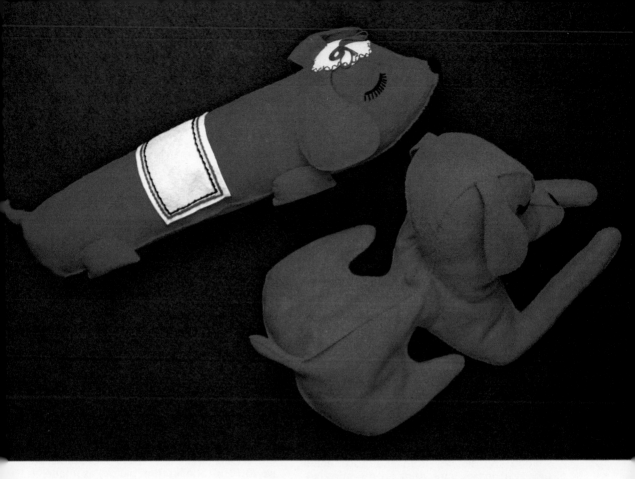

A sleepy dachshund

In a small size, like the one in the picture with the sleepy poodle (to make the poodle see p. 125), he is a cuddly soft toy; twice as big, he will lie on the floor to keep you company.

You will need :

A piece of felt 15 in. by 15 in. for the body; a rectangle of contrasting colour for a coat; some embroidery silk including black; matching sewing cotton; some kapok for stuffing.

He can be most easily made in felt. Any closely woven material can be used, but in this case remember to leave ½ in. turnings when cutting out the pieces. If thinner material is used then an inner lining of something like unbleached calico should be made.

He is fairly easy to draw for making a template (Fig. 10) because the outline has been simplified and the body is almost a sausage shape.

There are back and under gussets. For the under gusset measure the curve under the body from 2 in. below the tail to the nose, and cut the gusset this length, tapering at both ends and measuring 2 in. in the middle. The back gusset is different because the widest part comes at the top of the head. Measure the length from the nose over the back to 1 in. from the tail and mark where the top of the head comes. The widest part here should be 1½ in. then tapering gently to a point at the tail end and more sharply to the nose so that the face part will be triangle shaped (Figs. 11 and 12). The ears

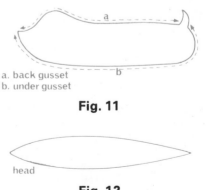

a. back gusset
b. under gusset

Fig. 11

head

Fig. 12

107

eye

Fig. 13

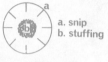

a. snip
b. stuffing

Fig. 14

are shaped like a stubby boot and the legs are semi-circular.

Cut out two body pieces, four ears, eight legs, one back gusset and one under gusset, and a rectangle in contrasting felt long enough to cross over his back and about 2½ in. wide. He will be about 15 in. long when finished.

Sew the two sides to the back gusset, taking care to match nose and tail, so that the second side matches the first, and starting the sewing from the nose each time. Put in any pins right on the edge so that stitching will cover up any marks. Sew one side to the under gusset starting from the nose. Pin the second side in position and start sewing it from the nose end. The two sides, under and back gussets should meet in a point at the nose.

Sew about a quarter of the gusset and then stuff the head. Push the kapok gently into the point of the nose and into the head seams to keep a good shape. Continue sewing and stuffing and sew the remainder of the under seam, over tail and the back.

Features

For the eyes, embroider a crescent shape in black chain stitch with straight stitches radiating from it for eye lashes (Fig. 13). Either embroider a nose in embroidery silk or cut a small circle about one inch in diameter, snip the edges, place a small ball of stuffing in the centre and gather up the edges (Fig. 14). Sew this on over the point.

Sew together two ear pieces round the curved edges for each ear. These are padded softly and flat in shape. Sew on to the seams just behind the widest part of the head with the 'toe' of the 'boot' pointing towards the nose.

Sew together two leg pieces round the curved edges for each leg, pad softly and flat and sew in position on the body so that the straight edges rest on the floor. Check that each side matches.

Embroider round the edges of the rectangle for the coat and sew it in place on the back.

To make him into a floor toy, double his length and make his width half as much again.

A wise old owl

You will need :

Felt for the body, for wings and eye sockets; some soft stuffing like kapok; embroidery silks.

His shape has been made simple so that he can be easily drawn or traced (Fig. 15). His head and body are made rounder by inserting gussets and the wings and feet are added separately when the seams are sewn. The one in the picture is made in chestnut-coloured felt with beige wings and eyes and bright orange feet.

Templates

Trace the pattern pieces on to thin card and trace round them on to the felt, reversing the pattern where necessary to keep all pencil marks on the wrong side.

Cut out two body pieces in the chestnut felt; four wings, two oval eye sockets in beige felt; two circles in orange felt (drawn round a button), two smaller ones in white and two slightly smaller in black for the eyes; two gussets in chestnut felt, one for the head which will stretch over the head from one side of the neck to the other, and the other one for the base; four feet shapes from the orange felt; a scrap of black makes the diamond-shaped beak with one rounded end (Fig. 16).

Embroidery first

Embroider a pair of wing shapes for left and right with scattered brown fly stitches (Fig. 17). For the eyes, sew a black circle to a white one and sew both on to an orange circle. Place them in the centre of an oval of beige and fasten this down with long black

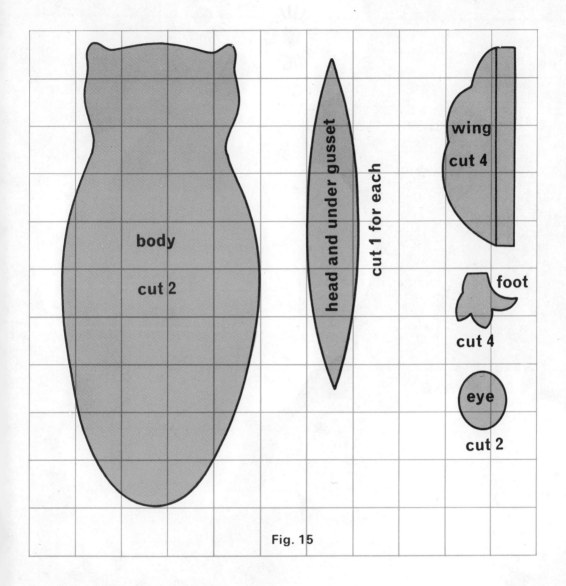

body

cut 2

head and under gusset

cut 1 for each

wing

cut 4

foot

cut 4

eye

cut 2

Fig. 15

straight stitches radiating from the edge (Fig. 18). They should be quite close together on the face. Embroider one of the body pieces below the neck in slanting lines of blanket stitch in yellow and brown (Fig. 19).

Sew a triangular beak between and slightly below the eyes. Sew the two corners A and B (Fig. 16), curving slightly in towards each other so that the pointed beak stands out from the face.

Sew a plain and an embroidered wing piece together round the curved edges, pad it softly to be slightly round but not hard and sew them on to each side of the front,

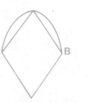

Fig. 16   **Fig. 17**   **Fig. 18**

Fig. 19

Fig. 20

matching the position of each, with the wider part of the wing at the top (Fig. 20).

Sew two felt pieces together for each foot, leaving the tops open. Stuff them with tiny pieces of kapok, pushing it gently and firmly into each claw, making the whole claw fairly hard. Sew them in position on the front piece.

Mark the centre of the top gusset edge, and the centre of the top of the head and pin the gusset in place starting from the centre marks. Check that the points of the gusset match on each side of the neck. Oversew the edges.

Repeat with the back body piece.

In the same way mark the centres of the base edge and the gusset and pin in place, checking the position of the gusset points. Sew it to the front body piece including the feet in the front seam. Sew the side seams of the body as far as the base gusset, including the wings in the seam.

Stuff the head, easing the stuffing into the ears and the seams, so that a good shape is made. Stuff the body. Sew half of the remaining gusset seam and complete the stuffing. Sew up the rest of the seam.

111

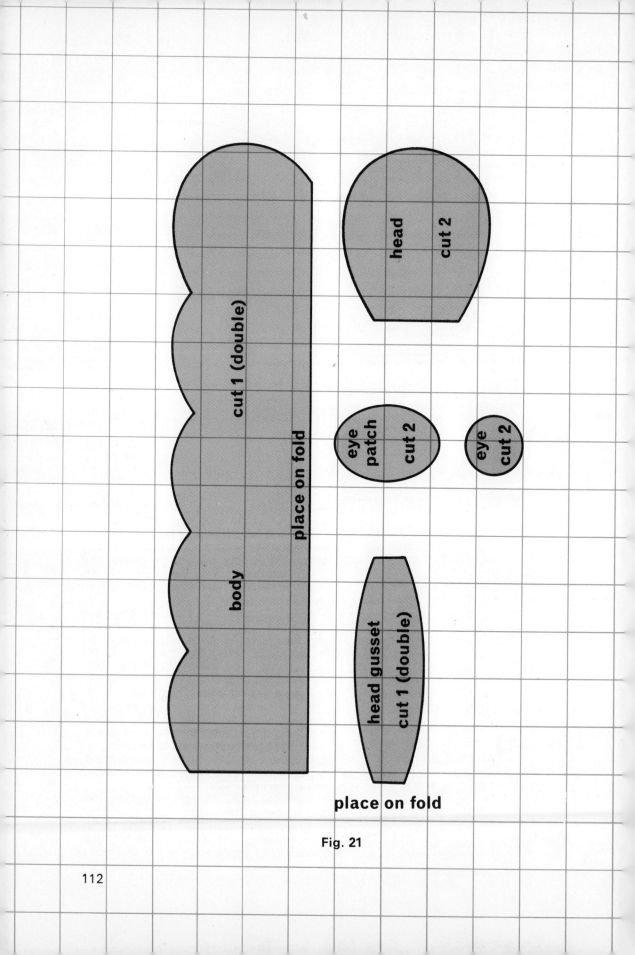

body

cut 1 (double)

place on fold

head

cut 2

eye patch

cut 2

eye

cut 2

head gusset

cut 1 (double)

place on fold

Fig. 21

A colourful caterpillar

You will need :

Felt ; kapok ; cotton ; black embroidery silks.

He, like the dachshund, can be a cuddly toy or, made longer and fatter, will lie on the floor. He is made from a green felt piece 13 in. by 6 in. and has an orange and yellow felt head, with circles of black and white felt for his eyes.

Trace the pattern shapes (Fig. 21) on to thin card and use as templates.

Cut out one body piece, two head pieces in orange, one head gusset in yellow, two black and two white circles.

Sew a black circle on to a white circle with the edges touching on one side (Fig. 22), repeat for the other eye. Sew them in place on each head piece, close to the rounded edge which is the front of the head, with the eye looking forward (Fig. 22a).

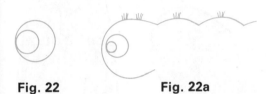

Fig. 22   **Fig. 22a**

Mark the centre of the curve in the head pieces and pin them to the head gusset, the narrow part of the gusset to the centre of each head piece. Sew them in place.

Fold the body piece in half and oversew the tail and the scalloped edges, leaving the front open.

Stuff the head firmly for a smooth round shape and fill the body, pushing the kapok well down into the tail with a blunted pencil. Pin the head to the body, with the scalloped top of the body pinned to the middle of the head gusset edge. Sew them together with ladder stitch (Fig. 23) — that

is, one stitch in the head and one stitch in the body, pulling the thread together fairly tight. Push in any extra stuffing before closing the seam.

Work a row of yellow wool tufts all along the back on both sides of the seam and a ring of them on the top of his head. The tufts are made by threading a needle with a double strand of wool and then taking a stitch in the felt leaving an end. Take a second stitch across the first and draw the end of wool and the needle through the loop pulling it tight (Fig. 24). Cut off the ends.

Cut two strips of felt ¾ in. wide and the length of the body. Cut out notches in one long side of each and sew them along the length of the body so that the notched side touches the floor resembling feet.

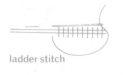

ladder stitch

Fig. 23

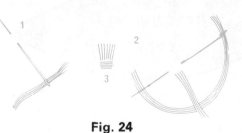

Fig. 24

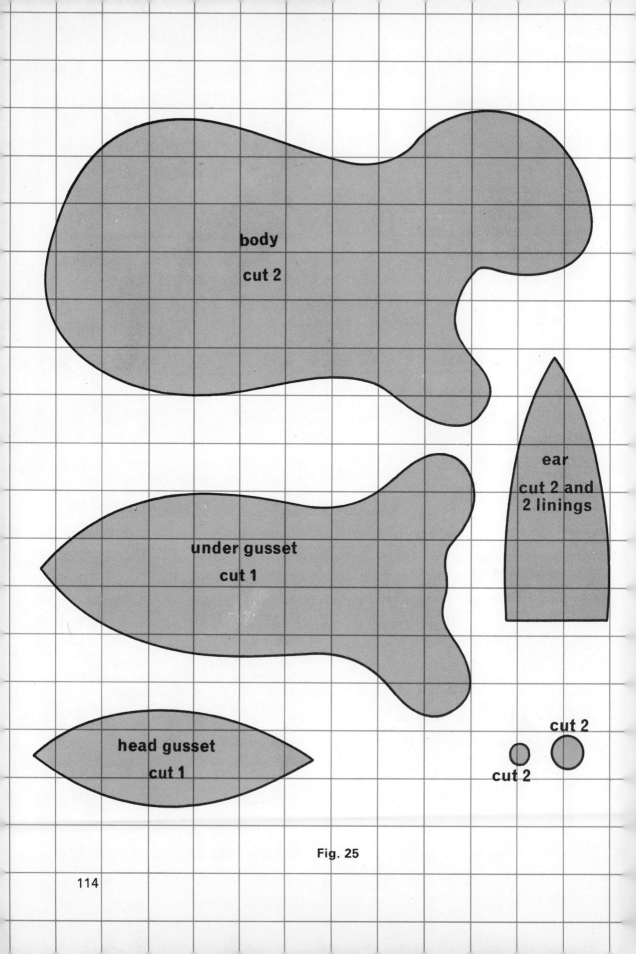

body
cut 2

ear
cut 2 and
2 linings

under gusset
cut 1

head gusset
cut 1

cut 2

cut 2

Fig. 25

114

A white rabbit

She is a pet rabbit sitting with one ear down and one ear up, listening and waiting for her little owner to bring her a crisp lettuce leaf. She has an under gusset to make her sit nicely and a head gusset to make the head rounder (Fig. 26).

You will need :
White fluffy man-made fibre 12 in. by 20 in.; pink felt for the ear linings; soft fluffy wool for the tail; kapok or similar stuffing; scraps of pink and black felt for eyes; a strand of black embroidery silk; some soft white wool.

The template is made from the silhouette of a sitting rabbit (Fig. 25). A line drawn from below the tail to the middle of the chest gives the shape of half the under gusset. The head gusset stretches from the point of the nose to the back of the neck. The widest part of this is not quite in the middle, so that it comes at the top of the head, is 2½ in. wide and tapers to a point at each end.

The ears are about 5½ in. long and are leaf shaped.

Trace the patterns on to thin card and trace round them on to the wrong side of the man-made fibre. Press down hard on the edges because the material stretches easily and will move about under the card unless held very firmly.

Cut two body pieces, one under gusset, one head gusset, two ears, out of the man-made fibre, two ears from the pink felt, two pink circles about ¾ in. in diameter, and two black ones slightly smaller for the eyes.

The sewing is done on the wrong side. Sew both pieces to the head gusset starting each time from the nose and stitching with

double oversewing, that is, taking two stitches into the same spot each time. Sew the under gusset to one side in the same way.

Pin the under gusset to the second side, but do not sew it.

Sew the front seam on the chest, from the nose to the gusset, and the back seam from gusset to gusset.

Take out the pins and turn the rabbit inside out. Sew in the under gusset as far as the paw. Use ladder stitch on this seam taking a stitch first in one side and then in the other.

Now fill the head with small pieces of stuffing, keeping it smooth and free from lumps, and a good shape. Continue sewing, stuffing as you go.

Sew a pink felt ear to the right side of a man-made fibre ear, leaving the straight side open. Turn it inside out and press out the seam. Repeat with the second ear. Fold the points into the centre and sew it on at the top of the head on the seam, using ladder stitch. Press one ear down as you sew it.

Sew the black felt circle on to the pink one and sew them on to the side of the head on the gusset seam.

Sew the nose and mouth in black embroidery thread in single chain stitch

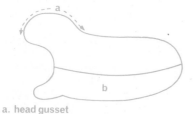

a. head gusset
b. under gusset

Fig. 26

Fig. 27

(Fig. 27). Sew a few whiskers on each side.
Lay a double strand of white wool along a piece of card 1 in. wide and wind the white wool round both card and strand of wool 30 to 40 times. Cut the loops of wool and tie round them tightly with the double strand over which they were wound. Trim the ends to make a fluffy ball and sew it on at the back where the under gusset ends.

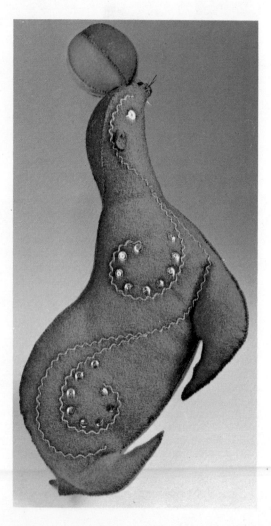

A circus sealion

Because he is a circus sealion doing his famous balancing act, he has to glitter and shine so he is embroidered with silks and sequins to give him this sparkle.

You will need :
Coloured felt ; stuffing ; embroidery silks ; sequins ; matching cotton ; some small scraps of felt for the ball.

The pattern (Fig. 28) is made from a silhouette drawing of a seal and a curving line drawn from mid-chest to just above the tail gives the shape of the under gusset, to include both pairs of flippers. This gusset must be fairly flat so that he will balance comfortably. A narrow gusset in the head from the top of the nose to the back of the neck makes his head rounder but still sleek. It is about 1 in. wide in the middle.

Trace from your templates on to the felt and cut out two side pieces, two under gussets, one upper gusset and two ears.

Embroider both side pieces, in a simple scroll design with a single line curving from the nose, over the eye down over the front flippers and up and over the flank. Two side scrolls curve, one up towards the shoulder and the second round towards the hind flippers.

To make such a design, trace the shape of the seal's side piece twice on thin tracing or tissue paper and draw the design in these shapes (Fig. 29). Pin them on to each side piece and work through the paper on to the felt with small running stitches in light coloured cotton. When the whole design has been transferred to the felt, tear away the paper.

Be sure to work the two side pieces for right and left sides. The actual working here is done in running stitch in golden yellow embroidery silk which is then threaded in and out with the same colour. Sequins in gold are sewn into the inner curves of the two scrolls. Sew gold sequins in place for the eyes.

Sew the head gusset on to each side piece starting each time from the nose ; sew the under gusset pieces together along curved seam on wrong side, then sew on to one side piece matching up the flippers ; the front neck seam from nose to under gusset and the back seam from the upper gusset to the tail end of the under gusset.

Stuff the head smoothly, not too hard, or

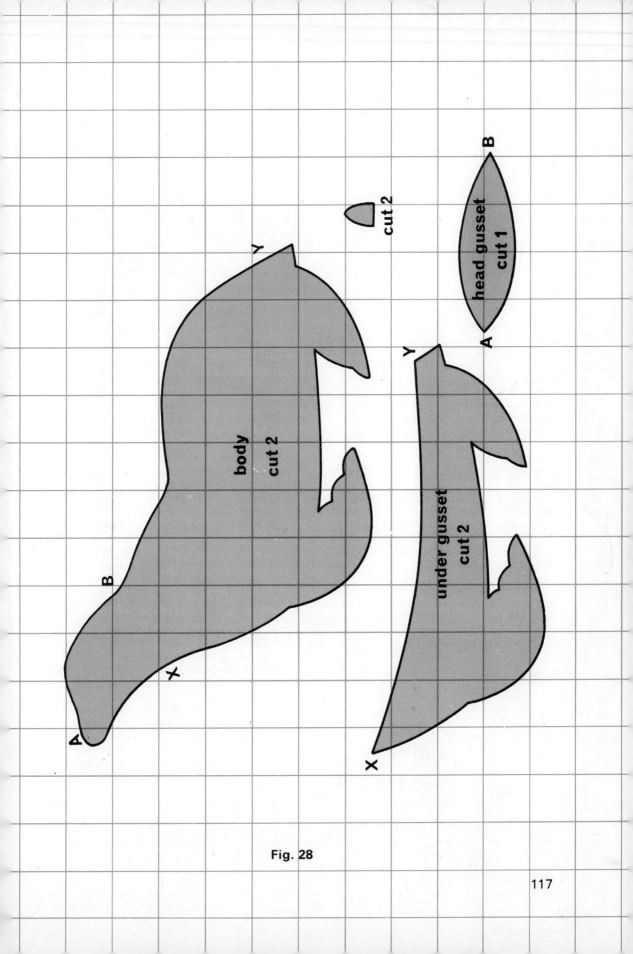

cut 2

B

head gusset
cut 1

A

Y

body
cut 2

B

X

A

Y

under gusset
cut 2

X

Fig. 28

117

Fig. 29

the sleek look will be lost, and stuff the two flippers which are sewn up.

Pin the under gusset to the second side and sew from the neck round the front flipper and fasten off the thread. Stuff this flipper and the neck, keeping it smooth.

Start sewing again at the tail end, and sew the seams of the back flipper. Stuff this flipper and the rest of the body.

Sew up the side seam.

Fold the points of the ears to the centre and sew the ears to the side of the head, keeping them flat to the head and pointing back.

Sew a single chain stitch in black each side of the nose for a nostril and sew in some whiskers in gold metal thread.

Cut six sections of felt, each a different colour, for the ball (Fig. 30). Each section measures 2½ in. by almost an inch. Join all the sections with oversewing, leaving the last two sides open for stuffing. Stuff firmly and not too hard and sew up the opening. Sew the ball to the top of his nose with invisible but strong stitches. Here he is, ready to perform for you.

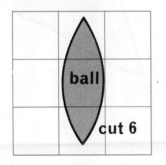

Fig. 30

The Three Bears

In chestnut-coloured felt with pinkish-coloured fronts, are a nice cuddly family to please any small child. Father Bear is twice as big as Baby Bear and half as big again as Mother Bear.

You will need :

A fairly large piece of chestnut-coloured felt, a 20 in. square should be big enough ; a smaller piece of the lighter colour felt for the fronts ; scraps of yellow and of black felt ; two or three strands of black embroidery silk ; chestnut-coloured cotton ; kapok or similar for stuffing ; a card template.

Trace off the three patterns on to thin card and cut them out. Each bear needs the same number of similarly shaped but different sized pieces to make it, and it is wise to cut out those bigger ones for Father Bear first (Figs. 31, 31a and 31b).

After the pieces are cut put them into plastic bags, label them and check all the pieces when you have finished cutting out. For each size you must cut two side pieces, a head gusset (Fig. 31), which is more shaped than the head gussets have been up to now, four ears from the chestnut felt, two under gusset pieces from the pinkish felt, two circles of yellow felt, two smaller black ones, and a black shield-shaped nose.

Sew the head gusset to both side pieces, the more shaped end of it being the face part. Sew each time from the nose. Join the two curved edges of the under gusset on to the wrong side and sew it to one of the side pieces matching up the paws. Sew together the nose and front neck seam as far as the beginning of the under gusset. Sew the back seam from the head gusset down to the tail end of the under gusset.

Fill the head, pushing stuffing well into the nose and cheek seams, but do not stuff too hard. Stuff the two paws which are sewn.

Pin the under gusset to the second side, matching the paws, and start sewing from under the chin and complete the first paw. Stuff the paw. Continue sewing, stuffing the body as you sew. Stuff the back paw, pushing in any extra stuffing needed in the body and sew up the opening.

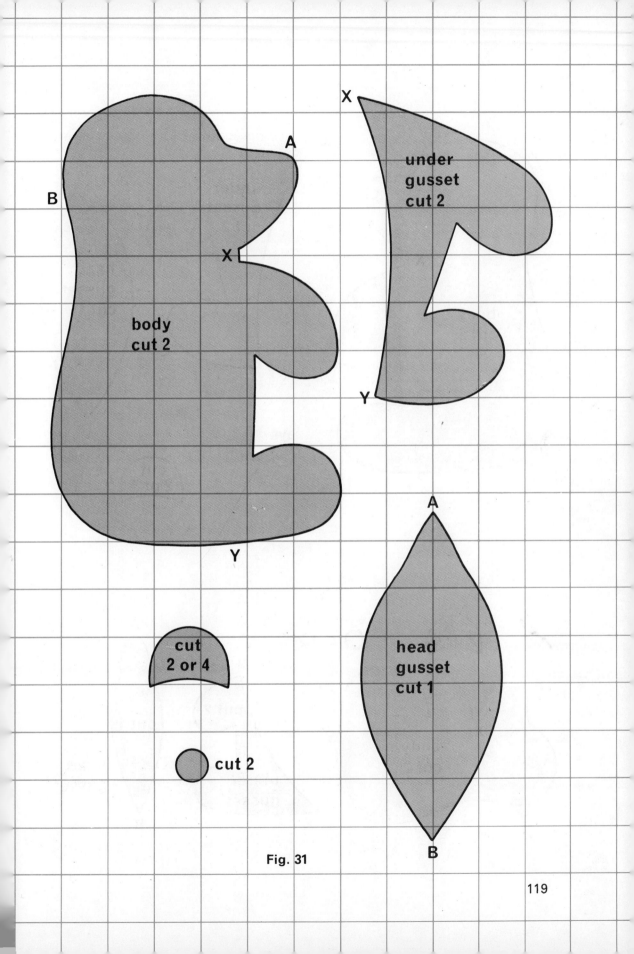

A

B

X

under
gusset
cut 2

Y

body
cut 2

X

Y

cut
2 or 4

cut 2

A

head
gusset
cut 1

B

Fig. 31

119

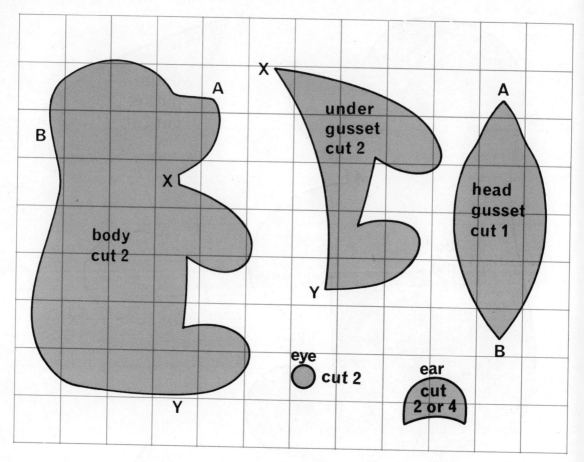

Fig. 31a

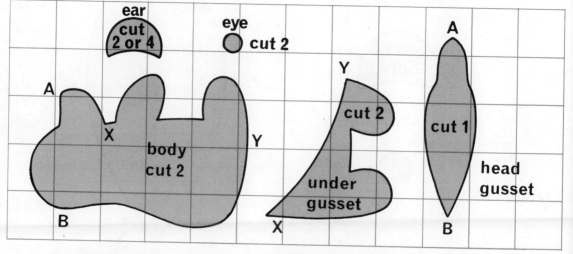

Fig. 31b

120

Sew together two ear pieces for each ear and sew them on to the side of the head in a horseshoe curve, the top edge of it on the head gusset seam. Use ladder stitch — taking a stitch in the ear and in the head alternately.

Sew a black circle on to a yellow circle for the eye, and sew it on the side of the face in a curve.

Sew the black nose in place and embroider two lines in black chain stitch curving away from the bottom of it, for the mouth.

Embroider black straight stitches on the outside of each paw for claws.

Each of the other bears is made up in the same way.

A baby sea-serpent

She is very colourful in her violet, blue and green, and her sharply-pointed rose pink ears which seem to be listening. She is pictured on p. 113.

You will need :
Violet-coloured felt for her two sides, a 12 in. square will be sufficient ; green felt for the under gusset ; royal blue felt for the head gusset ; bright pink felt for the ears ; orange, yellow and black felt pieces for eyes ; kapok or similar for stuffing ; sewing cotton ; black embroidery silk.

This, being an imaginary animal, can be as fanciful as you wish and the silhouette drawing for the pattern does not need to have a likeness to anything, but can be a combination of several animals.

Make a template in thin card (Fig. 32) for the shape of the side, and shape the under gusset as before, by drawing a curved line about ½ in. above the under body curve. The head gusset is more elaborately shaped to make an interesting head shape, the broad muzzle narrowing into a waist effect before swelling out into a rounded rather dome-shaped head. This is achieved by measuring the length needed — from the middle of the nose curve where the mouth would be — to the back of the neck, and marking three places — the widest part of the nose, the narrowest part of it, and the top of the head. Draw the gusset curve accordingly, tapering both ends to a point, a gradual one at the back of the neck and a sharper one over the nose (Fig. 33). The whole figure could be made rounder by continuing the gusset all along the back to taper off at the tail, but that could spoil the shape of the humps. Draw a long leaf shape for the ear, and three graduated circles for each eye, the largest about ¾ in. in diameter.

Cut two body pieces, two under and one top gusset, two ears in bright pink, two circles in orange, two smaller in yellow, and two smaller still in black felt.

Sew the black circles on top of the yellow ones and both on top of the orange ones, all to one side of the orange circle (Fig. 34), and sew them in place on the sides of the

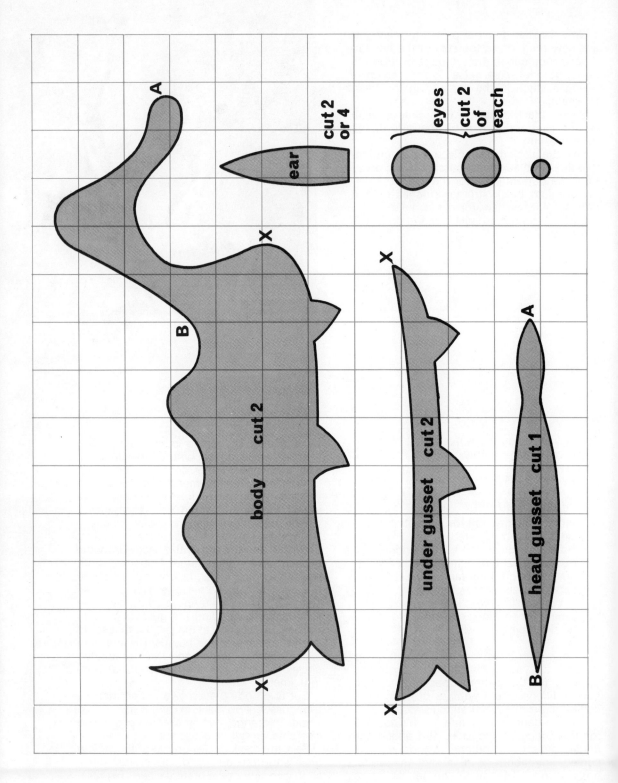

Fig. 32

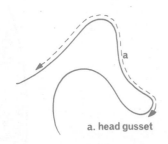

a. head gusset

Fig. 33

Fig. 34

head looking down towards the nose.

Sew the top gusset to the two sides, being very exact about matching up the curves. Sew two under gusset pieces together along curve on wrong side and sew one side to it.

Sew the seam under the nose and chin for about 1 in. and then stuff the nose very firmly, using small pieces to get a good shape. Continue sewing the seam an inch at a time, stuffing as you sew. It is important not to sew too much at a time. Stuff the flippers which are already sewn.

Sew the second side to the under gusset, stuffing the body as you sew and keeping it softer than the neck.

Fold the corners of the ears to the centre and sew them on top of the head on the gusset seam so that they stand upright.

Cut two wavy green felt strands and sew them on under the jaw for a beard.

Two single chain stitch nostrils in pink and some black embroidery silk whiskers complete the sea monster.

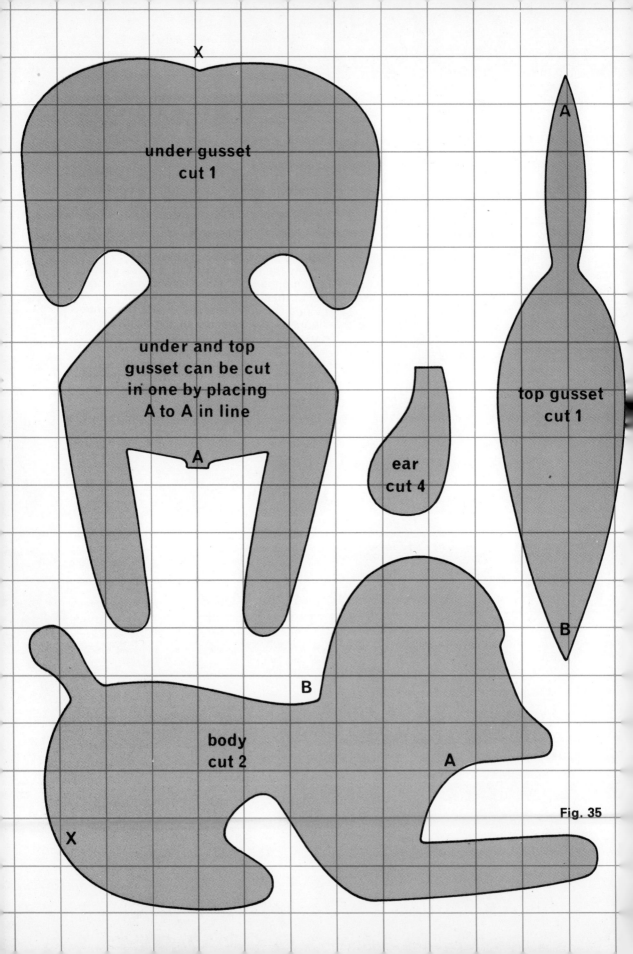

X

under gusset
cut 1

under and top
gusset can be cut
in one by placing
A to A in line

A

ear
cut 4

A

top gusset
cut 1

B

B

body
cut 2

A

X

Fig. 35

A sleepy poodle

He is relaxed, his nose droops down to his paws and his eyes are closed. Shh! His photograph is on p. 107.

You will need :

A piece of rose pink felt about 18 in. square; kapok; matching cotton; black embroidery silk; black felt for nose.

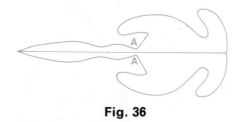

Fig. 36

The pattern is very similar to that of the sealion. His head is made rather more domed, to simulate the height of a topknot, and the shape of the legs has been simplified (Fig. 35). The side pieces are cut from a side view silhouette and the under gusset of the lower part from a line drawn across the middle of the side piece from just below the tail to below the chin. The tail is included in one with the body piece.

The head gusset is shaped to form a nose and narrow face, and stretches from the back of the neck to underneath the chin. Here it is joined to the under gusset (Fig. 36). It is a great advantage if the two gussets can be cut out in one piece avoiding the join under the chin. To do this, draw lines right through the centre of each gusset and lay them on the felt with the point A on the upper gusset joining point A on the under gusset and making sure that the two centre lines on them are in one continuous straight line. Cut out two body pieces, either one upper and one lower gusset, or one complete gusset, and four ears.

Pin the gusset to one side piece, matching paws, and nose, and oversew the seams.

Sew the back seam, over the tail, from one gusset to the other.

Stuff front and back legs which have been seamed, pushing kapok right into the corners but keeping them soft and not hard. Pin the gusset to the second side piece and sew, starting from the back of the neck over the head to the top of the chest.

Now stuff the head with small pieces of kapok, pushing it gently into the seams and particularly into the nose to make it firm but not hard, and keeping a good shape. Continue sewing round the front leg and stuff it too. Finish sewing the remainder of the gusset round the back leg, stuffing as you sew.

Sew two ear pieces together for each ear leaving the straight side open. Push a little kapok in to pad it softly, keeping a flattish look. Sew the straight edges to the gusset seam at the top of the head with the curved shape towards the nose.

Embroider a crescent-shaped line in chain stitch for each eye with a few straight stitches for lashes.

Cut a small shield shape in black felt and sew on the tip of the nose.

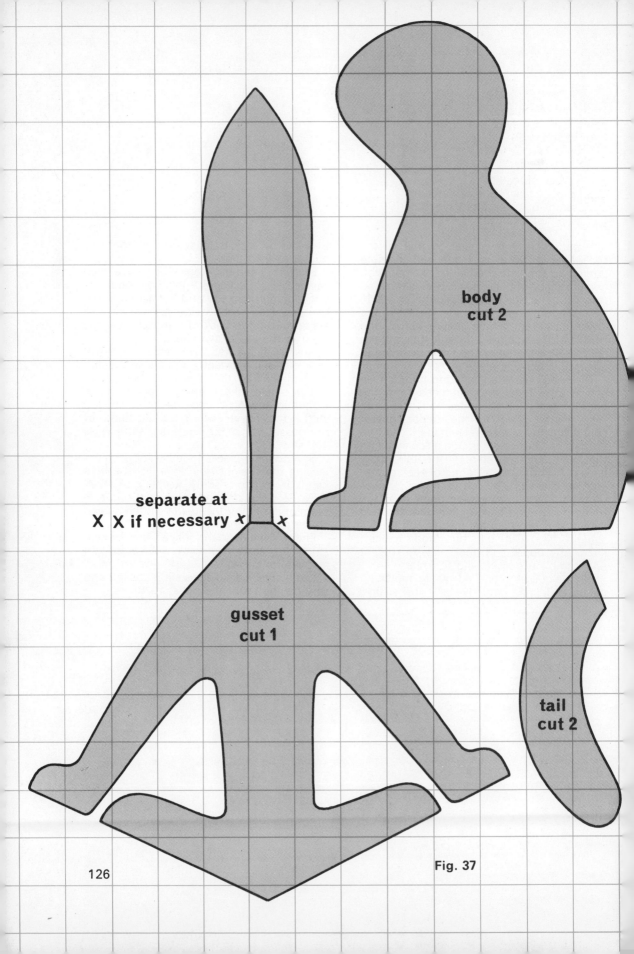

body
cut 2

separate at
X X if necessary

gusset
cut 1

tail
cut 2

126

Fig. 37

A sitting cat

Felt is suggested for making many of the toys because it is easy to cut, does not fray so needs no allowance for turnings, and being soft is easy to sew, so is especially good for children to sew.

The cat (Fig. 37) here is made in rose pink felt with green eyes, silver whiskers and a sequin 'jewelled' collar. She can be as big or as small as you like, according to how much you enlarge the pattern.

You will need :

Felt ; kapok ; embroidery silks ;
sequins ; silver metal thread ; cotton.

The main pattern is a side face or silhouette of a sitting cat with straight front legs. The tail is sewn in. If you are good at drawing, try a silhouette of your own cat, making the finished pattern to the size you want. On the drawing, mark the front neck, mouth, ear and back of neck. Draw the top gusset stretching from the front of the neck to the back of the neck in length, about 1 in. wide at the top of the head and pointed at each end.

The under gusset will be the shape of the front and back legs spread wide open. This shape is obtained by drawing a straight line from the chin to the tail. This pattern would be cut from the folded material, the straight line placed on the fold. If your material is long enough, cut the head gusset and the under gusset in one piece (Fig. 38), and so avoid the join under the chin. Your whole gusset will then look like the small drawing.

As well as the gusset, cut two body pieces and two ears (cut four if you want to make them double).

When using felt it is important to remember that pin and tacking marks sometimes show as dirty spots, so do any pinning or tacking as near to the edge as possible. Mark the position of ears, eyes and mouth with tacking stitches rather than with pins, which may fall out — do *not* use pencil.

With the right sides outside, pin the front feet of the gusset to the feet of the side pieces, and the back feet of the gusset to the back feet of the side pieces. Complete the pinning of the gusset from chin to tail on each side.

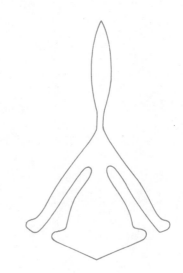

Fig. 38

Join them with oversewing or stab stitch.

Pin the head gusset to the sides of the head pieces, starting each time from the chin. Sew these seams, starting to sew each time from the chin.

Sew the two tail pieces together, stuffing it as you sew the second seam and leaving the short ends open. Stuff the front and back legs smoothly with small pieces of kapok, pushing it gently into the seams with a blunt pencil or small stick.

Stuff the head firmly, pushing stuffing well into the seams to keep the head a good shape. Keep looking at it from all angles to make sure of the shape.

Sew up the back seam starting at the neck and stuffing as you sew. Sew in the open ends of the tail with the last of the back seam and finish sewing the seam up to the under gusset.

Embroider the mouth and nose where marked and embroider slanting eyes on each gusset seam.

Make a small pleat in the straight edge of the ears and sew them on to the seams at the widest part of the head gusset.

Whiskers can be sewn in fine silver metal thread.

Embroider and sew sequins on to a narrow band of felt for a close fitting collar round her neck.

A sitting poodle

The pattern is based on the one for the sitting cat, with the following alterations. The head is higher and dome shaped, the face is curved in over the nose and under the chin to make a sharp little face. The front and back legs are shaped to make slender 'ankles', and a tail is added. The head gusset too, is more shaped, widening very gradually from the point at the nose, but still narrow in width, not more than ½ in. in the middle, and then broadening more to a width of 1¾ in. at the top of the head, and tapering to a point. The under body gusset starts at the base of the throat and ends just under the tail. The ears are almost circular at the bottom and 2¾ in. wide, narrowing to ½ in. at the top. When finished the poodle measures 12 in. The pattern (Fig. 39) is on page 130.

You will need :

A piece of white felt 15 in. by 24 in.; a strip of purple or bright coloured felt for a collar about ¾ in. by 4½ in.; some pearls, sequins, beads to ornament the collar; a dozen black sequins or two very big ones for the eyes; a scrap of black felt for a nose; some fluffy white nylon wool for the topknot, whiskers and tail; kapok for stuffing; white cotton for sewing.

Cut two side pieces, one head, one under and one tail gusset, four ears from the white felt.

Join the head gusset to the side pieces starting each time from the nose. Join one side piece to the under gusset, starting to sew from the chest, down the front seam of the front leg, round the foot and about 1 in. up the back of the front leg. Stuff the foot with *very* small pieces of kapok, pushing it in gently but very firmly so that it is quite hard without splitting the stitches. Continue to sew about an inch at a time and then stuff, keeping it smooth and firm all the way otherwise the legs will not stand firm but will bend. Continue sewing the side seam and along the back leg, sewing and stuffing as the front leg.

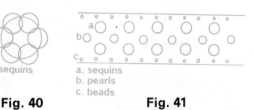

sequins

a. sequins
b. pearls
c. beads

Fig. 40   **Fig. 41**

Sew in the tail gusset, matching the sides exactly. Sew up the under part of the tail seam, between the two gussets. Stuff the tail smoothly and very firmly. Sew the top seam of the tail and stuff as you sew, keeping the tail as firm as possible. Continue sewing the back seam up to the head gusset.

Pin the second side to the under gusset, keeping all pins on the edges to avoid marks, and sew from the chest, round the leg, sewing and stuffing as before. Stuff the body pushing the stuffing well up into the neck and shoulders but not making it too hard. Sew the side seam, stuffing the body as well, and sew and stuff the back leg. Push in any extra stuffing needed before sewing the final length of seam.

Sew two ear pieces together for each ear, pad softly with a little stuffing and sew on to the seam at each side of the top of the head.

Sew loops of fluffy nylon wool on to the top of the head and cut the loops and trim the ends.

Sew on a shield-shaped piece of black felt for the nose and sew loops of nylon each side and trim them in shape for whiskers.

Cut a small circle round a coin and sew on six sequins overlapping in a ring (Fig. 40). Sew them on for eyes at each side of the gusset.

Sew nylon loops all over the ball of the tail and trim them short.

Sew a row of pearls down the middle of a purple felt strip for the collar, sew green sequins in a row each side of them, in the spaces, and a row of gold beads along each edge (Fig. 41). Sew it in place round her neck.

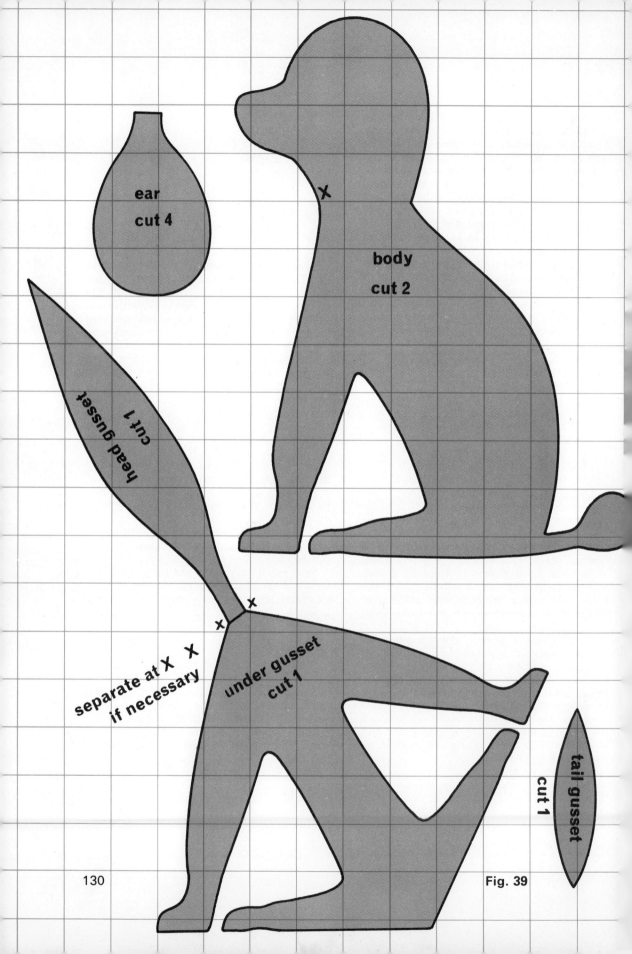

ear
cut 4

body
cut 2

head gusset
cut 1

separate at X X
if necessary

under gusset
cut 1

tail gusset
cut 1

130

Fig. 39

Kanga and little Roo

Kanga sits up very nicely and Roo makes himself comfortable in her pouch.

Roo is a rather flat shape made from two pieces, so that he fits easily into the pouch. Kanga has a head gusset and an under gusset which makes her a plump well-fed looking kangaroo. She is 12 in. high and her baby 2½ in.

The pattern for Kanga is Figs. 42 and 43. Roo's pattern is Fig. 45.

You will need :

A piece of felt 12 in. by 24 in.; some scraps of black and pink felt for eyes and nose; a strand of black embroidery silk; matching cotton; some kapok.

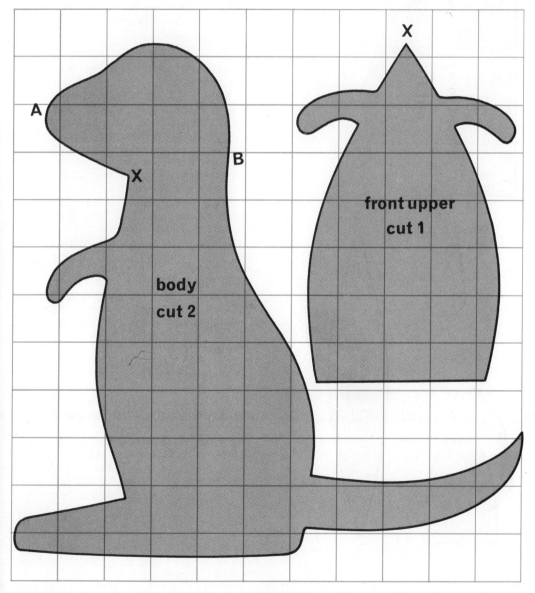

body
cut 2

front upper
cut 1

Fig. 42

Fig. 44

The under gusset is cut in two pieces, the lower part overlapping the top to form the pouch (Fig. 44). Trace the pieces from templates in thin card, which have been made from the pattern.

Cut two side pieces, one head gusset, one under gusset in two pieces, and four ear pieces, all from the large piece of felt; a shield-shaped nose and two small circles for eyes from the black felt.

Sew the head gusset in place on both side pieces from the nose to the back of the neck. Sew the top part of the under gusset to both side pieces matching up the little forearms. Sew the seam under the chin from nose to under gusset.

Stuff the head and the little forearms very firmly and stuff the forearms particularly with very small pieces of kapok, pushed in place gently with a blunted orange stick.

Pin the lower half of the under gusset in place matching up the hind legs, with the straight edge overlapping the upper half.

Start sewing from this edge over the upper part of the gusset seam and continue round the back leg for about 1 in. and then stuff it. Continue sewing the leg stuffing as you sew. Finish off at the back edge of the gusset. Repeat this with the second side of the lower gusset.

Sew the back seam starting from the back of the neck and sewing half way to the tail. Stuff the upper part of the body. Sew the rest of the back, and round the tail for about 1 in. Stuff this bit of tail and stuff the body. Continue sewing the tail about an inch at a time, stuffing very firmly. Push any extra stuffing needed in the body and sew the rest of the seam.

Sew together two ear pieces for each ear, fold the corners to the centre and sew them

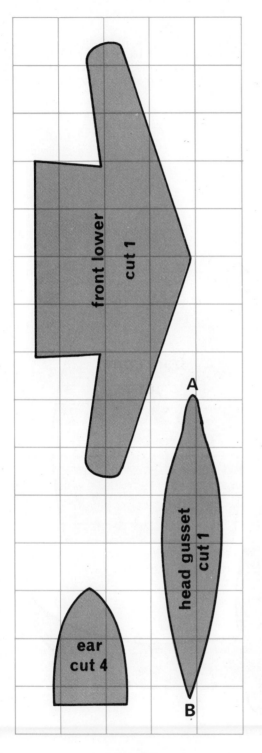

Fig. 43

front lower
cut 1

A

head gusset
cut 1

B

ear
cut 4

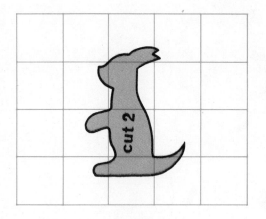

Fig. 45

in place on the seams at the top of the head with the folds outwards. Use ladder stitch for fixing them.

For the eyes, cut two pointed ovals in pink felt and sew circles of black in the centre of them and sew them on along the gusset seams.

Sew on a shield-shaped piece of black felt for her nose and embroider a curved mouth in stem stitch.

For Roo:

Trace round the template twice (Fig. 45) and sew the two pieces together starting at the ears, down the back and round the tail. Stuff the tail. Sew on round the hind leg and stuff; round the front leg and stuff; then the lower part of the body, keeping it flat rather than round. Sew to the top of the head and stuff then sew the rest of the ear, easing in the stuffing at the same time.

Embroider spots for the eyes and a little smiling mouth in stem stitch.

A penguin

He is smart in his traditional black and white with a brilliant orange flash above the eye, which is a shining black encircled with yellow. His beak is curved and down-pointing, the underside being yellow (Fig. 46).

You will need :

Black felt; white felt; small pieces of orange and yellow felt; a strand of yellow embroidery silk; kapok; a piece of firm wire for the feet; sewing cotton; two large or twelve small black sequins.

The pattern is more involved than any up to now, and the front gusset is quite a different shape. It is really the front half of the body and does not include the feet. The flippers have a ¼ in. extra allowance down the straight sides for insertion in the seams.

The pattern pieces are as follows :- the head, back and tail in one piece; the complete shape of the front; the flipper; eye patch; eye; head gusset; foot; two beak pieces, one the whole beak and the other the upper beak; and the triangular base. He stands 11 in. when finished.

Trace all the pattern pieces and cut them out in thin card. In black felt, cut out two back pieces, four flippers, two upper beaks and four feet. In white felt, cut out the complete front in one piece. Cut two orange flashes and two yellow whole beaks.

Sew the orange flashes on to each head piece with the point at the cheek and the rounded part curling up to the top of the head (Fig. 47). Sew the black felt eyes in place in the curve of the orange flashes. Work a ring of yellow chain or stem stitch round them.

eye flash

Fig. 47

134

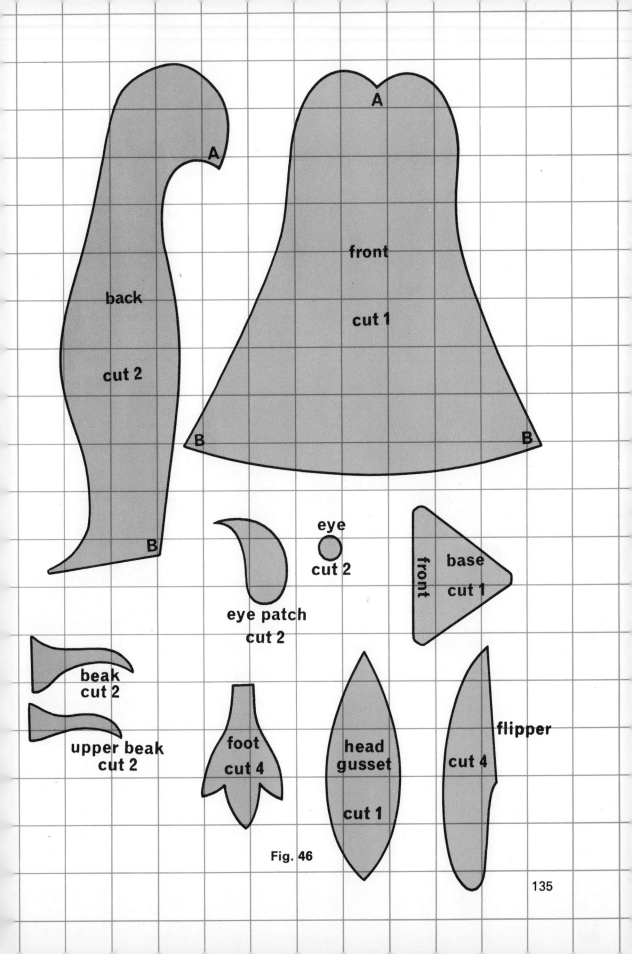

back

cut 2

A

B

front

cut 1

A

B

B

eye patch
cut 2

eye
cut 2

front
base
cut 1

beak
cut 2

upper beak
cut 2

foot
cut 4

head
gusset

cut 1

flipper

cut 4

Fig. 46

135

a. pipe cleaner chenille
wire shape for foot

Fig. 48

a. side seam

Fig. 49

Sew the head gusset on to the back pieces.

Sew together two flipper pieces for each flipper and push in a little stuffing to pad them softly. Pin them in place with the edge of the back piece pinned on to the small flap allowed for a turning, so that the flipper stands out from the back.

Twist each end of the wire into shape to fit into the feet, leaving the middle of it in a loop which will be buried in the body (Fig. 48). Sew together two feet shapes round the toes for each foot and push the wire in through the opening so that a 'toe' of wire fits into each felt toe. Push in some stuffing, keeping them fairly flat and sew up the rest of the side seams.

Pin the front gusset in place starting at the neck and taking great care to match the top curves, and keeping all pinning on the edge because of pin marks showing on the white felt.

Sew the gusset seams, sewing in the flippers as well (Fig. 49). Stuff the head firmly, keeping a good shape.

Sew down the back seam a little at a time, stuffing as you sew. When half way, pin the feet in position on the front, bending the feet at right angles at the toes and pinning at the top of the ankles. Continue sewing the back seam, and stuffing, packing the stuffing round the wire to bury it in the middle of the body. Push the stuffing gently but firmly into the point of the tail. Push in any extra stuffing needed to make the base firm.

Sew on the triangular base piece, starting with the front, stitching in the feet very firmly from both sides.

Sew the black and yellow beak pieces together. Sew the curved seams all round, stuffing when sewing the second curve, and making it very firm. Stuff firmly right up to the opening which should be kept open and should be oval in shape. Using ladder stitch sew the beak on to the face, yellow side down and keeping the oval shape at the end. Take care that the beak is held at right angles to the face all the time you are sewing, otherwise it may turn to one side or the other and spoil the effect.

He should stand quite well, balancing on feet and tail.

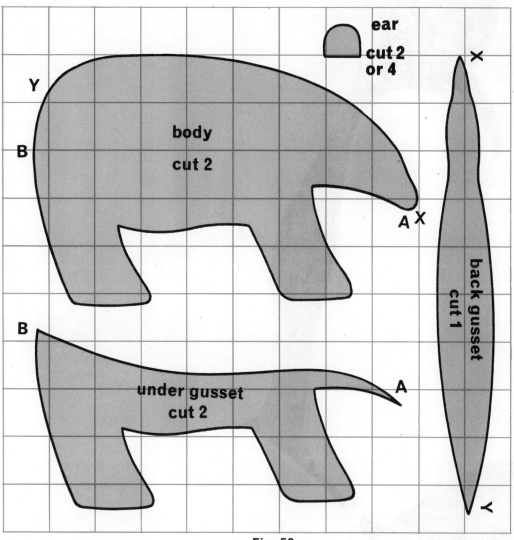

ear
cut 2
or 4

Y

B

body
cut 2

A X
X

back gusset
cut 1

B

under gusset
cut 2

A

Y

Fig. 50

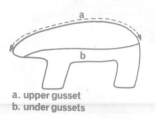

a. upper gusset
b. under gussets

Fig. 51

double oversewing

Fig. 52

A polar bear and her baby

You will need :

White fluffy man-made fibre or white felt which will give a good effect; some kapok or stuffing material; sewing cotton; a strand of black embroidery silk, or black cotton used double would do.

The pattern (Fig. 50) is made from a side view silhouette, the legs rather thick to simulate the thickness of fur. The under gusset is cut from the bottom half of the side shape, from a curving line drawn from under the tail and extended to a tapering point under the chin. The head gusset stretches from the top of the nose, is shaped for the face, its widest part being over the shoulders (Fig. 51).

Make templates in thin card and trace round them on to the wrong side of the man-made fibre, pressing down the edges of the card to keep the material in place, or the outline will waver and be distorted.

Cut two side pieces, two under gussets, two ears, the tail and one top gusset.

All sewing except for the final seam is done on the wrong side. Pin the top gusset to the two side pieces matching the curves, and sew the seams, using double over-sewing, that is, putting the needle twice into the same place (Fig. 52). Sew the two under gusset pieces together and pin to one side piece, matching feet, and sew it into place. Pin the second side in place, but sew only from the chin, round the front leg and fasten off. Then sew from the tail round the back leg leaving the middle seam between the two legs open.

Sew the short seam on the nose between the two gussets.

Turn it inside out and press the seams as flat as possible.

Stuff the head and legs fairly firmly but not too hard or the material will stretch out of shape. Stuff the rest of the body evenly, and sew up the remaining seam with ladder stitch.

Embroider the eyes in circles of straight stitch on the face just touching the gusset seams, and a nose. The mouth shape is in

Fig. 53

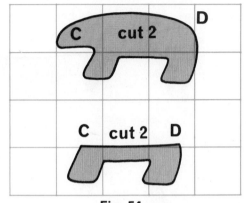

Fig. 54

single chain stitch as shown (Fig. 53). Eyes and nose can be cut from scraps of black felt or Vilene if wished.

Sew four or five straight stitches in black on the front of each foot for claws.

Sew two ear pieces together on wrong side round curved edge and turn right side out. Sew the straight edges of the ears on to the face near the gusset seam with ladder stitch, curving the edges into a horseshoe shape.

A rectangle of man-made fibre folded in half and seamed with one end turned under into a curve forms the tail, sewn on where the two gussets meet.

Her baby has an under gusset to make her stand, but has no top gusset, and needs only a small piece of material (Fig. 54). She measures just over 3 in.

Cut two side pieces, two under gussets, the tail and two ears.

Again sewing is done on the wrong side. Sew the joined gusset to both side pieces, leaving one middle seam open between the legs. Use double oversewing.

Turn it inside out and finish off like the big bear.

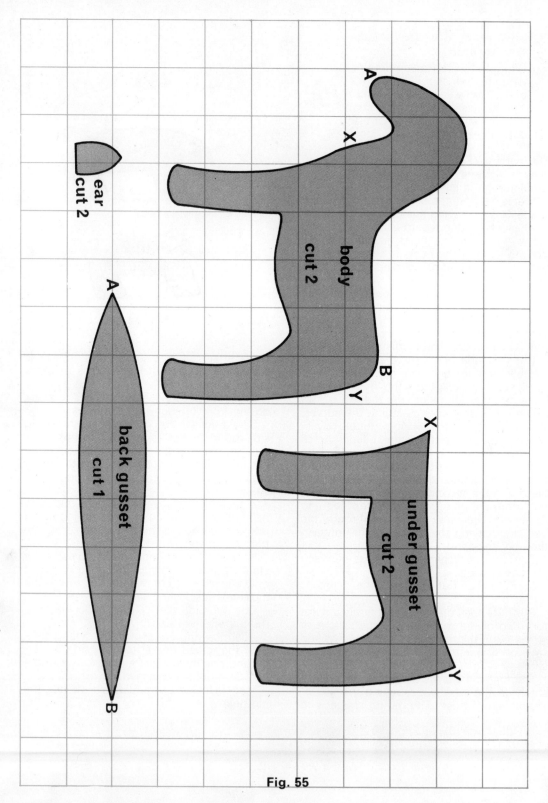

ear
cut 2

body
cut 2

back gusset
cut 1

under gusset
cut 2

Fig. 55

140

A little standing horse

He is made of pink felt with embroidered legs and trappings and stands just over 6 in. His mane and tail are of fringed black felt (Fig. 55).

You will need:

A piece of felt in the main colour measuring 8 in. by 16 in.; a small piece of black felt; an oval 2 in. by 3 in. for his saddle in a contrasting felt; some embroidery silks, including black; metal thread; sequins; kapok or similar for stuffing.

He has a long back gusset from nose to tail to give him a round back, and an under gusset to enable him to stand.

If you are making your own template, draw a silhouette with a straight front leg and a hind leg with a slight bend in it. On this side view draw a curved line from the middle of his chest to under the tail, the line following the curve under the body. The ear is a triangle shape with curved sides.

For the top gusset measure from just under the nose, over the head and back, to the tail, and cut the gusset this length tapering to a point at each end and about 1½ in. wide along the back (Fig. 56). The mane is a narrow double strip of black felt long enough to stretch from the forehead over the head down to the base of the neck.

Trace round the template on to the big piece of felt, with a very sharp pencil, reversing the templates for the second sides so that all pencil marks can be kept on the wrong side.

Cut two side pieces, two under gussets, two ears and one top gusset.

Do the embroidery before any sewing up.

For embroidering, draw a simple design on thin paper on to a traced outline of the sides of the horse.

Pin this to the body pieces and sew the design through the paper and felt with small running stitches in contrasting cotton. When the whole design has been sewn, carefully tear away the paper and embroider over the running stitches. If not wholly covered by the embroidery they can be pulled out. Be careful to work the pieces for right and left sides.

Sew the back gusset to both side pieces starting each time from the nose and working

a. upper gusset
b. under gusset

Fig. 56

141

Fig. 57

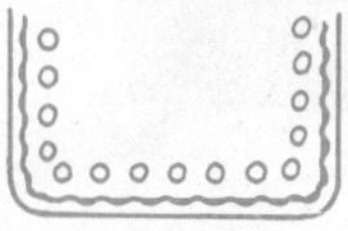

Fig. 58

on the right side. Sew the two under gussets together along the curved seam, on the wrong side, and sew it to one side of the body, matching feet and tops of legs. Sew the seam of the body pieces from the nose to the point of the under gusset.

Stuff the head smoothly, and the two legs already sewn, firmly. Pin the second side to the under gusset and sew round both legs, leaving the seam open between the legs. Stuff the two legs firmly especially at the top so that there are no weak places or the horse will not stand up. Stuff rest of the body evenly with small pieces of stuffing. Sew up the remaining seam.

Embroider an eye (Fig. 57) each side in stem stitch, with straight stitches for eye lashes, a single chain stitch for each nostril, and a mouth in stem stitch.

Fold the mane in half along its length and snip into a fringe. Sew it down on each side of the fold so that it will stand up on the head and neck. Use ladder stitch to sew it.

Cut a long narrow piece of black felt into a long fringe for a tail and sew it on where the two gussets meet.

Sew the ears on either side of the mane in a horseshoe shape so that they stand upright.

Embroider round the edge of the oval of felt for the saddle (Fig. 58). This one has an edge of pink running stitches threaded with silver metal thread and a row of pink sequins sewn inside it. Lay it over the back of the horse and attach it with tiny invisible stitches. The embroidery on the legs is a wavy line of threaded running stitch in turquoise silk (to match the saddle cloth) and inside one row of blanket stitch in silver metal thread. Bridle and reins could be added if desired.

A giraffe

He is tall with long slender legs. He is cut out in natural-coloured felt with chestnut-coloured markings. His colouring has been made with separate irregular diamond-shaped pieces sewn on to sides and back.

You will need :

Natural-coloured felt ; chestnut-coloured felt ; kapok or similar stuffing ; beige and chestnut-coloured sewing cotton ; black embroidery silk, or double black cotton ; light brown wool for tail.

The actual pattern pieces (Fig. 60) are not complicated — an upper gusset, shaped over the pointed head, narrowing for the long neck and broadening out over the back to taper to a point at the tail, and the usual under gusset of lower part of body and legs, cut from a curved line from tail to base of neck (Fig. 59).

Trace the shapes on to the felt very carefully, especially round the legs, holding the template firmly so that it does not move, and reversing the templates for the second pieces.

Cut two side pieces, two under gussets, two ears, and one back gusset from the beige or natural-coloured felt, and a number of ½ in. wide strips, cut into diamond

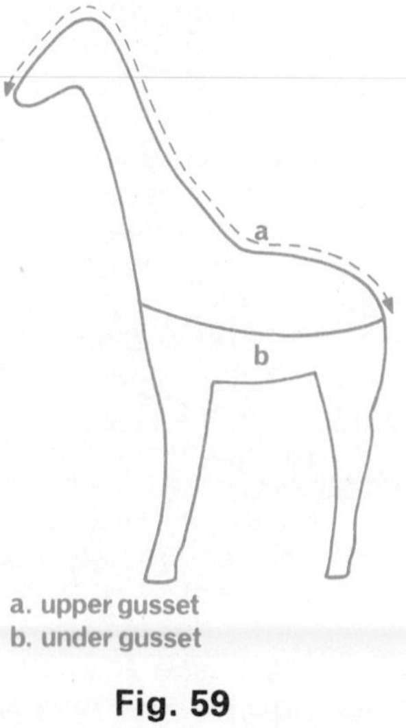

a. upper gusset
b. under gusset

Fig. 59

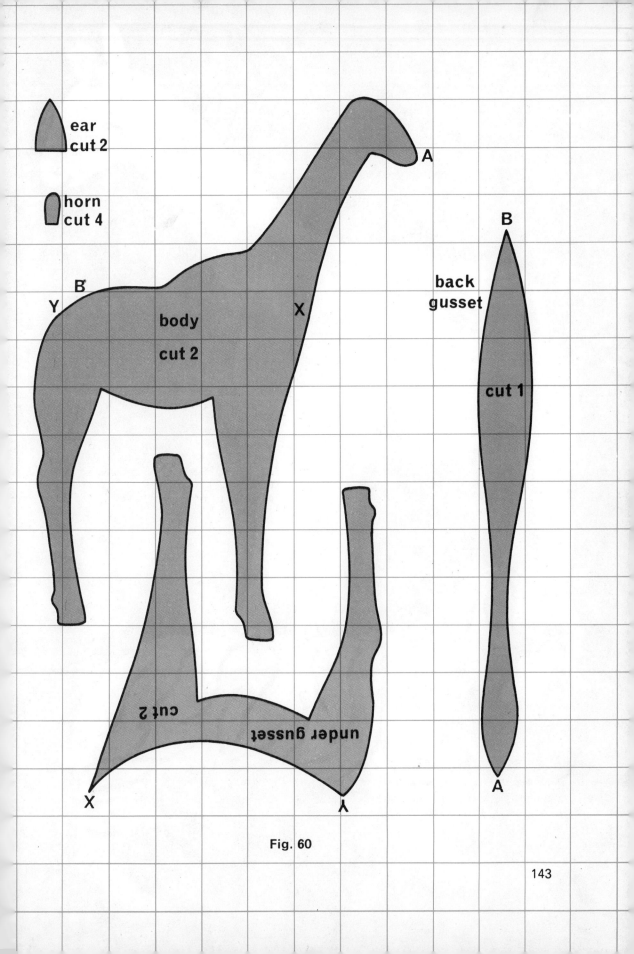

ear
cut 2

horn
cut 4

A

B

back
gusset

body

cut 2

cut 1

B

Y

X

cut 2

under gusset

X

Y

A

Fig. 60

143

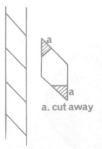

a. cut away

Fig. 61

shapes (Fig. 61), and four horn shapes from the chestnut felt. Cut the strips of felt diagonally and trim some of the corners off the pieces to make them irregular in shape.

Sew them in position in three rows, spaced apart, starting with a middle line of them from high on the neck, across the centre of the side and down the back leg. A row of them each side of this, one row across the body and down the front leg, and a second row down the front of the neck and the front of the front leg should be enough. Repeat this on the second side, reversing the side piece so that you have a pair.

Pin the back gusset in place carefully and sew it onto both sides with right sides outside. Stitch some chestnut shapes down the neck and back of the upper gusset taking one or two over the seams. Join the under gusset pieces along the curved seam, on the wrong side. Pin it to one of the side pieces, matching the feet. Start sewing from the neck down the leg and about 1 in. along the inner leg seam.

Because his legs are so slender, they must be stuffed very carefully or the shape will be spoiled. Stuff the leg with *very* small pieces of stuffing, pushing them down into corners and seams with a blunted orange stick, and making it as firm as possible without pulling the stitches. Continue sewing an inch at a time, stuffing as you sew. Continue with the hind leg in the same way. Sew the seam under the chin and about ½ in. down the neck. Stuff the head. Continue sewing the neck seam stuffing as you sew.

Make a short cord for the tail by twisting the doubled wool together, sew the ends to keep them in place and fringe them. Push the end under the point at the end of the top gusset and sew in securely.

Pin the second side to the gusset and sew round both legs, stuffing very carefully and very firmly, leaving the seam open between the legs. Stuff the rest of the body keeping it smooth but not so hard as the legs. Sew up the opening.

Fold the corners of the ears to the centre, and sew them on the sides of the head with ladder stitch so that they stand out at each side. Sew the curved seams of the two little horns, stuff them firmly and sew them on top of the head with ladder stitch, keeping them in an upright position as you sew.

Sew spots in satin stitch for eyes (Fig. 62), with straight stitches for the long eyelashes, and two nostrils and mouth in black embroidery silk.

Fig. 62

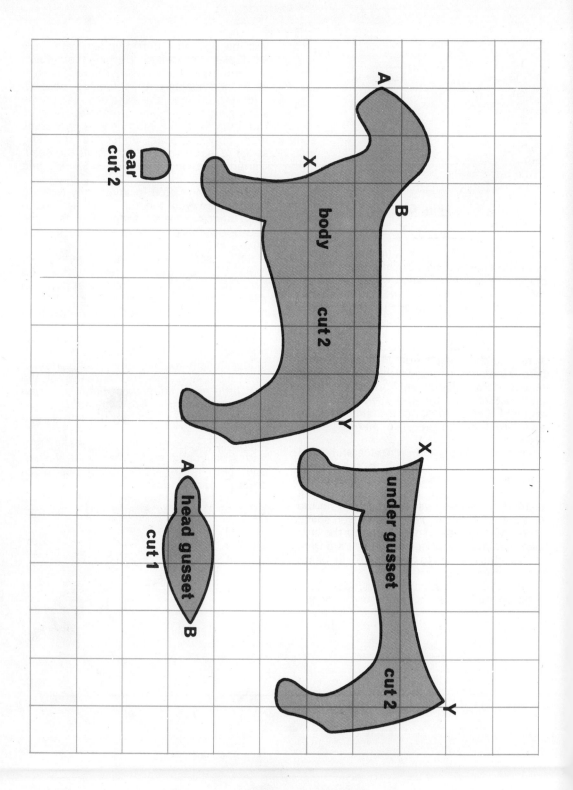

ear
cut 2

body
cut 2

A

X

B

Y

head gusset
cut 1

A

B

under gusset
cut 2

X

Y

Fig. 63

A tiger

You will need :

Orange felt; black and green embroidery silk; kapok for stuffing; orange and white cotton.

The template (Fig. 63) is similar to that of the horse. It is made from a silhouette of the tiger, with a small head gusset from the top of the nose to the back of the neck, cut to give a slightly oval shape to the top of the nose, and tapering to a point at the back of the neck. The under gusset consists of the front and back leg, the top being a curving line from the chest to the tail, following the under body curve.

Make the templates in thin card and trace round them on to the felt, reversing them for the second pieces.

Cut two body pieces, two under gussets, one head gusset and two ears, all in orange felt.

Embroider, using chain stitch, the two side pieces in wavy stripes from the back downwards, in black embroidery silk (Fig. 64). Pair them for left and right.

Join the two sides to the head gusset on the right side, starting each time from the nose with the more oval end, and matching the finishing point at the neck.

Embroider more lines on the top and back of the head gusset, extending them over the seams in some cases.

Join the curved sides of the under gusset on the wrong side, and sew one body side piece on to it starting from the neck. Sew down the front seam of the front leg, along the sole, and about 1 in. of the back seam.

Now stuff the foot very firmly with small pieces of kapok. Finish the leg seam and stuff the rest of the leg. Continue along the under body and sew the back leg in similar manner as the front leg.

Make a cord for a tail with orange cotton, and fringe the end. Pin it in position at the top of the gusset.

Sew the back seam between the two gussets. Sew the seam from the nose to the top of the neck, and stuff the head, pushing stuffing carefully into the seams and keeping the head a good shape.

Pin the under gusset to the second side, matching pinning points at the feet and the tops of the legs.

Sew and stuff the front leg, and then the back leg, leaving the middle of the body seam open for stuffing. Fill the rest of the body, pushing the stuffing well into the tops of the legs to keep them firm. Sew the tail in with the final seam.

The eyes are an open-ended single chain stitch in black embroidery silk with a green spot in the middle. Embroider in black stem stitch lines each side of the nose, down the nose at the end of the gusset, to within ⅜ in. of the bottom, then curl the line round to make the mouth (Fig. 65). Embroider white cotton loops for whiskers, cutting the loops to leave about ¾ in. of whisker.

Fold the corners of the ears to the middle and sew them on the side of the head, touching the head gusset at its widest point.

Fig. 64

nose embroidery

Fig. 65

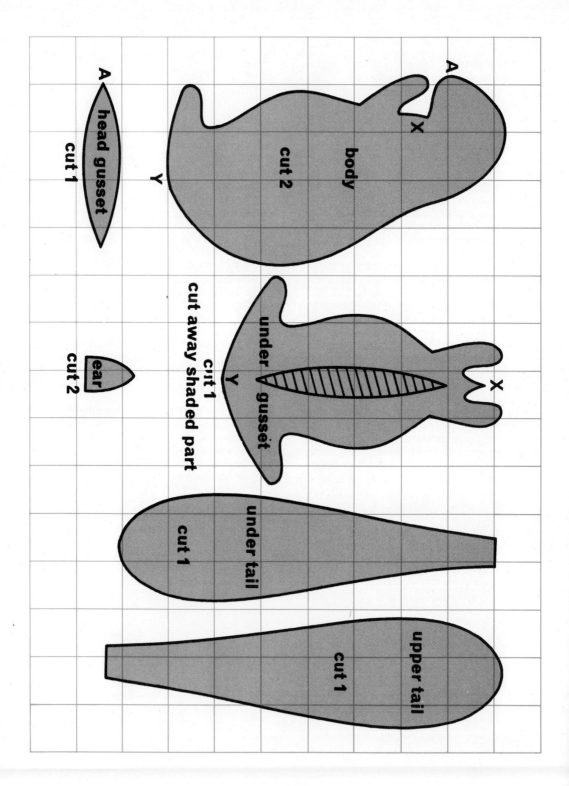

Fig. 66

The squirrel

In shape he very much resembles the kangaroo. See him on the colour plate facing p. 111.

You will need :

chestnut coloured felt ; chestnut coloured silky wool ; dark orange felt for the tail and nut ; kapok ; a strand of black embroidery silk ; matching chestnut coloured cotton.

The template is again cut from a silhouette drawing, and the under gusset has a curved line following the body line to give a more shaped gusset. The head gusset stretches from the nose to the back of the neck, is pointed at each end and almost 1 in. wide on the top of the head. The tail is cut in two parts, the outer piece a ¼ in. shorter to make it curl over (Fig. 66).

Cut two side pieces, one under gusset, one head gusset and two pointed ears from the chestnut-coloured felt.

Sew the head gusset to the two sides, starting each time from the nose. Sew the inner curved edges of the under gusset together on the wrong side. Sew under gusset to one side piece, matching legs. Sew the back seam between the gussets. Sew the front seam from the nose, under the chin as far as the gusset.

Stuff the head and the two sewn legs. Sew the second side to the under gusset, stuffing as you sew.

Embroider two biggish black spots, each surrounded with four straight stitches in a diamond shape, for eyes (Fig. 67).

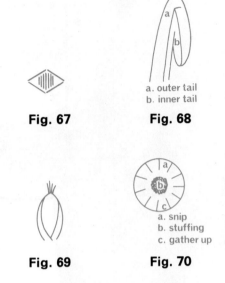

Fig. 67

Fig. 68

a. outer tail
b. inner tail

Fig. 69

Fig. 70

a. snip
b. stuffing
c. gather up

Sew loops of chestnut-coloured cotton for whiskers, and cut and trim them.

Sew together the curved sides of the tail, making a fold across the top so that the wider end curls over (Fig. 68). Stuff softly and evenly, keeping it flat. Sew it on at the base of the back so that the end curls outwards, away from the head. With cotton, sew loops of apricot-coloured wool all up the back and over the top of the curled part of the tail. Cut all the loops, and tease out the wool carefully for a fluffy effect.

Unravel a short length of wool and thread a needle with a single ply of it. Sew small tufts on the pointed ends of the ears (Fig. 69). Sew the ears on top of the head on the gusset seams, in a horseshoe shape so that they stand upright, with the curve towards the back.

Cut a small oval of orange felt and snip round the edges. Place a ball of stuffing in the centre, gather up the edges and draw up into a ball (Fig. 70). Sew it between the paws for a nut.

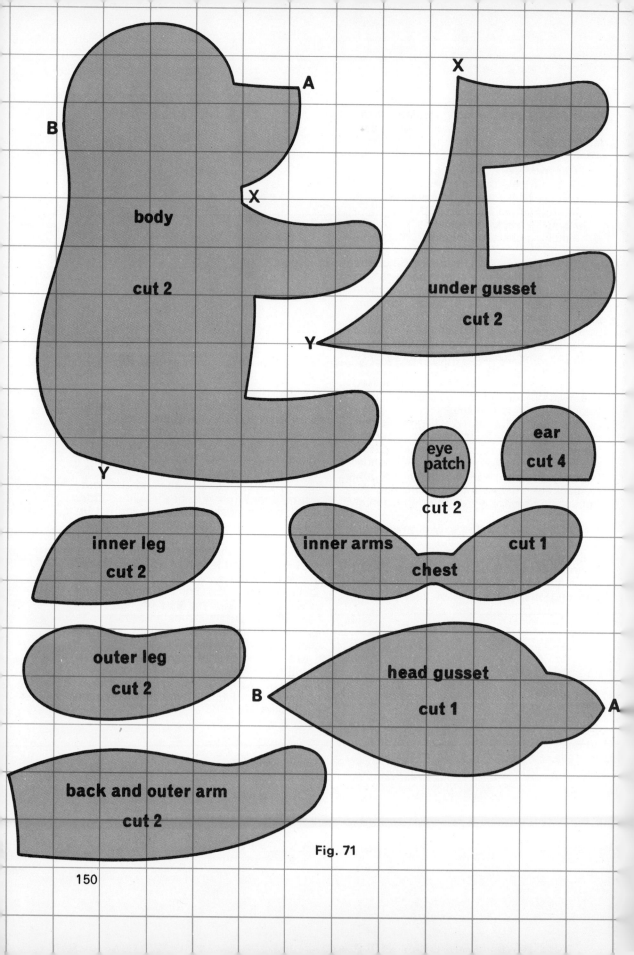

body

cut 2

A

B

X

X

Y

under gusset

cut 2

Y

eye patch

cut 2

ear

cut 4

inner leg

cut 2

inner arms

chest

cut 1

outer leg

cut 2

B

head gusset

cut 1

A

back and outer arm

cut 2

Fig. 71

150

The panda

The panda shape is very similar to that of the sitting three bears. She is made in white felt with black legs and features.

You will need :

Black, white and pale yellow felt; some kapok ; a strand of black and light brown embroidery silk ; black and white cotton.

The sides are a silhouette view of her, and the under gusset is made with a curved joining line to give a softer shape (Fig. 71). The head gusset stretches from the top of the nose and then widens sharply to give width to the face and head. It finishes in a point at the back of the neck. Separate templates are made for the legs. An outer forearm which extends right across the back to the centre join, an inner forearm which stretches across the chest in a narrow band and an outer and inner back leg. The eyes (Fig. 72) are a black circle, traced round a button, placed on a slightly larger pale yellow or beige circle, both placed on a large oval-shaped black piece. The ears are semi-circular in shape.

Cut the complete figure in white felt and sew the black limbs on to it, afterwards cutting away the surplus white felt. Or cut the head and body side pieces separately in several parts and join together by the outer arms, but these many seams weaken the toy.

Cut two side pieces, two under gussets, and one head gusset in white felt, and two outer forearms, two outer hind legs, one inner forearm (complete for both arms), two inner hind legs, two large eye ovals, two small circles, one shield shape nose piece, and four ears all from black felt.

Sewing is done on the right side. Sew both side pieces to the head gusset starting each time from the nose, and taking great care to match up at nose, eyes and back of neck. Sew up half of the back seam. Seam the straight edges of the forearm outer pieces. Pin them on over the white shape. Cut away most of the white arms level with the body. Pin on the outer hind legs and sew round the curve. Cut away the white legs. Sew the forearm pieces on to the shape. Sew the inner hind legs on to the gusset pieces, pairing them for left and right sides, and cut away the white legs level with the body. Sew the curved edges of the under gusset together on the wrong side. Sew the

black inner arms and chest piece to the right side of the gusset. Pin the under gusset to one side piece. Sew it on. Finish sewing the back up to the tail. Sew the front seam from the top gusset, under the chin as far as the under gusset.

Stuff the head and the sewn paws. Sew the second side front leg and stuff the leg and top part of the body. Sew the back leg and stuff it, and stuff the rest of the body. Sew up the opening.

Sew the small black circle into the centre of the pale coloured circle so that a rim of the pale colour surrounds the black one and sew them both on the bottom half of the black oval. Sew the ovals on the face, lapping them over on to the head gusset where it widens out sharply.

Sew the shield shape on to the front of the nose and embroider a short line down the seam from the bottom of the nose in close chain stitch. A curved line each side of it, also in chain stitch, forms a mouth.

Sew two ear pieces together round the curved edges and sew them on to the head at the widest part of the gusset, in a horse-shoe shape (Fig. 73), half on the gusset and half on the side piece.

Embroider claws in single chain stitch in light brown silk.

a. eye patch

Fig. 72

horseshoe curve of ear base

Fig. 73

CHAPTER EIGHT

All kinds of dolls

It is a very interesting hobby to make a collection of dolls from different kinds of materials and then to dress them in national costume of different countries.

Because felt does not fray, it needs no turnings; but if you make your doll in fabric, then you must allow ½ in. extra for turnings.

Dolls from felt

These dolls are easy to make because felt is so easy to work with. It is soft, and presents no difficulty in cutting, or sewing, and does not fray when it is cut, so no turnings are needed in its making up.

Felt is easy for children to use for dressing their dolls too – its colours are gay and very varied and when the dolls are small, like peg dolls, it is the most successful means of dressing them.

Things to remember
Be careful when pinning felt because pale colours do mark easily, and always pin as near to the edge as possible so that any marks will be hidden by the sewing.

When leaving unfinished work, always stick the needle in on the edge or in some stitching or embroidery already done.

When transferring designs for embroidering to felt, trace the design on to thin paper, place this in position for the embroidery and work running stitch in contrasting cotton through paper and felt, afterwards tearing away the paper. The stitching or embroidery will hide the running stitches, if they cannot be pulled out.

When tracing round templates as for instance, for a doll, use a sharply-pointed pencil and do not press down too heavily. You may find that the resulting outline is a smudgy thick line, so always trace on the wrong side of the material, and cut out the shape, if possible, inside the traced lines, otherwise seams may appear grubby and soiled.

Most of the dolls are sewn together on the right side, either with oversewing or stab stitch, which in appearance is rather like running stitch. Running stitch itself should not be used because when putting the needle in and out in one motion, the thickness of the felt will tend to stretch one side more than the other, resulting in a puckered finish. Stab stitch is sewn by inserting the needle at right angles from front to back, and then at right angles again from back to front. In this way, both edges of material are kept together, one not moving more than the other.

The simple doll
The template of it is all in one with arms and legs (Fig. 1).

You will need:
Felt; some soft stuffing material like kapok; embroidery silks; wool or silk for making hair; material for dressing.

There are two ways of sewing up felt dolls, either by oversewing or by stab stitch. If you are going to oversew, then trace round the template twice and cut out the pieces, cutting just inside the pencil lines.

Pin the two pieces together matching the heads, hands and feet, and then oversew, starting from the top of a leg, round the legs, arms and head, leaving one side open for stuffing.

If using stab stitch, fold the felt in half and trace one outline. Tack round the outside of the shape (Fig. 2), and stab stitch

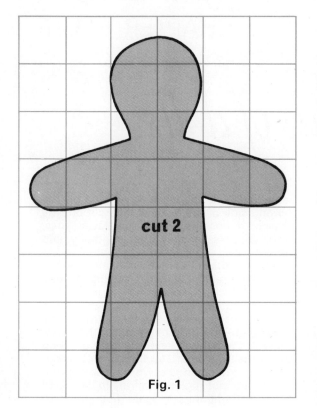

cut 2

Fig. 1

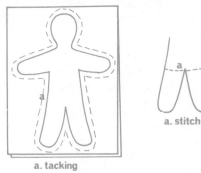

a. tacking

Fig. 2

a

a. stitch

Fig. 3

Fig. 4   Fig. 5

it together leaving one side open. When finished, trim off the surplus felt as close as possible to the stitching.

Legs

Stuff the legs first, pushing the stuffing gently into the feet with a blunted pencil or orange stick. Stuff thinly near the tops of the legs if you are going to make a jointed leg so that the doll can sit. To do this, sew a row of close stab stitch or backstitch across the tops of the legs (Fig. 3).

Head and arms

Stuff the head and arms, keeping the parts flat rather than round, otherwise the stitches may pull. Take care too, not to pull too hard on the corners of the opening or the felt may tear. Stuff the rest of the body and sew up the opening.

Features

Embroider the features with embroidery silks; felt-tip pens are not very successful on felt, because the hairy surface makes the outline smudgy.

Hair

Hair can be made in several ways — for straight hair, or braids, cut lengths of wool to reach from shoulder to shoulder over the head (Fig. 4). Spread them out over the back of the head and catch them down the centre with back stitch, like a parting. Bunch them together at the side and tie with bows, or braid the ends. Curls can be made by threading a darning needle with brown or yellow wool; take a stitch through the head on a previously marked hair line across the forehead, place a finger on the strand of wool close to the head and wind it two or three times round the finger. Slip the loops off and catch them down on the head with a couple of stitches through all the loops. Repeat this, sewing the loops close together all along the hairline, then filling in the rest of the head (Fig. 5). Separate the loops by ruffling the hand through them.

Dress

Make a little Spanish bib dress from a piece of material 4 in. by 10 in. using the directions for it on p. 162.

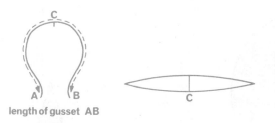

length of gusset AB

Fig. 6   **Fig. 7**

Small doll with head gusset

The pattern for the simple doll can be used for a little doll which has a much rounder head, by adding a gusset, from the neck one side to the other, and using oversewing to make it up.

Measure the length from the neck, over the head to the neck at the other side, and cut a gusset this length, pointed at each end and ½ in. wide at the widest part at the top of the head (Figs. 6 and 7).

Pin the gusset in place on one piece and oversew it in place. Pin the second side, matching points with the first side and oversew it. Make up the rest of the little doll like the other one, leaving an opening for stuffing and finishing it off in the same way.

Features

Features for it can be made from two small circles in blue felt, sewn on with straight stitches for eyelashes, and a small crescent shape for a smiling mouth.

Hair

Hair can be made in a fringe of felt. Cut a piece long enough to stretch across the forehead and about ¾ in. wide. Cut it into a fringe and sew it across the forehead. Cut two more strips long enough to encircle the back of the head from cheek to cheek. Cut both lengths in a fringe and sew one piece across the back of the head just above ear level and the other piece on the top of the head almost folded together so that the join makes a parting and the fringed side covers the top of the lower fringed piece.

Kewpie doll

A larger size flat felt doll has a slightly different shape. The arms stand out to the side and the hands are shaped with a suggestion of a thumb, like a Kewpie doll.

You will need :

Felt ; embroidery silks ; wool or silk for hair ; some kapok or other soft stuffing.

This one too can be sewn up either with stab stitch or oversewing. If stab stitching it, then fold the felt in half and trace the template (Fig. 8) once on to one half and tack the two pieces together round the outside of the shape. Do not cut off any of the surplus material until the sewing is completed.

Leave one side of the doll open for stuffing. Complete the stuffing and sewing up as for the other doll, remembering to keep it flat rather than round because it is only in two pieces.

Embroider features in coloured silks or wool, or cut shapes for eyes and mouth from felt, and sew on wool for hair.

Kewpie doll with head gusset

A doll with a rounder head can also be made from this same template out of pale flesh-coloured felt, by sewing in a gusset over the head from one side of the neck to the other.

Measure the distance and cut a strip of felt this length and about ¾ in. wide in the middle and tapering to a point at each end.

Sew the gusset to both of the head pieces, taking care to match starting and finishing points exactly. Sew up the rest of the doll, leaving an opening. Finish the stuffing and sewing up as before.

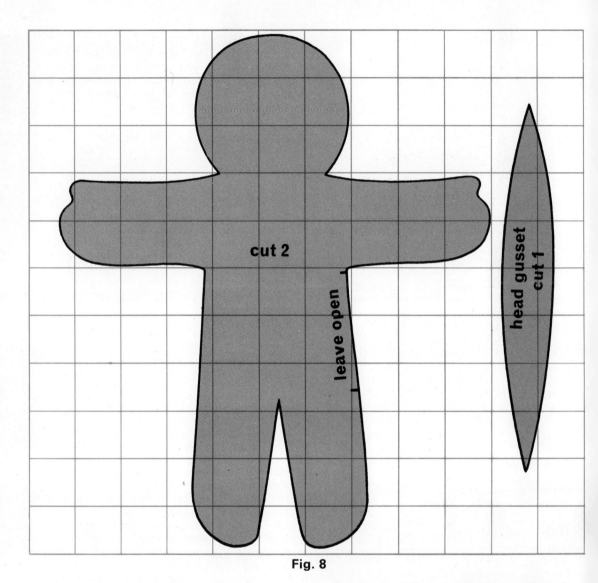

cut 2

leave open

head gusset cut 1

Fig. 8

Mexican peon doll

in the picture is made up and finished off exactly as the other dolls.

You will need :

Reddish brown felt for the doll ; black felt for trousers, red felt for waistcoat, soft white nylon or cambric for blouse ; tiny pearl buttons ; lace ; ribbon ; silver ricrac braid ; kapok ; natural-coloured raffia ; a medium crochet hook ; black embroidery silk and cotton.

Cut this blouse with very full sleeves gathered into the wrists, with a frill of narrow lace and tiny pearl buttons down the front.

To cut it, measure from the tip of one hand to the other, and from the top of the shoulder to below the waist, and fold a piece of cambric to these measurements (Fig. 9). Measure from side to side of the waist and allow an extra inch for turnings and cut out the triangle from each lower corner (Fig. 10), the fold of the material being at the top. Turn it inside out and sew the seams and gather up the wrists with a narrow turning. Cut down the front from neck to hem and sew lace and buttons down one side — make a turning at neck and hem.

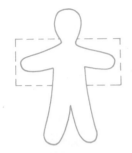

Fig. 9

fold

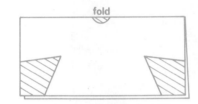

cut away all shaded parts

Fig. 10

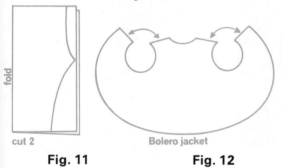

fold

cut 2

Fig. 11

Bolero jacket

Fig. 12

The trousers

Measure from waist to foot for length and all round the waist for width, allowing extra for turnings if not using felt. Cut two pieces (Fig. 11). Sew the two leg seams, then sew the seam joining the two fronts and backs from the waist in front to the waist at the back. Make small turnings on the legs and waist. Finish off round the waist with a narrow fringed ribbon sash.

Waistcoat jacket

(Fig. 12)
Make this in red felt with a curved front, buttonholed round the edges and with stripes of silver ricrac braid sewn across the fronts.

Features

His features are worked in black embroidery silk, eyes narrow and rather slit-like, and three or four strands to make a drooping thin moustache. His hair is worked with thick black embroidery cotton in long and short straight stitches.

Hat

His pointed wide brimmed hat is crocheted from natural coloured raffia, starting with the brim, making a big ring of chain, and working double crochet into every stitch without decreasing until about ¾ in., then decreasing until it fits his head. Decrease very gradually for the crown until very few stitches are left. Sew them all together.

157

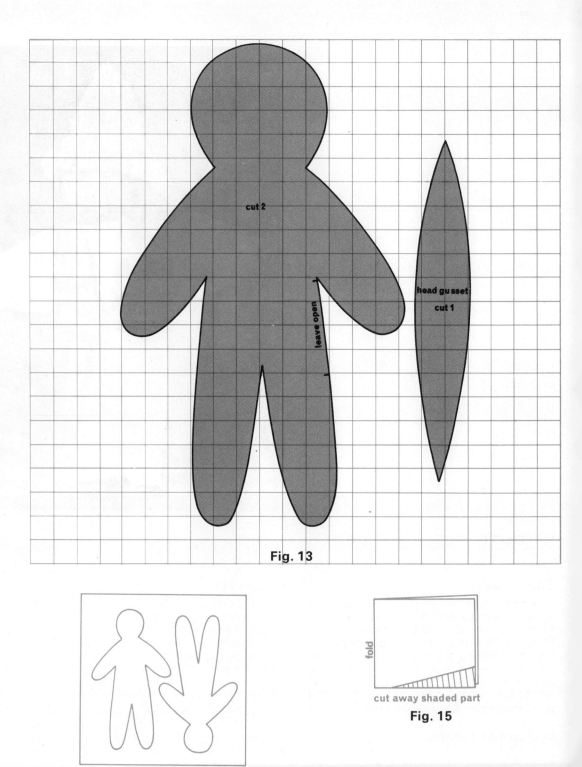

cut 2

leave open

head gusset

cut 1

Fig. 13

24 in. square

Fig. 14

fold

cut away shaded part

Fig. 15

158

Two larger dolls

Here are two larger felt dolls. Both can be made in two pieces rather flat, or with their heads rounder and more plump by inserting a gusset from one side of the neck over the head to the other side.

Little girl doll

The first doll (Fig. 13) is a more natural little girl shape with the arms pointing down to the sides. When finished she is about 20 in. high. Cut the head gusset as in the other dolls with head gussets, but make this one about 1¾ in. to 2 in. wide in the middle. (Vary the width of the gusset according to the size of the doll).

Sew the doll in the same way as for the little ones, which were given in detail.

Be careful not to stuff the doll too hard if not inserting a gusset, or all the seams at the edges will pucker.

You will need :

A 24 in. square of felt in natural or flesh colour to cut the doll, fitting in the template by turning it upside down and reversing it for the second piece (Fig. 14).

The gusset if used, will fit in over the pieces if you place them near the edge of the felt.

As she is a bigger doll, her clothes can be made to take off and on, so that she can have a change of wardrobe. You will find too that the first size knitting patterns for baby clothes will also fit her.

Doll's clothes

For panties you will need : a piece of cotton material 7 in. by 8½ in.

Fold it in half lengthwise and then in half across the width, so that the long fold is at the left side and the other fold in front of you (Fig. 15). Cut off the corner as shown, open it out and seam the two sides. Make a half inch hem at the top and insert elastic. Make narrow hems on the legs, and add a frill of lace or embroidery.

Another shape of knickers can be made by folding the material (Fig. 16) and cutting up the long fold for ½ in. to ¾ in. Then sew the side seams and the inner leg seams and finish off in the same way as for the panties.

The dress

A dress with a gathered skirt and a belt or sash round the waist can be made from any cotton, gingham or silk material. The bodice is cut from two pieces of material one 6½ in.

by 6 in. for the front, and 8½ in. by 6 in. for the two backs.

Fold both pieces in half lengthwise and cut out the neck and armholes (Fig. 17). The wide neck line in the piece for the backs is to allow for turnings on the back opening. Cut down the fold in the back.

Sew the side and shoulder seams. Make a turning on the neck and bind it with bias binding. Turn in 1 in. on each back fastening. Make a small turning on the armholes and sew a frill of ribbon or lace round each one.

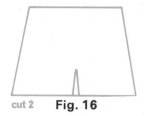

cut 2   **Fig. 16**

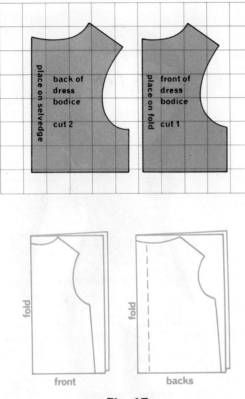

Fig. 17

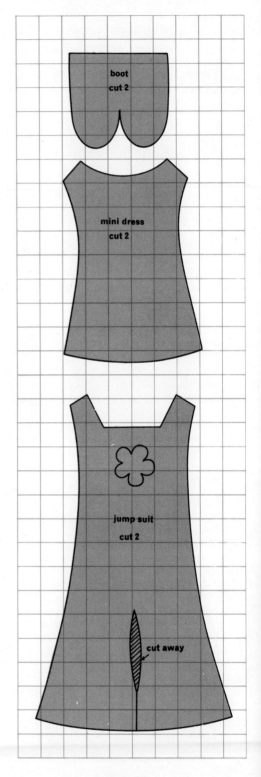

Skirt

The skirt is a straight strip of the same material cut to the length you wish, measuring from the waist and allowing extra for turnings and about 24 in. to 30 in. wide.

Join the seam (which will be at the back) leaving a quarter of it open. Make a hem along the bottom edge and embroider it with a decorative running stitch, or sew on braid or coloured tape.

Gather or pleat the other edge to fit the waist of the bodice and sew them together.

Sew press studs at neck, waist and the middle of the back opening.

Finish off the waist with a tie belt of the material or coloured binding or ribbon.

Boots, mini dress and jumpsuit

Patterns for these are given in Fig. 18.

Fig. 18

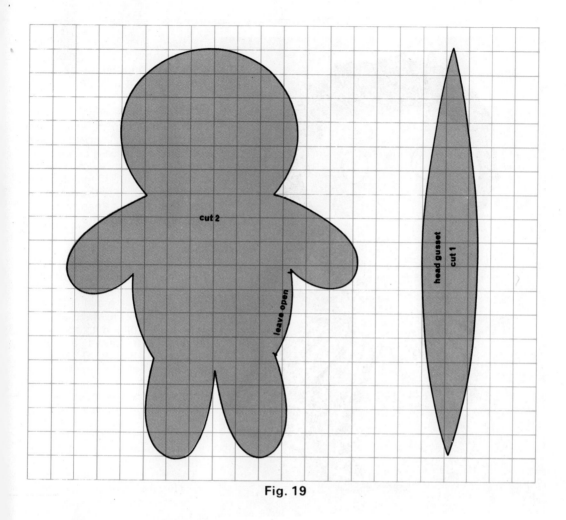

cut 2

leave open

head gusset
cut 1

Fig. 19

Baby doll

The second doll (Fig. 19) with its short fat little body and large head makes a very good baby doll. It too, can be made in two pieces and flat, or have a gusset inserted in the head to make it rounder. It looks better with the gusset, but be careful not to make the gusset too wide in the middle because of size of the the head.

Features

When embroidering the features, set them in the lower half of the face to give it a real baby look. Make its hair in soft fair or brown curls (Fig. 20). Thread a needle with the wool, take a stitch on the previously marked hair line along the forehead, place a finger close to it and wind the wool round it three or four times. Sew all the loops together to

Fig. 20

the head, and continue making and sewing loops fairly close together all along the forehead and over the rest of the head.

Clothes

Little panties can be made from the previous doll's pattern and you can make an easy Spanish bib dress for her from a straight strip of material about 30 in. wide, the length according to the measurement from neck to knee plus turnings, about 2½ in. extra.

Spanish bib dress

Fold the material in four and make a crescent-shaped cut from the folded side, curving up to the neck. This will make little cap sleeves (Fig. 21). Make an inch wide hem along the top with a heading and thread a ribbon through it (Fig. 21a). Make a similar hem on the bottom edge but without the heading, and embroider it or bind it with a contrasting colour of bias binding. Either sew blanket stitch embroidery round the armhole edges or bind them with similar bias binding.

The bib can be made into a dress by sewing up the back seam as far as the top hem, leaving that open.

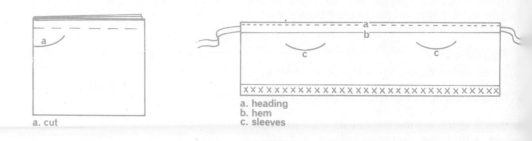

a. cut

a. heading
b. hem
c. sleeves

Fig. 21

Fig. 21a

Sock dolls

Jack and Jill

Jack and Jill here have been made from a very small pair of socks, the smallest size obtainable. You can make a sock doll from an old sock, which should be a white or pale-coloured one (it could be dyed pale pink) and it must not have any darns or holes in the back of the heel because this will be the doll's face.

You will need :

A sock ; some kapok or other soft stuffing (cut up old nylon stockings very fine) ; some wool to make the hair ; embroidery silks ; cotton for sewing ; some pieces of felt or fabric and white lawn for clothes.

Cut off the toe of the sock across the instep (Fig. 22) and fold the sock so that the back of the heel is on top and the cut instep at the back. See that it is folded evenly, and then cut up the middle of the ribbed welt to make legs (Fig. 23). Turn it inside out and backstitch round the legs (Fig. 24). Turn it right side out.

Stuff the legs smoothly and backstitch across the tops of the legs to give some movement and enable the doll to sit. Stuff the body and tie a thread around the neck. To make the neck and head firmer, fold a pipe cleaner in half and twist it a little and enclose this in a little stuffing in the neck so that half of it is in the body and half in the head (Fig. 25). Be sure that it is entirely enclosed in stuffing. Stuff the head very

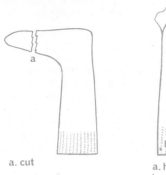

a. cut

Fig. 22

a. heel
b. welt
c. cut

Fig. 23

a. wrong side
b. cut

Fig. 24

a. pipe cleaner

Fig. 25

163

a

a. toe cut to make arms   back view

Fig. 26   **Fig. 27**

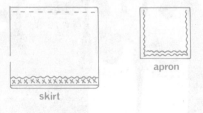

skirt

apron

Fig. 28   **Fig. 29**

bolero

Fig. 30

a

a. fold

hat

Fig. 31

firmly and gather up the cut ends of the instep and sew them down at the back of head.

For arms, cut the toe pieces in half lengthwise, turn them inside out and backstitch (Fig. 26). Turn right side out, stuff them, not too hard at the top, and sew them on across the shoulders.

Both boy and girl dolls are made in the same way.

Features

Embroider the features with embroidery silks or cotton. Drawing or painting them on the sock fabric is not very successful because the result is generally smudgy.

Hair

Jill's hair is yellow wool. A fringe of straight stitches is sewn on the forehead (Fig. 27). For her braids, cut ten or twelve strands of wool long enough to reach from her waist at one side, over the top of her head to her waist at the other side. Lay these across the head and sew down the middle parting with back stitch. Braid them to fall each side of the face.

Dress

She is dressed in felt; her apron, embroidered jacket and cap giving her an Austrian or Swiss look.

The skirt is a straight piece of felt, embroidered at the hem and gathered round the waist (Fig. 28).

A small rectangle of contrasting coloured felt makes the apron, embroidered at the bottom and sides and sewn over the skirt at the waist (Fig. 29).

Little gathered white sleeves made from straight strips of white lawn are sewn on at the shoulders.

Jacket

The jacket or bolero is cut in one piece of black felt, embroidered in a scroll design on front and back and joined at the shoulders (Fig. 30). The cap is an oblong of felt, folded in half to fit round the head, and the two sides oversewn (Fig. 31). Sew it on the head round the edge with crossed oversewing in a contrasting silk.

cut away shaded part

shoe back   front

Fig. 32

Fig. 34

stitching for boy's hair

Fig. 33

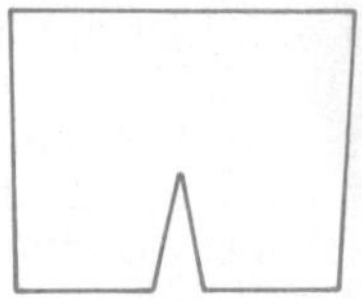

Fig. 35

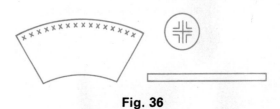

Fig. 36

Shoes

Her strap shoes are cut in two pieces for back and front. Cut four pieces — draw a shape round the flattened foot — and cut out the centres of two of them (Fig. 32). Sew the curved edges together, pull on over the foot and sew on round the top.

Hair

Jack's hair is embroidered in brown wool in long and short stitches each side of a parting (Fig. 33). The second row stitches are all the same length, joining with, and if necessary overlapping the first row. Continue in this way until the head is covered.

Trousers

His trousers are cut in two pieces, the front with a bib (Fig. 34) and the back to the waist (Fig. 35). Sew a contrasting patch pocket to the front of each leg and embroider the bib in a simple design. Oversew the side seams and inside leg seams with contrasting silk and oversew the edges of the trouser legs. Sew them on to the doll round the waist. Cut two strips of felt matching the pockets, long enough to reach from the waist in front, over the shoulder and crossing the back to the trousers waist. Embroider the strips and sew them on.

Pail

The pail is made from a shaped piece of felt, embroidered along the top edge, and on the circle of felt for the bottom (Fig. 36). Oversew the side seams, sew the circle to the base, and sew a strip at each side for a handle. Fasten it to the boy's hand with invisible stitches.

165

Fabric dolls

All of the patterns used for the felt dolls can be used for dolls made from fabrics such as calico, poplin, gingham or any other firmly-woven material.

They can also be made from used material. Make quite sure that you use only the best and strongest parts, discarding anything which is thin or worn, or your finished doll will not last for very long, which would be a great pity after you had put so much work into it.

Trace round the templates on to the wrong side of the material, folded in half, and tack the shapes together outside the pencil edge.

Machine stitch or back stitch firmly all round the pencil line, leaving one side open for stuffing.

Trim off all surplus material and cut out small 'v's in all curved edges and snip into all corners, at neck, under arms and legs, as close as possible to the stitching, but without cutting it (Fig. 37). If in doubt about the strength of the stitching at these points, do a second row touching the first or almost on top of it. Do not leave a space between the rows or the edge on the right side will be pulled too tight and will pucker. Turn the stitched and trimmed shape inside out, and press the edges flat.

Stuffing and make up is the same as for the felt dolls.

A more flexible arm movement can be obtained if the arms near the shoulders are stuffed sparingly and a line of back stitching worked across the shoulders to give the same kind of arm movement as in the legs when this is done (Fig. 38). A variation can

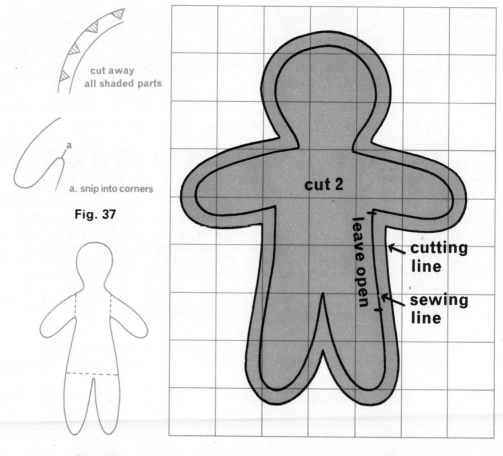

cut away
all shaded parts

a. snip into corners

Fig. 37

Fig. 38

cut 2

leave open

← cutting
line

← sewing
line

Fig. 39

also be made in the pattern to give a doll with more flexible arms, by cutting the arms separately and making them up and stuffing them — keeping stuffing thin at the open ends — and sewing them on across the shoulders so that they hang loosely at the side of the doll.

Small doll

This little one made in pale pink poplin can be made in just two pieces for a very easy and quickly made doll. Or she can have a head gusset just like the big dolls, but because of her size, the very small corners of the head gusset need very careful manipulating. Because the doll is so small too, it is easier to sew by hand than by machine. (Template Fig. 39).

If you are machining, allow generous turnings and tack the pieces together *very* firmly outside the pencilled line. If sewing by hand, use a small backstitch or double running stitch, which is done by doing a second row of running stitch over the first one, in the spaces.

Snip 'v's in all curves, and snip into the corners very carefully. Trim off all the surplus turnings before turning it inside out.

Use a little blunted skewer for pushing small pieces of stuffing into legs and arms and take care not to pull too hard on the seams.

Finish off the features and hair in similar way to the felt dolls. Felt-tip pens can be used quite successfully on these smooth-faced dolls.

Little panties for her can be made from a rectangle wide enough to go round the waist plus allowance for turnings, and length from waist to thigh (Fig. 40). Make a small hem on one long side and sew lace on the other side. Join the seam and insert elastic in the top hem. Join the middle of the two edges of the lacy side to make the two legs of the panties (Fig. 41).

The Spanish bib (see earlier) made into a dress is simple to make for the small dolls.

a. fold

Fig. 40

Fig. 41

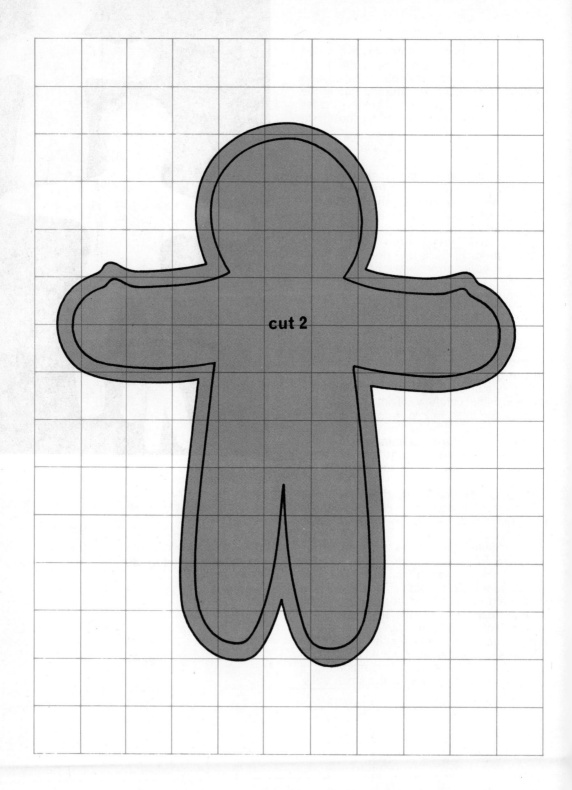

cut 2

Fig. 42

Medium-sized Bavarian doll

This is made from unbleached calico. The template (Fig. 42) is traced on to the wrong side of the folded material, tacked together outside the pencil line, and machined or back stitched along the pencil line leaving one side open for stuffing. It can have a rounder head by stitching in a gusset. Legs and arms can be jointed by stuffing thinly at shoulders and hips and either machining or back stitching across the joints.

Clothes

The one in the picture is dressed in a type of Bavarian national costume. She is wearing thick white knitted cotton stockings, which have been made from discarded cotton socks, and felt or bonded interlining shoes. Her black skirt is full and embroidered on the edge with braid. An embroidered white blouse with puff sleeves has over it a sleeveless bolero jacket, laced together with a coloured lace in the front. Her apron is patterned — it could be embroidered — and is lace edged to match her head scarf which is a triangle edged with lace to frame the face.

Features

Her features are drawn with felt-tip pens; the brows, lashes and mouth are done in embroidery silks. Her hair under the scarf is of strands of yellow wool sewn down with a centre parting and made into short braids each side.

169

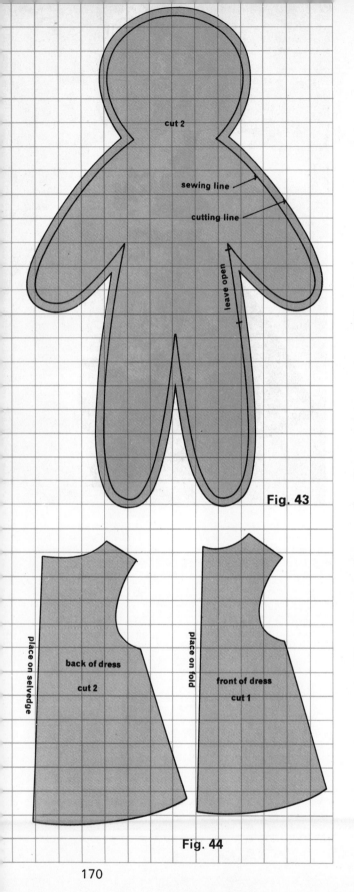

cut 2

sewing line

cutting line

leave open

Fig. 43

place on selvedge

back of dress

cut 2

place on fold

front of dress

cut 1

Fig. 44

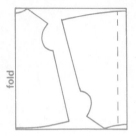

fold

Fig. 45

Larger dolls

These two bigger dolls can be made in pale pink poplin, with or without head gussets. One which measures 19 in. when finished (Fig. 43) can be a little boy or girl doll. The other shorter one, 15 in. and more squat looking, with a big head, makes a very good baby doll (Fig. 46).

A flared skirted dress

A pretty flared skirted dress, fastened up the back with press studs, can be made from the given pattern.

To make it big enough for the 19 in. doll you must make your pattern four times bigger than Fig. 44. The squares on this grid measure ¼ in., so make your grid of one in. squares. Mark dots on it where the lines of the pattern cross the grid lines and when the dots are joined up you will have the larger pattern.

Fold the pattern in half and cut it down the centre. Use one piece to cut the front of the dress, laying the straight edge of the pattern on the fold of the material, because the straight line will be the centre front of the dress. To cut the backs, place the straight edge of the pattern one in. in from the selvedges to allow a turning for fastening the

Fig. 47

dress. If your material is plain, or with an all-over pattern which has no up and down to it, you can lay the patterns on the material (Fig. 45), which then takes less material — ¼ yd. of 36 in. width should do it easily.

Join the backs to the front at side and shoulder seams. Bind the neck, armholes, and hem with bias binding and fasten the back with press studs. Sew a button on over each press stud.

The baby doll

Just a variation on the felt baby doll (Fig. 46), but the features here can be drawn on the smooth surface with felt-tip pens. It is a good idea to practise drawing the features on a scrap of material — the same kind of material as for the doll and the same size as the doll's face — so that they can be placed in exactly the right position. Mistakes made with felt-tip pens will spoil the doll, so before painting or drawing the features make quite sure that you know what you are doing (Fig. 47). Remember also, to put baby features in the bottom half of the face.

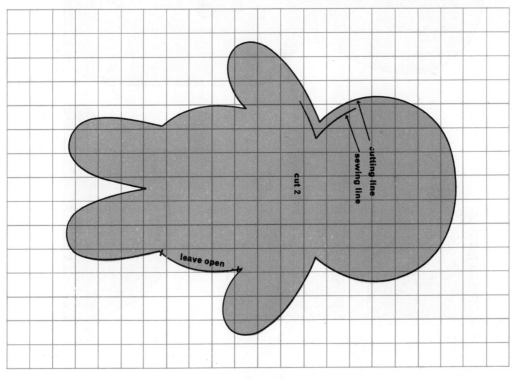

cutting line

sewing line

cut 2

leave open

Fig. 46

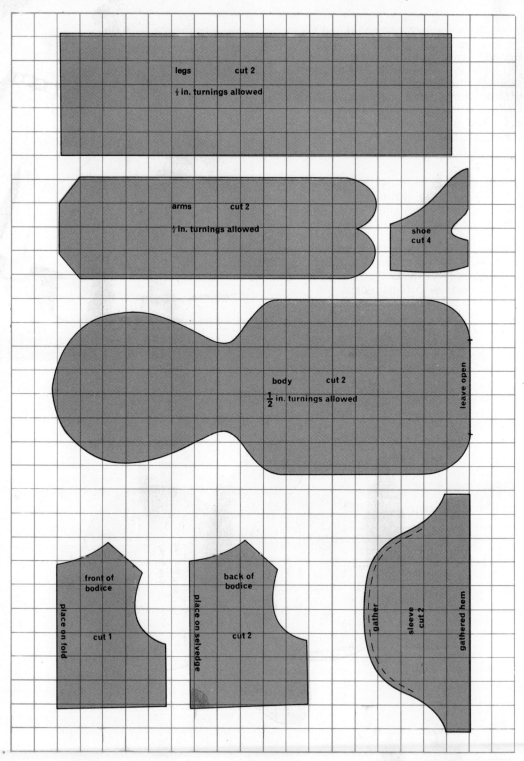

Fig. 48

Jemima Jane

A Victorian miss with long legs and demure ringlets. She has on long lace-edged pantalettes, showing underneath her full-skirted embroidered check gingham dress, with short puffed sleeves and ribbon tie belt. She too, is cut out of pale pink poplin (Fig. 48). The pattern is in four pieces, body, arms, legs and shoes.

You will need:

Any smooth closely-woven material for the doll's body; one yd. of white cambric for pantalettes and waist slip; three yd. of narrow white lace; 1½ yd. of check gingham; 4½ yd. of medium width ricrac braid in white; 3 yd. of mauve seam binding (to match the dress which is of mauve check gingham); some embroidery silks; kapok, blonde-yellow thick soft wool for hair; black felt or imitation leather for shoes.

Trace round the pattern templates on the wrong side of the material and cut out two body pieces, two arms, two legs, and four shoes from black felt or imitation leather. Allow turnings on the doll pieces when cutting them.

Machine or backstitch on the pencil lines, leaving the bottom of the body open for stuffing, and the tops of the arms and legs.

Snip out 'v's in all the curved edges and snip once or twice into all corners (neck etc.). Turn it inside out and press all the seams.

Turn right side out and fill with stuffing, not too hard, and sew up the openings. Sew the arms and legs in place. Sew two shoe pieces together for each shoe and sew them on to the legs round the ankle.

Pantalettes

Her pantalettes (Fig. 49) are made from two rectangles of cambric 20 in. by 10 in. Fold them in half lengthwise and stitch the side seams for 14 in. Pin the rest of the edges together from waist front to waist back for back and front seams. Make a small hem in the top and insert elastic. Make small turnings on the legs and sew on two rows of lace.

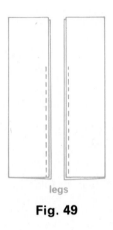

legs

Fig. 49

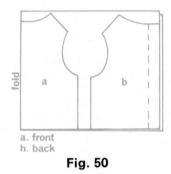

a. front
b. back

Fig. 50

Slip

For the waist slip, cut a piece of cambric 16 in. by 36 in. Seam the two short edges. Make a small hem at the top for elastic, and sew a frill of lace all round the bottom edge.

Dress

The dress has a fitted bodice with a very full gathered skirt. Fold the bodice pattern in half and cut it down the middle. Place the piece for the front on folded material with the straight edge to the fold. Place the piece for the backs with the straight edge 1 in. in from the selvedges (Fig. 50). Seam the side and shoulder seams.

173

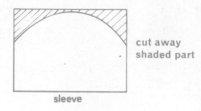

cut away
shaded part

sleeve

Fig. 51

Fig. 53

Sleeves

Cut two sleeves from folded material 6½ in. by 18 in. Curve the tops (Fig. 51). Gather up the curved edge to fit the armhole and sew it in place. Make a turning on the bottom edge, gather it to fit the arm tightly and sew ricrac braid over the gathers.

Skirt

Cut two pieces of material for the skirt each measuring 18 in. by 36 in. Join the selve-edges together for front and back seam, leaving open 3 in. at the top of the back seam. Gather the top edge and join on to the waist of the bodice (Fig. 52). Make a hem on the bottom and sew a row of white ricrac over it on the right side. Sew a second row 2½ in. above it and in between sew a strip of mauve seam binding with white ricrac on top of it.

Sew a 'V' of seam binding from each shoulder to the middle of the waist in front, with white ricrac on top of it (Fig. 52). Bind the neck on the wrong side and sew ricrac round it on the stitching. Fasten the back with press studs, with pearl buttons sewn on top and tie a strip of mauve seam binding round the waist with long ends in front.

Features

Embroider or draw features with felt-tip pens.

Cut strands of silky wool long enough to reach from shoulder to shoulder over the head. Spread them over forehead and back of the head sewing them down the centre parting with back stitch. Loop them over the forehead down the cheeks and tie in a bunch at each side of the face with mauve ribbons (Fig. 53).

Fig. 52

Cotton-Knit dolls

Directions for making a doll from T-shirts or other knitted fabric are given in Chapter Eleven. Different sizes of doll can be made in this material, just as in others, once you have the basic measurements. Dolls twice as big or half as big can be made by doubling or halving these measurements. Features on these dolls must be worked in embroidery silks or coloured cottons, *not* painted or drawn with felt-tip pens, because the material is not smooth enough and lines will be smudgy.

The little doll

Here in the knitted cap is a fun doll, both happy and sad at the same time, for one side of her head has a happy smiling face and the back (which is hidden by her hat) has a miserable turned-down mouth and she looks ready to cry (Fig. 54).

It is fun too to make an upside-down doll (Fig. 55), particularly good in calico, by cutting out on double material two bodies joined at the waist, and four limbs. Dress both dolls in different characters as girl dolls, for instance, a schoolgirl at one end and a baby at the other. The dress of one doll will hide the other doll. So, you have two dolls in one and can have a quick change whenever you wish.

Fig. 54

Fig. 55

175

Dolls on wire frames

The little prince riding on his elephant (in Chapter Ten) is made on a wire frame and the making is fully described there. He is small in size, and for larger dolls you must increase your length of wire, but the method of making them is the same. If you don't have a polystyrene ball to use for a head, then pad the loop of wire with wadding or screwed up tissue paper and cover that with strips of soft material or bandage and finally with pale-coloured nylon stocking which will stretch easily into shape. Pad the arms, legs and body with strips of material and finally with nylon stocking. Keep the loops in the wire for hands and feet.

The clown

Bobbing up and down on elastic the clown has been made on one of these wire frames, but only his head needs to be padded, because the rest of the frame is hidden by his baggy dress. Only his hands and feet are showing.

Fig. 56

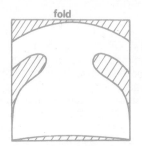

fold

cut away all shaded parts

Fig. 57

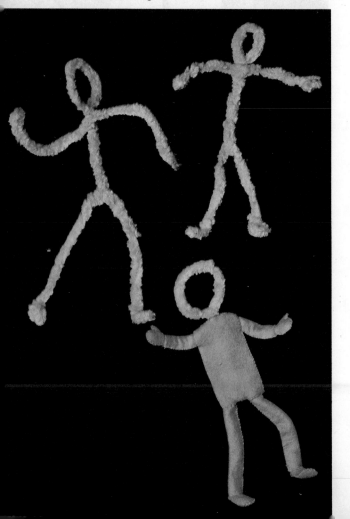

He can be made from pipe cleaners twisted together to make the required length which is about 72 in., but it is much easier to twist and form into shape if you have a continuous length of wire with no joins. The most comfortable kind of soft flexible wire to use is pipe cleaner chenille, which is like an extra soft and fluffy pipe cleaner.

The clown's feet and hands can be covered with old nylon stocking.

Features

His face has an oval red felt mouth and a red felt nose cut as a circle. His eyes are embroidered black wool crosses and the eyebrows inverted 'v's of black felt or inter-lining (Fig. 56). His pointed hat is cut from a segment of felt — about ¾ of a circle, the straight edges joined and the hat sewn on round the head.

Dress

His dress is cut in two pieces from two 8 in. squares, and cut as in Fig. 57. Sew the side seams and shoulder seams leaving a neck opening. Make a turning on the sleeves and gather them up. Make a small turning along the bottom.

Fit the dress on, sewing the neck closely to the wire and sew the front and back edges of the bottom together, sewing in the legs with it. Cut a strip of white Vilene, about 1 in. wide and 10 in. long. Draw blue and red stripes on each long edge with felt-tip pens, gather it up along the middle and sew on at the neck.

Hat

He could have wool pom-poms (made like those for the Pierrot in Chapter Nine) for his hat, dress and shoes. Sew a piece of round elastic in his hat, with a loop to hold at the end and he will bounce beautifully for you.

Two little dolls

Made from cut lengths of wire, so if you have some shorter pieces left over from making other things, you can use them up like this.

The first doll can be made from two pieces, a 20 in. piece for head, body and legs, and a 7 in. piece for the arms. Fold the long piece in half, make the head loop and twist the remaining wire together for the body, leaving the last 4 in. for the legs. Twist a small loop at each end for the feet. Twist the ends of the shorter piece of wire for hands, and thread it through the body twist, just below the head loop. Bend the right one to the left, and the left one to the right to lock them in place.

The second doll frame

Made from three short lengths, the head and body from a 15 in. length, legs from a 12 in. strip and the arms from a 9 in. one.

Make the head and body and leave about 1½ in. of the body wires untwisted. Make loops for the feet on the leg wire, mark the centre of it and twist the body wires round it, one on each side of the centre mark. Make the arms in similar way to the first doll. Pad the head loops for a soft padded head, or cut the wires, make a hole in a polystyrene ball and push in the wires.

The small felt-covered doll

Made on the same type of frame, but legs, arms and body are covered with felt, which dresses him sufficiently, especially if a suitable colour of felt is chosen.

Cut two strips of felt 1 in. wide and long enough to reach from hip to ankle, and two similar strips for the arms from shoulder

Fig. 58

to wrist (Fig. 58). Fold each piece round a wire limb and oversew the edges, turning the seams to the inside of legs and arms. Pad the body wire with strips of wadding or bandage. Cut two pieces of felt to reach

177

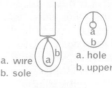

cut 4

a. wire
b. sole

a. hole
b. upper

Fig. 60   **Fig. 61**

Cut four hand shapes in felt. Sew them together round the sides and fingers, slip them over the wire loops and sew round the wrist felt with thumbs pointing upwards (Fig. 60).

Draw round the foot loop on a piece of felt and cut four ovals slightly bigger than the pencilled outline. Two pieces will be for the soles and two for the uppers. Make a small cut down the narrower end of the uppers and cut out a very small circle only big enough to take the wire (Fig. 61). Oversew the curved edges together, slide them over the slightly padded footloops so that the cut out circle fits over the wire. Sew up the back seam and sew the leg felt over the upper.

The four costume dolls

The Japanese lady, the Chinese coolie lad, the Pakistani lady and the Eskimo boy have all been made on wire frames.

Make your chosen dress by drawing the pattern shape you need round your finished doll frame, allowing good turnings.

Many books on national costume will give you ideas.

The Japanese lady

Her kimono with its very wide sleeves is in yellow thick silk, with a roll collar extending in a fold all down the front. Cuffs and lining of the wide sleeves are of grey and red striped silk and this also makes the obi — the wide sash bound round her waist in the traditional manner. Her inner sleeves and the neck band folded inside her kimono are of black and gold silk. Her feet have been padded and mounted on little leather soles with thick black silk thongs to hold them on.

Hair

Hair has been stitched in long and short stitches in black wool with a big chignon of the black wool entwined with a black and gold band and a decorative pin thrust through.

from shoulder to shoulder covering the tops of the felt arms and from shoulder to hips to cover the leg felts (Fig. 59).

Sew the body inside these two pieces, oversewing the side seams and sewing in the arms and legs. Fold over the top corners on the shoulders and sew them down.

Pad the head and cover the whole with a piece of nylon stocking, tucking the ends down inside the neck edge of felt and sewing them in.

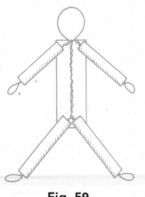

Fig. 59

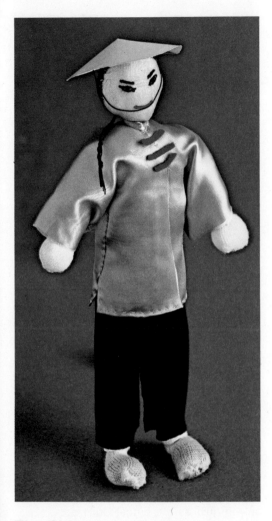

The Pakistani lady

She has wide swathed green chiffon trousers and a blue close fitting top, and a filmy long green chiffon scarf across her shoulder.

Her hair is of long strands, to below the shoulder, of black embroidery silk, the face having been covered with a dark nylon stocking.

On her feet are little turned up pointed Moorish-type blue felt slippers.

The Chinese coolie lad

He has long black heavy silk trousers and kimono type hip length jacket in blue, high at the neck and fastened with three red clips, and with a rampant red dragon across the back.

His hair is sewn in long and short stitches in black sewing cotton ending in a fine pigtail.

His hat is a shallow cone of yellow card, cut from a segment of a circle.

179

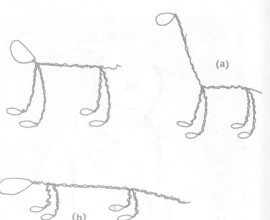

Fig. 62

The Eskimo boy

He has had his wire frame well padded so that he appears to be warmly dressed. He has trousers and and a longish coat with a hood in a furry white material banded on all edges and round the hood with a different kind of fur, and fur mitts on his hands.

His head has been covered with a brown nylon stocking and his straight fringe of hair showing under his hood has been worked in black wool. His moccasins are of thick grey felt.

Animals

These same wire frames, made in exactly the same way, can be used, with small adjustments, for many animals. These you might like to put with your dolls as pets. Or you can make a model or scene using several dolls and some background to illustrate it.

Dog

A dog can be made from the completed doll frame by bending the head up at right angles to the body (Fig. 62) and the arms and legs down to make the animal's four legs.

Larger animals would need longer lengths of wire just as the bigger dolls do.

Giraffe

A giraffe (Fig. 62a) would need extra wire to twist into his extra long neck.

Crocodile

A crocodile (Fig. 62b) needs extra wire in his long snout and body but less in his short strong legs.

Dolls from old-fashioned dolly pegs (clothespins)

Whole families and sets of these little dolls can be made very quickly — in fact, as a wet holiday afternoon occupation it is a wonderful pastime.

You will need :

Old-fashioned pegs or clothespins ; some pipe cleaners to make arms ; some scraps of material for dressing them ; a little padding for the head ; an old nylon stocking for covering the head padding and the arms ; small piece of modelling clay to stand them on.

Cover the small knob with little pieces of wadding peeled in half to mould it better (Fig. 63), or small pieces of kapok moulded round it, and cover it all with a piece of nylon stocking.

Wind a piece of wire round the neck, the ends forming the arms, with small loops turned over for hands.

Glue or sew on wool for hair, draw or embroider the features and it is ready to be dressed.

In this little group of peg dolls are a *little girl* who is dressed ready for a party, in a very gay dress.

A cheeky-looking *Irish leprechaun* in

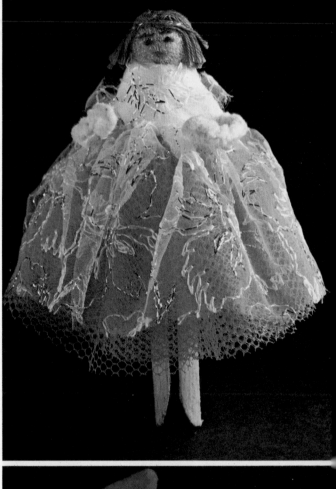

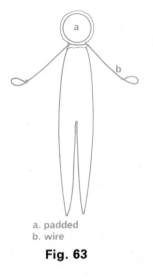

a. padded
b. wire

Fig. 63

long red trousers, bright green tail coat and pointed fairy hat. His features have been drawn with felt-tip pens and his beard of fine white cotton jersey stuck on. Little flesh-coloured felt hands have been sewn over the hand wires.

With him is a little lady from Russia.

The little *Russian peasant doll* has a very full-sleeved gathered blouse and a full gathered green woollen skirt embroidered round the hem. Her apron is black and also embroidered. Over her yellow wool hair she wears a head scarf in green, embroidered to match the skirt.

Ever so dignified is the little *Dutch lady doll* who is really very grand in her stiff black silk best dress and apron. Her fichu and apron are of Dutch lace, as is her bonnet with its traditional ruched braid along the back of it. Under it you can see her yellow braided hair (of embroidery silk). In her hand she carries a jewelled net purse with a tiny silver Dutch coin. She is probably ready to go to church.

CHAPTER NINE

Knitted dolls

knit on
army dad
For Jimmy

Points to remember

The basic plan for the knitted dolls in this chapter is a straight strip of garter stitch knitting, the design so simple that small children can learn how to knit from it, the finished doll being much more fun to have than a knitted square for a pot holder or blanket or dish cloth.

The finished strip is folded over at the top of the head and joined up at each side. Knitting begins with the front half of the front legs, up the front of the body, the face and head, and then down the back of the body and the legs (Fig. 1).

To make up the doll, fold the strip in half with the right side inside, and oversew the edges (Fig. 2) backstitching where the corners are to be rounded off for head and feet, and leaving an opening at one side for stuffing. Join the arm pieces in the same way, leaving the top open.

When changing colours in the knitted strip, be careful to make all joins of the new colours on the same side of the strip to give a right and wrong side (Fig. 3), and in joining up be careful to match up the colours on each edge.

You can strengthen the neck of a knitted doll in the following way : fold a pipe cleaner in half, twist it, and insert it when stuffing the head so that half of it is in the head and half in the body. Keep it in the centre of the neck with stuffing all round it (Fig. 4).

If a 'jointed' leg is required, then stuff the top of the leg thinly and backstitch right across the top of the legs for a joint and the doll will be able to sit (Fig. 5).

Other types of knitting stitch as well as garter stitch can be introduced, both for the clothes and the doll itself.

Additions of clothes for dressing can vary in ply and make. In fact, this often adds interest to the finished doll.

Three sizes of doll are given so that families of dolls can be knitted, and dressed. All sizes and directions for the medium and smallest ones are in the brackets. Small amounts of wool can be used for them, but the main body part should be made of the same ply and make of wool, otherwise the finished doll will be irregular and thinner in parts.

The basic measurements (Fig. 6) for the whole strip for the dolls is as follows :

Front of legs 4½ (3 ; 2¼) in.
Body 14 (10 ; 7¼) in. made up as follows :
  body front 4½ (3 ; 2¼) in.
  face and head 5 (4 ; 3) in.
  body back 4½ (3 ; 2¼) in.
Backs of legs 4½ (3 ; 2¼) in.
Abbreviations : k = knit. tog = together. St(s) = Stitch(es).

Small children enjoy a change of colour and so a golliwog is quite a useful inducement for the beginner to keep on knitting.

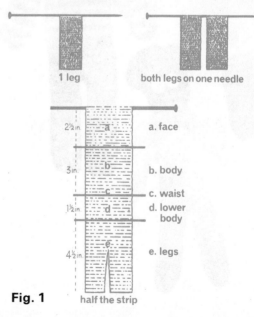

1 leg   both legs on one needle

2½in. — a —   a. face
3in.   — b —   b. body
       — c —   c. waist
1½in. — d —   d. lower body
4½in. — e —   e. legs

Fig. 1   half the strip

Golliwogs

You will need :

1 oz. each of red, black, royal blue 4 ply or double knitting wool ; three No. 10 knitting needles (U.S. size No. 3) ; a pipe cleaner ; scraps of black, red, white and yellow felt for trimming ; kapok for stuffing.

N.B. Colours must be joined on the same edge each time with the right side of the strip facing you. Directions are given for three sizes of golliwog but the amount of wool given here is for the largest sized one only.

Legs

With black wool cast on 10 (8 ; 6) stitches.
Knit for ½ in.
Change to blue wool.
Knit 4 (2½ ; 1¾) in.
Break off wool and leave sts. on needle.
Knit a second leg to match and knit both sets of sts. on to one needle giving 20 (16 ; 12) sts.

Body

Still with blue wool, knit 1½ (1 ; ¾) in. for rest of trousers.
Break off blue wool and join on red wool for jacket front.
Knit 3 (2 ; 1½) in. and break off red wool.

Head

Join on black wool.
Knit 5 (4 ; 3) in.
Break off black wool and join red wool.

Body

Knit 3 (2 ; 1½) in. for back ot jacket.
Change to blue wool.
Knit 1½ (1 ; ¾) in. for top of trousers.
Divide stitches.

Legs

On the first 10 sts. knit in blue wool for 4 (2½ ; 1¾) in.
Change to black wool.
Knit ½ in.
Cast off.
Rejoin wool to second 10 sts. and finish second leg to match.

Arms

Cast on 16 (14 ; 12) sts. in black wool.
Knit for ½ in.
Change to red wool.
Knit 2½ (2 ; 1½) in.
Cast off.
Knit a second arm to match.

Making up

Fold the strip in half with right side inside and take care to match the stripes of colour.
Oversew the head seams, backstitching round the corners to round them off, and continue round the edges as in Fig. 2, again rounding off the corners of the feet and leaving one side open for stuffing.
Turn inside out.

Head

Stuff the head very firmly being careful not to stretch the knitting unduly, and insert a twisted pipe cleaner half in the head and half in the body, to keep the head and neck firm. Pad stuffing carefully round the pipe cleaner to keep it in the centre of the neck.

Tie a thread tightly round the neck.

Legs and body

Stuff the legs next, keeping stuffing thin at the top of the legs and backstitching across the top of the legs to give them a 'joint'. Use a blunted pencil to push the stuffing into small openings like legs and arms. Stuff the body and sew up the opening.

Arms

Sew up the arms on the wrong side, rounding off the corners. Turn inside out and stuff firmly. Sew them on across the top of the shoulder.

Sew ½ in. loops of black wool all over the head, then cut the loops and trim the ends for a close mop (Fig. 7).

Features

Cut two white felt circles for eyes and sew them on the face, cut a smiling crescent of red mouth and sew on invisibly.

Cut a belt and big buttons from black felt and sew in place.

Finish with a white felt collar and a big yellow bow.

The smaller golliwogs can have shorter trousers and striped jerseys for a change.

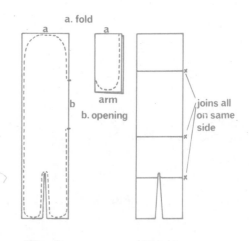

a. fold
b. opening
arm

Fig. 2

joins all on same side

Fig. 3

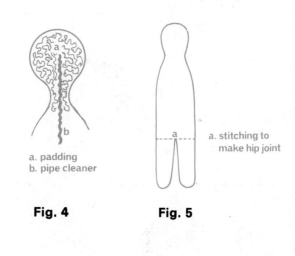

a. padding
b. pipe cleaner

Fig. 4

a. stitching to make hip joint

Fig. 5

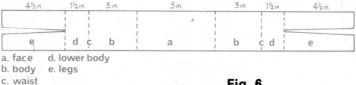

4½ in.   1½ in.   3 in.   5 in.   3 in.   1½ in.   4½ in.

e   d c   b   a   b   c d   e

a. face   d. lower body
b. body   e. legs
c. waist

Fig. 6

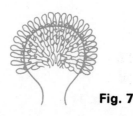

Fig. 7

a. opening

Fig. 8

a. corners gathered
up for ears

Fig. 9

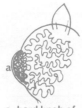

a. hard knob of
stuffing for nose

Fig. 10

Fig. 11

The Three Bears

You will need :

3 oz. of 4 ply or double knitting wool in a speckled golden yellow will make the set of three; three No. 10 knitting needles (U.S. size No. 3) ; brown tapestry or embroidery wool ; kapok for stuffing. (Directions for Mother Bear and Baby Bear are given in the brackets).

Cast on 10 (8 ; 6) stitches.
Knit plain for 4½ (3 ; 2¼) in.
Break off wool and leave sts. on needle.
Knit a second leg to match.
Knit both sets of sts. on to one needle, 20 (16 ; 12) sts.
Knit plain on these sts. for 14 (10 ; 7½) in.
Divide for the legs and on the first 10 (8 ; 6) sts. knit 4½ (3 ; 2) in.
Cast off.
Rejoin wool to the remaining sts. and complete to match the first leg.

Arms

Cast on 16 (14 ; 12) sts.
Knit plain for 3 (2½ ; 2) in.
Cast off.
Knit a second arm to match.

Making up

Fold the strip of knitting in half, right side inside.
For Father Bear put marker pins for the neck 2½ in. from the fold.
(For Mother Bear mark 2 in. from the fold).
(For Baby Bear 1½ in. from fold).
Oversew the head and leg seams and one side of the body, rounding off the leg corners for paws but *not* rounding off the head corners. Leave one side open for stuffing (Fig. 8).
Turn it inside out.
Push the corners of the head well out and sew across the corners, gathering them slightly for ears (Fig. 9).

Head

Stuff the head firmly to make a good shape, and then push a hard ball of stuffing into the front of the face to form a nose (Fig. 10).
Finish the rest of the stuffing as for the golliwog.

Arms

Sew and stuff the arms. Do not stuff the arms too hard at the top and then they will hang at the sides instead of sticking out.

a. sequins

Fig. 12   **Fig. 13**

Features

Embroider a square block of straight stitches for the nose and mouth. Embroider the eyes taking the wool from one to the other through the head and pulling slightly together to form features. Embroider lines in the ears to make them curl in, and straight lines for claws on each paw (Fig. 11).

A pirate

You will need :

1 oz. each of black, red, oyster wool in 4 ply or double knitting ; a small quantity of white, green, yellow wool ; a scrap of black felt for his eye patch and belt ; fine silver metal thread ; three No. 10 knitting needles (U.S. size No. 3) ; kapok for stuffing.

Cast on 10 stitches in black wool.
   Knit 2½ in.
   Change to red wool.
   Knit 2 in.
Break off wool and leave sts. on needle.
   Knit a second leg to match and put both on to one needle.
   Knit 1½ in. in red wool.
   Change to black and white wools.
   Knit jersey for 3 in. in alternate stripes of black and white.
   Change to oyster wool.
   Knit 2 in. for his face.
   Change to black wool.
   Knit 3 in
   Knit the back of the striped jersey for 3 in. beginning with the same colour that ended at the neck of the jersey.
   Change to red wool.
   Knit 1½ in.
   Divide for legs and complete them to match the front.

Arms

Cast on 16 sts. in oyster wool.
Knit 1½ in. in oyster wool and 1½ in. in black and white stripes to match the body of the jersey.

Head scarf

Cast on 2 sts. in yellow.
   Knit 4 rows.
   Increase in the first stitch in the next and every 4th row till 20 sts. are on the needle.
   Knit 3 rows.
   Knit together the first 2 sts. in the next and every 4th row till 2 sts. remain.
   Cast off.

Neckerchief

Cast on 2 sts. in green.

Knit 6 rows.

Increase at beginning of next and every 6th row till 12 sts.

Knit 5 rows then decrease at the beginning of the next and every 6th row till 2 sts. remain.

Cast off.

Make up is the same as the golliwog ; again care should be taken to match the stripes.

Embroider the features with wool. Cut an oval patch in black felt and stitch in place for one eye Cut a strip of black felt for a belt and sew on with a big buckle worked in fine silver metal thread. Tie the neckerchief on with the two ends in the front. Tie the head scarf to one side with the ends over one ear and the point over the other. Sew a small ear ring on to one side of the head.

Puss-in-boots

You will need :

1 oz. each of black, red, yellow
4 ply or double knitting wool ;
1 oz. of lime colour in 3 ply wool,
or in wool and fine metal thread
mixture ; green, gold, silver metal
thread ; strands of black wool ;
small feathers ; sequins ; two pipe
cleaners ; three No. 10 knitting
needles (U.S. size No. 3) ; kapok
for stuffing ; green and red felt.

Cast on 10 stitches in red wool.

Knit 2 in.

Change to black wool.

Knit 2½ in.

Break off wool and leave sts. on needle.

Knit second leg to match and knit both sets of sts. on to one needle.

Knit 14 in. in black, then divide sts. and knit legs to match the front ones.

Cast on 16 sts. in black wool for arms.

Knit 3 in.

Boot tops

With red wool cast on 41 sts.

Knit ½ in

Next row. k 2, k 2 tog. *k 4, k 2 tog*.
Repeat from* to * to last stitch, k 1 (34 sts.).

Knit for ½ in.

Next row. K 1 k 2 tog., *k 3, k 2 tog.*
Repeat * to * to last st. k 1 (27 sts.).

Knit ½ in.

Next row. K 1 k 2 tog *k 2 k 2 tog.*

Repeat * to * to end (20 sts.).

Knit ½ in.

Cast off.

Tail

Cast on 5 sts. in black wool and knit 9 in.

Cast off.

Hat brim

With yellow wool cast on 80 sts.

Knit 3 rows.

Next row. *k 2 k 2 tog.* all along the row (60 sts.).

Knit 3 rows.

Next row. *k 1 k 2 tog. all along row (40 sts.).

Knit 3 rows.

Next row (**Hat crown**) k 3 k 2 tog. *k 6 k 2 tog.* Repeat * to * to last 3 sts., k 3 (35 sts.).

Knit 3 rows.

Next row. k 3 k 2 tog. *k 5 k 2 tog.* Repeat * to * to last 2 sts. k 2. (30 sts.)

Knit 3 rows.

Next row. k 2 k 2 tog. *k 4 k 2 tog.*
Repeat * to * to last 2 sts. k 2. (25 sts.)
Knit 3 rows,
Next row. K 2 k 2 tog. *k 3 k 2 tog.*
Repeat * to * to last stitch, k 1. (20 sts.)
Knit 3 rows.
Next row. K 1 k 2 tog. *k 2 k 2 tog.
Repeat * to * to last stitch, k 1. (15 sts.)
Knit 1 row.
Next row. *k 1 k 2 tog.* Repeat * to * to
end of row. (10 sts.)
Knit 1 row.
Next row. K 2 tog. all along the row.
(5 sts.)
Run a thread through the 5 sts. and fasten
off.
Sew up the side seam.

Cloak

With lime wool and fine green metal thread
knitted together, cast on 60 sts.
Knit plain for 3¼ in.

Next row. K 3 tog. all along the row.
(20 sts.)
Knit 5 rows.
Cast off.

Waist scarf

With lime wool and fine green metal thread
knitted together, cast on 4 sts. and knit 9 in.
Cast off.
Make a fringe on each end.
Make up the doll in the same way as the
bear, sewing across the corners for ears
and pushing in a hard ball of stuffing in the
front of the face for a nose.
Join the seams of the boot tops, and sew
the narrow end on to the legs on the last
row of purple knitting. Turn up the brim of
the hat and sew a small bunch of curled
feathers at one side.

Features

Cut two oval-shaped pieces of green felt
and embroider all over with green metal
thread, or sew on green sequins (Fig. 12),
and sew to the face with a vertical bar of
stitching in black wool.
Whiskers can be made from silver metal
thread. Thread this into a darning needle,
insert the needle in the cheek and bring
out at the nose, then take a backstitch and
bring the needle out on the other cheek.
Repeat four or five times. Cut the loops of
thread.
Embroider a few vertical stitches in black
wool for a nose.
Cut a small crescent shape in red felt for
a tongue and sew it on under the nose.

For the tail

Twist two pipe cleaners together to make a
9½ in. length. Bend the ends back for a ¼ in.,
and lay it on the strip of tail knitting. Oversew
the seam, enclosing the pipe cleaner. Sew
the tail on to the back so that it curls up the
back and round to the front.
Tie the fringed scarf round his waist.
Decorate the boot tops with silver thread
and sequins.
Embroider a medal (Fig. 13) on the left
side of the chest with a sequin chain round
the neck to simulate a decoration.
Sew on the hat with invisible stitches,
giving it a sideways tilt, covering one ear
so that the feathers droop over one shoulder.

Red Riding Hood

You will need:

1 oz. each of red, pale pink, blue, white 4 ply or double knitting wool; a small quantity of black, brown, amber wool; four No. 10 knitting needles (U.S. size No. 3); size 12 crochet hook; two pipe cleaners; kapok for stuffing; ribbon.

Cast on 8 stitches in black wool.
Knit ½ in. for the front of the shoe.
Change to white wool.
Knit 1 in. for the sock.
Change to pink wool.
Knit 3 in. for leg.
Break off wool and leave sts. on needle.
Knit a second leg to match and put both lots of stitches on to one needle. (16 sts.)
Leave them on the needle and knit the **pantie frill**

Cast on 48 sts. in white wool.
Knit 2 rows, knitting the first row into the front and not the backs of the sts. to give a frilly edge.
Next row. K 3 tog. all along the row. (16 sts.)
Knit the pantie frill on to the legs as follows —
Place the needle with the pantie frill on it in front of the one with the leg sts. on it and knit *together* 1 stitch from each needle. (16 sts.)
Knit in white wool for 1½ in.
Break off wool and leave.

Skirt

Cast on 40 sts. in blue wool.
Knit for 2 in.
Next row. k 2 tog. all along the row. (20 sts.)
Next row. K 1 k 2 tog. *k 3 k 2 tog.* Repeat * to * twice, k 2. (16 sts.)
Knit the skirt on to the main doll in the same way as the legs were knitted on to the panties.
Knit in blue wool for 2½ in.
Change to pink wool.
Knit 2 in. for the face.
Cast off.
Repeat the above for the back of the body as far as the end of the blue wool for the body.
Join on the brown wool for hair.
Knit 2 in.   Cast off.

Cloak

Cast on 60 sts. in red wool.

Knit for 2¾ – 3 in.
Next row. K 3 *k 2 tog. k 4*. Repeat * to * to last 3 sts., k 2 tog. k 1. (50 sts.)
Knit 5 rows plain.
Next row. K 2 *k 2 tog. k 3*. Repeat * to * to last 3 sts., k 2 tog. k 1. (40 sts.)
Knit 5 rows plain.
Next row. *K 2 k 2 tog.* Repeat * to * to end of row. (30 sts.)
Knit 5 rows plain.
Next row. *K 1 k 2 tog.* Repeat * to * to end of row. (20 sts.)
Knit 5 rows plain.

Hood

Next row. *K 1, increase in next st.* Repeat * to * to last stitch, k 1. (30 sts.)
K 3 in. plain.
Cast off.

Arms

Cast on 14 sts. in pink wool.
Knit ½ in. for the hand.
Change to blue wool.
Knit 2 in.
Cast off.
Knit a second arm to match.

Making up

Sew seams on the wrong side leaving an opening for stuffing. Turn inside out. Sew up skirt side seams.
Stuff body and finish sewing up; stuff arms and sew on across the shoulder.
Embroider features keeping them on lower half of face (Fig. 14). Sew strands of brown wool across the top of the head, for hair, and finish in braids at the sides of the face.
Seam the hood and tie the cloak round the neck with a ribbon.
Sew the hood to the head invisibly.

Fig. 14

a. wool
b. raffia   **Fig. 15**   **Fig. 16**

Basket

With amber wool and size 12 crochet hook make a ring of 4 chain and work into it 6 double crochet.

In the next two rounds work 2 double crochet into each stitch.

In next work 2 d. c. in alternate sts.

Continue working rounds with an occasional 2 d. c. into 1 stitch to keep the work flat, until it measures 2¼ in. across.

Continue for five or six rounds without increasing, for the sides.

In the last round, work the stitches over a pipe cleaner to give a firm edge.

For a handle, insert the second pipe cleaner from side to side, bend up the ends and twist round. Bind wool all round it tightly to cover the cleaner. Attach it to the doll's arm with a few stitches.

Hawaiian girl

You will need:

3 oz. light brown 4 ply or double knitting wool; black wool or silk for hair; three No. 10 knitting needles (U.S. size No. 3); scraps of white and coloured felt; beads; raffia for skirt; kapok for stuffing.

For legs: cast on 10 stitches.

Knit 4½ in.

Break off wool and leave sts. on needle.

Knit a matching second leg, and put both sets of sts. on one needle (20 sts.).

Knit 14 in. and then divide for legs, and knit them to match the front halves.

For arms knit 3 in. on 16 sts.

Make up the doll as for the golliwog.

Skirt

Cut a length of wool about 16 in. long. Cut the raffia into 10 in. lengths (Fig. 15), double each strand and knot it over the wool, pulling the two ends through the loop, and continue until it is sufficiently long to fit round the waist. Tie it tightly round the waist; secure in place with a few stitches.

Hair

Cut the wool or silk into 12 in. lengths and lay it over the head from shoulder to shoulder. Spread it out over the back of the head and backstitch it down the centre parting.

Cut simple flower shapes and leaves from felt (Fig. 16) and sew in a garland round one side of the head and face.

Features

Cut two oval shapes in white felt for eyes and sew on with a flat blue bead in the centre.

Red felt or embroidery shapes the mouth.

Sew a small brass ring on the side of the head opposite the flowers.

Bead necklaces, anklets and bracelets can be made to match.

An English guardsman

You will need:

1 oz. each of black, red, royal blue, pink (pale) in 4 ply or double knitting wool; four No. 10 knitting needles (U.S. size No. 3); strips of white felt; fine metal thread; kapok for stuffing; 4 paper fasteners.

Colours must be joined on the same edge each time, with right side of work facing you.

Cast on 10 stitches in black wool.
Knit ¾ in. in black wool.
Knit 3¾ in. in blue wool.
Break off wool and leave sts. on needle.
Knit a second leg and put all the stitches on one needle. (20 sts.)
Knit as follows on these 20 sts.;
Blue 1½ in.;
Red 3 in.;
Pink 1½ in.;
Black 7 in.;
Red 3 in.;
Blue 1½ in.;
Here divide for legs and on the first 10 sts. knit 3¾ in. in blue and ¾ in. in black.
Repeat for second leg.

Arms

Cast on 16 sts. in pink wool.
Knit ½ in. in pink wool and 2½ in. in red wool.
Cast off.
Knit a second arm to match.

Bottom of coat

Cast on 60 sts. in red wool.
Knit 2 in.
Cast off.

Making up

Oversew all seams on the wrong side, leaving a side opening. Turn inside out and stuff. (Ease stuffing into arms and legs with a blunted pencil). Finish sewing up. Stuff the arms and sew on across the shoulder.

Insert four paper fasteners down the front of the jacket for buttons.

Sew the bottom of the coat on at the waist, slightly overlapping the fronts. Cover the join with a strip of white felt for a belt.

Embroider a buckle with gold thread, and a red line down the outside of each leg in stem or backstitch. Embroider features and moustache.

Cut a narrow strip of red felt to fit round the neck and embroider a motif each end and fasten it to the neck with invisible stitches, so that the two ends meet and the collar stands upright.

An English sailor

You will need :

2 oz. of navy blue, 1 oz. each of black, pink and a small quantity of white all either 4 ply or double knitting wool; about 6 in. of narrow black ribbon; a black felt strip for a headband; silver metal thread; four No. 10 knitting needles (U.S. size No. 3); kapok for stuffing.

Legs

With black wool cast on 10 stitches.
Knit 3 in.
Break off wool and leave.

Bell bottom (See Fig. 17)

With navy blue wool cast on 25 sts.
Knit ½ in.
Next row. K 2 k 2 tog. *k 8 k 2 tog.* Repeat * to * once, k 1. (22 sts.)
Knit ½ in. without decreasing.
Next row. K 1 k 2 tog. *k 7 k 2 tog.* Repeat * to * once, k 1. (19 sts.)
Knit ½ in.
Next row. K 2 k 2 tog. *k 5 k 2 tog.* Repeat * to * once k 1 (16 sts.)
Knit ½ in.
Next row. K 1 k 2 tog. *k 4 k 2 tog.* Repeat * to * once, k 1. (13 sts.)
Knit ½ in.
Next row. *K 2 k 2 tog.* Repeat * to * twice k 1. (10 sts.)
To knit the bell bottom on to the leg, place the needle with the bell bottom in front of the needle with the leg stitches and knit *together* one stitch from each needle. (10 sts.)
Knit for 1½ in.
Break off wool, and leave sts. on needle.
Knit a second leg to match, and put both sets of stitches on one needle. (20 sts.)
Knit 4½ in. for body, then 2 in. in pink wool and ½ in. in brown wool.
Cast off.
Repeat all the above for the second half to the end of the blue knitting.
Change to brown wool and knit 2½ in. for the back of the head.
Cast off.

Arms

Cast on 16 sts. in pink wool.
Knit ½ in.
Change to navy blue wool.
Knit 2½ in.
Cast off.
Knit a second arm to match.

Collar (See Fig. 18)

Cast on 16 sts. in navy blue wool.
Knit 2 in.
Next row. K 5 sts. cast off the next 6 sts. and on the last 5 sts. knit as follows —

Knit 3 rows.
On next row k 2 tog. at the neck edge.
Knit 2½ in. on these 4 sts.
Cast off.
Rejoin wool to the **neck** edge of the remaining 5 sts. and knit 2 rows.
Next row K 2 tog. at the neck edge and knit 2½ in. on remaining 4 sts.
Cast off.

Bib (See Fig. 19)

Cast on 12 sts. in white wool.
Knit 3 rows.
*Next row. K 2 tog. at beginning and end of row.
Knit 3 rows.*
Repeat * to * till 2 sts. remain.
Cast off.

Hat top

Cast on 8 sts. in white wool.
Knit into the front and back of the first stitch in every row until 24 sts. are on the needle.
Knit 8 rows without increasing.
Knit 2 tog. at the beginning of each row until 8 sts. remain.
Cast off.
Knit a second piece to match.

Making up

Sew all seams on the wrong side, leaving an opening at one side for stuffing and rounding off the corners for head and feet. Turn inside out and stuff. Finish sewing up.
Embroider features and a lock of brown wool over the forehead.
Sew and stuff arms and sew on to shoulders. Sew the bib to the chest under the chin.
Couch a line of white wool just inside the edge of the collar and sew it on to cover the edge of the bib.
Sew an end of the narrow ribbon each side under the collar and knot it in front.
Join the hat tops with the lines of knitting crossing each other and oversew the edges.
Cut a narrow strip of felt to fit the head.
Embroider the name in silver, join it into a

ring and sew on the underside of the hat top. Fasten it to the head with small stitches.
Sew the side seams of the bell bottoms.

Santa Claus

You will need :

2 oz. of dark red wool ; 1 oz. each of white, black, pink, oatmeal colour wool in 4 ply or double knitting ; three No. 10 knitting needles (U.S. size No. 3) ; a strip of black felt ; kapok for stuffing.

Legs

Cast on 10 stitches in black wool.
Knit 2½ in.
Change to red wool.
Knit 2 in.
Break off wool and leave sts. on needle.
Knit a second leg to match and put both sets of sts. on to one needle. (20 sts.)
Knit in red wool for 4½ in.

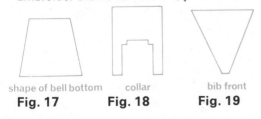

shape of bell bottom   collar   bib front

Fig. 17   **Fig. 18**   **Fig. 19**

Join pink wool and knit 5 in.
Knit 4½ in. in red wool.
Divide for legs and knit them to match the front halves.

Arms

Cast on 16 sts. in pink wool.
Knit ½ in.
Change to red wool and knit 2½ in.
Cast off

Coat bottom

Cast on 54 sts. in red wool.
Knit 3 in.
Cast off.

Hood

Cast on 30 sts. in red wool.
Knit 3¾ in.
Cast off.

Sack

Cast on 8 sts. in oatmeal coloured wool.
Knit 1 row.
Next row. Knit into the front and back of each stitch. (16 sts.)
Knit 6 in.
Next row. K 2 tog. all along the row. (8 sts.)
Knit 1 row.
Cast off.
Make a cord or chain in the oatmeal coloured wool to thread through the top of the sack.

Making up

Sew up all seams on the wrong side, leaving an opening for stuffing and rounding off the corners of head and feet. Turn inside out and stuff.
Sew and stuff arms and sew on at shoulders. Use a blunt pencil to ease the stuffing into the arms and legs.
Embroider thick white eyebrows and a bushy white moustache. Eyes are straight stitches in black wool.
Sew the coat bottom on to the waist, overlapping slightly in front. Cover the join with the strip of black felt for a belt.
Seam the hood along the top and attach at the neck.
Surround the face with two or three rows of ¾ in. loops in white wool. Cut the loops and trim. Attach the hood to the face and head behind the white fringe.
Join the side seams of the sack, thread the cord through the top and hang it over one shoulder.

A Dutch boy

His body is knitted in two parts — a front and a back.

You will need :
1 oz. each of black, blue, red and flesh pink in 4 ply or double knitting wool ; a small quantity of brown wool for hair ; three No. 10 knitting needles (U.S. size No. 3) ; kapok for stuffing.
Cast on 10 stitches in black wool.
Knit ½ in.
Change to blue.
Next row. Increase in every stitch. (20 sts.)
Knit 5 in.
Break wool and leave sts. on needle.
Knit a second leg to match and put all sts. on to one needle. (40 sts.)
Knit one row.
Next row. K 2 tog. all along the row. (20 sts.)
Knit till work measures 6½ in.
Change to red wool.
Knit 3 in.
Knit 2 in. in pink wool.
Knit ½ in. in brown wool.
Cast off.
Knit a second piece to match, finishing at the end of the red knitting.
Join on brown wool and knit 2½ in.
Cast off.

Arms

Cast on 16 sts. in pink wool.
Knit ½ in.
Change to red wool.
Knit 2½ in.
Cast off.

Hat

Cast on 20 sts. in black wool.
Knit 5 in.
Cast off.

Scarf

Cast on 5 sts. in black wool.
Knit 12 in.
Cast off.
Make a small tassel and sew on to each end of it.

Making up

Oversew all seams on the wrong side, leaving an opening in one side for stuffing, and rounding off corners for the head. Turn inside out. Stuff the body and sew up the opening. Sew and stuff the arms and sew them at shoulders.

Fold the piece for the hat in half, join the seams and sew it on to the head slightly at a tilted angle. Tie the scarf round the neck.

Embroider the features.

Ballerina or Christmas fairy

You will need:

1 oz. each of white, flesh pink 4 ply wool; a small quantity of blonde or brown wool for hair; Three No. 10 knitting needles (U.S. size No. 3); some white Tarlatan; some silver cord; kapok for stuffing; embroidery silk.

Cast on 10 stitches in white wool.
Knit 1 in.
Change to pink wool.
Knit 3½ in.
Break off wool and leave sts. on needle.
Knit a second leg.
Put both sets on to one needle (20 sts.) and knit 1½ in.
Change to white wool.
Knit 2 in. for the bodice.
Change to pink wool.
Knit 7 in.
Knit 2 in. in white wool.
Knit 1½ in. in pink wool.
Divide for legs and knit to match the front halves.

Arms

Cast on 14 sts. in pink wool.
Knit 3 in.
Cast off.

Skirt

With white wool cast on 150 sts.
Knit 2¼ in.
Next row. K 3 tog. all along the row. (50 sts.)
Knit 1 row.
Next row. K 2 tog. all along the row. (25 sts.).
Cast off.

Making up

Sew seams on the wrong side, rounding off corners of feet into points and rounding corners of the head. Turn inside out and stuff firmly. Finish sewing up. Sew and stuff arms and sew on to shoulders.

Embroider features with fine wool or embroidery silk.

Hair

Cut brown wool into 8 in. lengths, lay it across the head from shoulder to shoulder (Fig. 20) and fasten down the middle of the head with backstitch. Spread out to cover the back of the head, draw down in two wings each side of the face and take the ends to the back of the neck. Twist them into a knot and sew them down to the head.

Skirt

Cut three or four lengths of net or tulle or Tarlatan 2 in. wide, place them all together and gather them along one side with double cotton. Gather it up tightly and sew on round the waist. Pull the frills out separately. Sew the seam of the skirt and sew it in place on top of the net skirt.

Sew silver cord in a wavy design round the edge of the skirt, and in zigzags along the bodice finishing in front with a bow.

Make a small wreath of silver cord and sew on the head like a coronet.

A long-legged circus clown

He is one with the very large, long boots whose clothes are all too big for him.

You will need:

2 oz. of black wool; 1 oz. each of rust colour, jade, white, yellow and orange 4 ply or double knitting wool, three No. 10 knitting needles (U.S. size No. 3); scraps of red and black felt for features; kapok for stuffing.

back of head

Fig. 20

trousers

Fig. 21

Boots

With black wool cast on 8 stitches.

Knit 5 rows.

Increase each end of the next and every sixth row till 16 sts. are on the needle.

Decrease each end of every sixth row till 10 sts. are left.

Knit on these 10 sts. till work measures 8½ in.

Break off wool and leave sts. on needle.

Knit a second leg to match and put both sets of sts. on to one needle. (20 sts.)

Knit 1½ in. in black wool.

Change to orange and yellow wool.

Knit 2 rows each in orange and yellow wool starting with orange, for 3 in.

Change to white wool.

Knit 2 in. for the face.

Knit 3 in. in black wool.

Change to orange and yellow wool.

Knit 3 in. reversing the stripes from those on the front and finishing with orange.

Knit 1½ in. in black wool and divide for legs.

Knit 4½ in. on first 10 sts.

Next row. Increase at each end of the next and every sixth row till 16 sts.

Decrease each end of every sixth row till 8 sts. remain.

Knit 5 rows.

Cast off.

Rejoin wool to other 10 sts. and complete it to match the first leg.

Cast off.

Arms

With white wool cast on 16 sts. and knit 1 in.

Change to orange and yellow wool and knit in stripes for 2½ in.

Cast off.

Trousers

With rust-coloured wool cast on 25 sts.

Knit 4 rows.

Knit 2 tog. at the beginning of the next and every 4th row till 14 sts. remain.

Knit 1 row.

Break off wool and leave sts. on needle.

Knit a second trouser leg to match.

Put both sets of stitches on to one needle with the straight edges together and the slanting edges on the outside.

Knit on these 28 sts. for 1½ in.

Cast off.

Knit a matching piece for the back of the trousers (Fig. 21).

Coat back

Cast on 36 sts. in jade wool.

Knit 14 rows.

Join on black wool.

Knit 2 rows.

Break off black wool.

Repeat these 16 rows once.

Knit 10 rows in jade wool finishing on the wrong side.

Cast off 4 sts. at the beginning of the next 2 rows for the armhole and cast off 2 sts. at the beginning of the following 2 rows. (6 each side.)

Join black wool.

Knit 2 rows.

Knit 13 rows in jade wool.

Cast off.

Coat — left front

Cast on 20 sts. in jade wool.

Knit 14 rows.

Join black wool.

Knit 2 rows.

Repeat these 16 rows once.

Knit 10 rows of jade wool.

Cast off 4 sts. at the beginning of the next row.

Knit 1 row.

Cast off 2 sts. at the beginning of the following row.

Knit 1 row.

Knit 2 rows in black wool.

Knit 13 rows in jade wool.

Cast off.

Coat — right front

Knit as for left front as far as the armhole, but knit 11 rows instead of 10.

Next row (wrong side). Cast off 4 sts. knit 1 row.

Cast of 2 sts. at the beginning of the following row.

Knit 2 rows in black wool.

Knit 13 rows in jade wool.

Cast off.

Mark along the back of the jacket edge in squares and with black wool work stem stitch or backstitch from neck to hem of the jacket to give a plaid design.

Work a row right down the centre of the fronts.

Hat brim

With black wool cast on 72 sts.

Knit 2 rows.

Next row. *K 2 k 2 tog.* Repeat * to * to the end of the row. (36 sts.)

Cast off.

Making up

Sew all seams on the wrong side leaving one side open for stuffing. Turn inside out and stuff firmly and sew up the opening. Sew and stuff arms and sew on at the shoulder.

Pinch up a tuck over each instep and sew firmly to give some shape to the feet.

Sew the trousers seams. Make a chain or cord with wool and fasten it to the trousers top, over the shoulder and down to the back for a single support.

Join the side and shoulder seams of the coat and fasten it in front with a big black felt bow. Coat and trousers are purposely made too big for him.

Features

Cut two ovals in black felt for eyes. Work several straight stitches in blue in the ovals slightly to the sides and sew them in place with small stitches.

Cut a kidney-shaped large oval in red felt and trim away a slit in the middle, and stitch on for his mouth.

A pear-shaped piece of red felt makes a nose for him.

Hat

Join up the seam of the hat brim and sew it on round the top of the head.

With orange wool make a wispy fringe of hair sticking out over the hat brim.

A Pearly King and Queen

They are resplendent in their best clothes covered with pearl buttons.

The body for each is knitted in two parts — a front and a back.

Pearly King

You will need:

2 oz. black, 1 oz. of flesh pink, brown 4 ply or double knitting wool; about 150 small pearl buttons; a little red fine wool for a neckerchief; four No. 10 knitting needles (U.S. size No. 3); kapok for stuffing.

Legs

Cast on 10 stitches in black wool.
Knit 2 in.
Break off wool and leave sts. on needle.

Bell bottoms

Cast on 16 sts. in black wool.
Knit 4 rows.
Knit 2 tog. at each end of the next and every 4th row till 10 sts. are left.
Knit 1 row.
Knit it on to the legs as follows — Place the needle with the bell bottom in front of the needle with the leg sts. and knit *tog.* 1 stitch from each needle to the end. (10 sts.)
Continue knitting till leg measures 4½ in. from the beginning.
Break off wool and leave sts. on needle.
Knit a second leg to match and put both sets of sts. on to one needle. (20 sts.)
Knit 4½ in.
Change to pink wool.
Knit 2 in.
Knit ½ in. in black wool.
Cast off.
For the back — repeat all the above directions to the end of the body knitting.
Change to brown wool.
Knit 2 in.
Knit ½ in. in black wool. Cast off.

Arms

Cast on 16 sts. in pink wool.
> Knit ½ in.
> Change to black wool.
> Knit 2½ in.
> Cast off.

Coat bottom

Knit the two big patch pockets first.
> Cast on 16 sts. in black wool.
> Knit 1½ in.
> Break off wool and leave.
> Cast on 36 sts. in black wool.
> Knit 2 in.
> Next row. Knit 10, now knit pocket flap on by placing it in front of the coat and knitting tog. 1 stitch from each needle till all the pocket sts. are used, then knit the remaining 10 sts. of the coat. (36 sts.)
> Knit until the work measures 2¼ in. from the beginning.
> Next row. *K 1 k 2 tog.* Repeat * to * to end of row. (24 sts.)
> Cast off.
> Knit a second one to match.

Cap brim

Cast on 16 sts. in black wool.
> Knit 1 row.
> Next row. K 14, turn.
> K 12, turn.
> Continue, knitting 2 sts. less in each row till 2 sts. are left.
> Knit to end of row.
> Cast off.

Neckerchief

Cast on 2 sts. in red wool.
> Knit 2 rows.
> Increase in next and every 5th row till there are 5 sts.
> Knit till work measures 4½ in. from the beginning.
> Decrease in every 5th row till 2 sts. remain.
> Knit 4 rows.
> Cast off.

Making up

Sew all seams from the wrong side leaving one side open for stuffing and rounding off the corners of head and feet.

Turn inside out, and sew on the pearl buttons in a pattern before doing any stuffing. He has ten sewn across the chest in a pattern of two fives (Fig. 22), a big one just above them, and six each side up to the shoulders like lapels. Sew them round three sides of the pocket flaps and a double row down what will be the front of the pieces for the coat bottom.

Sew twelve more in the fives pattern on the waist and the rest in two pyramid shapes on the bell bottoms, starting with five on the bottom and decreasing to one as they go up the leg.

Keep twelve to sew in smaller pyramids on the arms, and about 30 of the smallest to sew on the cap.

Stuff the body firmly and sew up the opening. Sew and stuff arms and sew in place.

Features

Embroider these in wool or silk.

Sew on the coat bottoms to overlap at front and back with buttoned piece in the front.

Sew up bell bottom seams.

Sew cap brim on to the first row of black knitting over the face.

Tie his red neckerchief round his neck with the two ends in front.

Pearly Queen

> *You will need :*
> 2 oz. of black wool, 1 oz. of flesh pink wool (you will probably have enough left over from the pearly king) ; some fine pink wool or silk for her scarf ; and some brown for her hair ; some small white feathers ; about 80 small pearl buttons ; four No. 10 knitting needles (U.S. size No. 3) ; kapok for stuffing.

Legs

Cast on 10 stitches in black wool.
> Knit 4½ in.
> Break off wool and leave sts. on needle.
> Knit a second leg to match.
> Put both sets of stitches on to one needle and knit 1½ in. on these 20 sts.
> Break off wool and leave.

Skirt

With black wool cast on 36 sts.
> Knit 3 in.
> Next row. K 2 k 2 tog., *k 4 k 2 tog.* Repeat * to * 4 times, k 2. (30 sts.)
> Knit 1 in. without decreasing.
> Next row. K 1 k 2 tog., *k 3 k 2 tog.* Repeat * to * 4 times, K 2. (24 sts.) .
> Knit 1 in.

Next row. K 2 k 2 tog. *k 4 k 2 tog.* Repeat * to * twice, k 2. (20 sts.)
Knit ½ in.
Join the skirt on to the body in the same way as the bell bottoms on to the trousers in the pearly king.
Knit in black wool on these 20 sts. for 3 in.
Change to flesh pink wool.
Knit 2 in.
Knit ½ in. in brown wool.
Cast off.
For the back — repeat the above directions to the end of the body knitting.
Change to brown wool and knit 2½ in.
Cast off.

Arms

Cast on 16 sts. in pink wool.
Knit ½ in.
Knit 2½ in. in black wool.
Cast off.

Bottom of coat

Cast on 60 sts. in black wool.
Knit 2 in.
Next row. *K 1 k 2 tog.* Repeat * to * to end of row. (40 sts.)
Cast off.

Hat brim and crown

Cast on 80 sts. in black wool.
Knit 3 rows.
Next row. *K 2 k 2 tog.* Repeat * to * to end of row. (60 sts.)
Knit 3 rows.
Next row. *K 1 k 2 tog.* Repeat * to * to end of row. (40 sts.)
Knit 3 rows.
Next row. K 3 k 2 tog., *k 6 k 2 tog.* Repeat * to * 3 times k 3. (35 sts.)
Knit 3 rows.
Next row. K 3 k 2 tog., *k 5 k 2 tog.* Repeat * to * 3 times, k 2. (30 sts.)
Knit 3 rows.
Next row. K 2, k 2 tog., *k 4 k 2 tog.* Repeat * to * 3 times, k 2. (25 sts.)
Knit 3 rows.
Next row. K 2 k 2 tog. *k 3 k 2 tog.* Repeat * to * 3 times k 1. (20 sts.)
Knit 3 rows.
Next row. K 1 k 2 tog. *k 2 k 2 tog.* Repeat * to * 3 times k 1. (15 sts.)
Knit 1 row.
Next row. *K 1 k 2 tog.* Repeat * to * to end. (10 sts.)
Knit 1 row.

Next row. K 2 tog. five times. (5 sts.)
Run a thread through the 5 sts. and fasten off.

Neckerchief

With pink wool cast on 2 sts.
Knit 5 rows.
Increase in the first stitch in the next and every 6th row till 13 sts.
Knit 5 rows.
Decrease at the beginning of the next and every 6th row till 2 sts. are left.
Cast off.

Making up

Oversew seams on the wrong side leaving one side open for stuffing, and rounding off corners for head and feet. Turn inside out and stuff firmly. Sew side seams of skirt on wrong sides. Sew the bottom of the coat on at the waistline.

Sew pearl buttons on bodice and skirt and bottom of coat in pattern. Sew a pyramid of them on the arms, and some on the back also.

Sew the hat seam and decorate the brim with small feathers. These can be curled slightly by pulling the feather smartly between the thumb and the open blade of a pair of scissors.

Embroider the features with wool or silk. Twist strands of wool into a chignon and sew to head at the back.

Attach the hat to the head with invisible stitches.

Tie scarf round her neck.

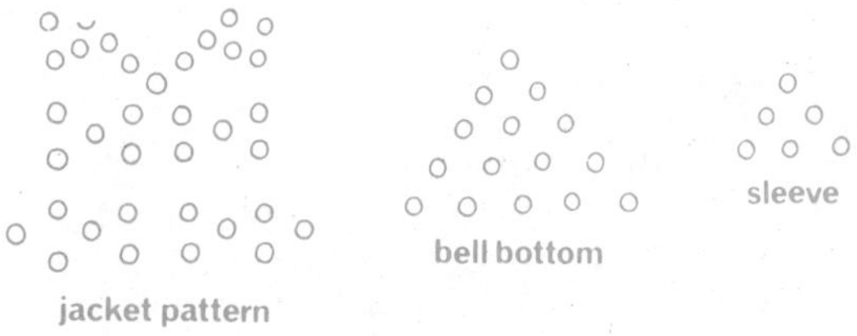

jacket pattern

bell bottom

sleeve

Fig. 22

203

Pierrot

You will need :

3 oz. of white 4 ply or double knitting wool ; small quantities of red, orange, green, black wool ; three No. 10 knitting needles (U.S. size No. 3) ; small piece of red felt ; kapok for stuffing.

Cast on 10 stitches in black wool.
Knit 1½ in.
Change to white wool.
Knit 3 in.
Break off wool and leave sts. on needle.
Knit a second leg and put both on to one needle. (20 sts.)
Knit 6½ in. in white wool.
Knit 3 in. in black wool.
Knit 6½ in. in white wool.
Divide for legs and knit them to match the front ones.

Arms

Cast on 16 sts. in white wool.
Knit 3 in.
Cast off.

Making up

Sew seams on the wrong side, leaving an opening for stuffing and rounding off the corners of head and feet. Turn inside out and stuff. Finish sewing up. Sew and stuff arms and sew on at the shoulders.

Cut a long oval in red felt and cut a slit in the middle, and sew in place for the mouth.

Embroider two big crosses in black chain stitch for the eyes.

Nose

Cast on 4 sts. of red wool.
Knit 1 row.
Increase at the beginning and end of the next row.
Knit 1 row.
Repeat the last 2 rows. (8 sts)
Knit 4 rows.
Decrease at the beginning and end of the next row.
Knit 1 row.
Repeat these 2 rows. (4 sts.)
Cast off.
Run a gathering thread round the edge of the knitting, put a hard ball of stuffing in the middle, draw it up tightly into a ball and sew it in the centre of the face.

Dress

Front.
Cast on 10 sts. white wool.
Knit 1 row.
In the next row increase twice in every stitch by knitting into the front, the back and then the front again. (30 sts.)
Knit 2¾ in. on these sts.
Break off the wool and leave.
Knit a second leg to match and put both sets of stitches on to 1 needle .(60 sts.)
Knit 1 in.
Next row. K 5 k 2 tog. *k 10 k 2 tog.* Repeat * to * 3 times k 5. (55 sts.)
Knit 1 in. including decrease row.
Next row. K 4 k 2 tog. *k 9 k 2 tog.* Repeat * to * 3 times. (50 sts.)
Knit 1 in.
Next row. K 4 k 2 tog. *k 8 k 2 tog.* Repeat * to * 3 times. (45 sts.)
Knit 1 in.
Next row. K 3 k 2 tog. *k 7 k 2 tog.* Repeat * to * 3 times. (40 sts.)
Knit 1 in.
Next row. K 3 k 2 tog. *k 6 k 2 tog.* Repeat * to * 3 times. (35 sts.)
Knit 1 in.
Next row. K 3 k 2 tog. *k 5 k 2 tog.* Repeat * to * 3 times. (30 sts.)
Knit on without further decreasing until work measures 9 in. from the beginning
Next row. *K 1 k 2 tog.* Repeat * to * to end of row. (20 sts.)
Cast off.
Knit a second piece for the back of the dress.

Neck and ankle ruffles

With orange wool cast on 60 sts.
Knit 1 row.
Change to white wool.
Knit 4 rows.
Change to green wool.
Knit 2 rows.
Change to white wool.
Knit 2 rows.
Next row. Slip 1 k 2 tog., pass slipped stitch over. Repeat this to the end of the row. (20 sts.)
Cast off.
Knit two more ruffles for the ankles.

Sleeve ruffles

With orange wool cast on 48 sts.

Knit 1 row.
Break off wool.
Change to white wool.
Knit 4 rows.
Change to green wool.
Knit 2 rows.
Change to white wool.
Knit 2 rows.
Next row. Slip 1, knit 2 tog., pass slipped stitch over. Repeat this to the end of the row. (16 sts.)
Cast off.
Knit a second one to match.

Hat

With white wool cast on 48 sts.

Knit 1½ in.
Next row. *K 6 k 2 tog.* Repeat * to * to end of the row. (42 sts.)
Knit 3 rows.
Next row. *K 5 k 2 tog.* Repeat * to * to end of row. (36 sts.)
Knit 3 rows.
Next row. *K 4 k 2 tog.* Repeat * to * to end of row. (30 sts.)
Knit 3 rows.
Next row. *K 3 k 2 tog.* Repeat * to * to end of row. (24 sts.)
Knit 3 rows.
Next row. *K 2 k 2 tog.* Repeat * to * to end of row. (18 sts.)
Knit 3 rows.
Next row. *K 1 k 2 tog.* Repeat * to * to end of row. (12 sts.)
Knit 3 rows.
Next row. Knit 2 tog. all along the row. (6 sts.)
Knit 3 rows.
Next row. K 2 tog. 3 times. (3 sts.)
Next row. Slip 1, knit 1, pass slipped st. over.
Cast off.

Pom-poms

Cut two strips of cardboard ½ in. wide. Place them together with a thread of wool between them lengthwise (Fig. 23). Wind orange wool round them about 50 times. Cut through the wool between the cards and tie very tightly round the middle to form a ball. Trim off the ends to the required size. Make two or three for the hat and three for the dress.

Make up

Sew together the inside leg seams.

Pin the centre of the neck of the dress to the doll's neck, similarly pin the back. Pin the trouser legs together at the ankles. They should be slightly baggy.

Oversew the side seams on the right side. Catch down to the doll at neck and ankles. Join shoulder seams.

Join seams of ruffles and sew them round neck and ankles and the two smaller ones round the wrists.

Sew three pom-poms down the front.

Sew seam of hat, turn brim back in a roll (Fig. 24) and catch down. Sew on pom-poms, stuff lightly to keep shape and stitch to the head through the brim.

Fig. 23

Fig. 24

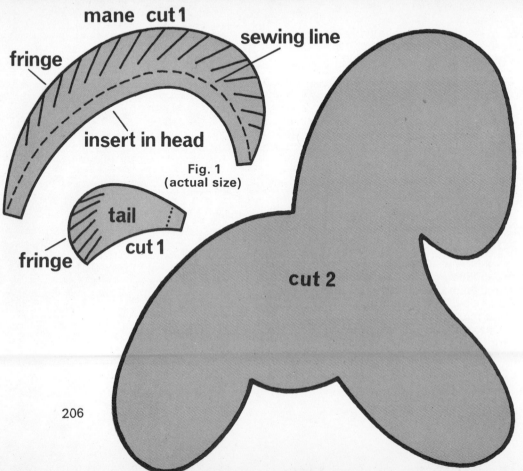

mane cut 1

fringe

sewing line

insert in head

Fig. 1
(actual size)

fringe

tail

cut 1

cut 2

Decorated toys

Mobiles

Mobiles are attractive, not just for any colour or interesting shape they may have, but because they have movement as well, and this, like tropical fish in a tank, or flying birds, holds attention and interest. Mobiles can be gay and exotic with birds or butterflies or dragonflies; comical with faces and masks; abstract with wood or wire shapes; even musical with metal shapes or figures.

A mobile merry-go-round

Here are gaily-coloured little horses and cocks swinging round under a circus ring-like top, bright with embroidery and sparkling with sequins and beads. They are, like the flat toys described in Chapter Six, cut in two pieces without a gusset and joined together to make flattish figures. There are three cocks and three horses all in different colours.

You will need :

Fairly small pieces of many different-coloured felts, for cutting the bodies (here the horses are sky blue, orange, mauve, and the cocks royal blue, rose pink and emerald green) ; small scraps of other colours in felt for manes and tails, legs, and wings ; a larger piece in one colour for the ring they are swinging on ; embroidery silks ; sequins ; beads ; metal thread ; kapok or similar for stuffing ; some thick cardboard, a piece of firm wire about 25 in. long and some gilt cord.

Horses

The template for the little horses is in three pieces, for body, tail and mane (Fig. 1). From them cut two body pieces, one mane and tail in a different shade. Reverse the template always when tracing the second pieces and cut inside the pencil lines to avoid a grubby looking seam on pale colours.

Embroider the pieces before sewing together. Work a line of chain stitch in embroidery silk all round the outline of the horse, about ¼ in. in from the edge (Fig. 2). Over this sew continuous fly stitch in bright metal thread. Sew a sequin at the end of it on the forehead. The eye is a curved line of silver chain stitch with straight stitches raying out from it. In the centre of the triangle of embroidery formed by legs and neck sew a fairly large sequin, with three lines of silver fly stitch pointing in to the legs and neck. Sew a sequin at the end of each.

Embroider the second piece for the other side.

Cut the round end of the tail piece in a fringe and pin it on to one side piece so that it sticks out jauntily (Fig. 3).

The mane is cut in a curve to follow the line of the head and stretches from just above the eye to the base of the neck. Fringe the edge and pin in place on the same side piece. Place the two pieces together with right sides outside, placing pins carefully through the embroidery so that they won't leave marks on the felt.

Oversew the edges starting from the chin, up the head to the beginning of the mane. Sew in the mane with the head seam using stab stitch, inserting the needle at right angles from front to back through the three thicknesses of felt and then inserting at right angles from back to front through the mane only and close to the edge of the head felt. When finished it will resemble the oversewing.

Sew to the base of the neck. Stuff the head with small pieces of stuffing, keeping it smooth and softly rounded. Continue sewing round the back leg, and then ease the stuffing in place with a blunt pencil end.

207

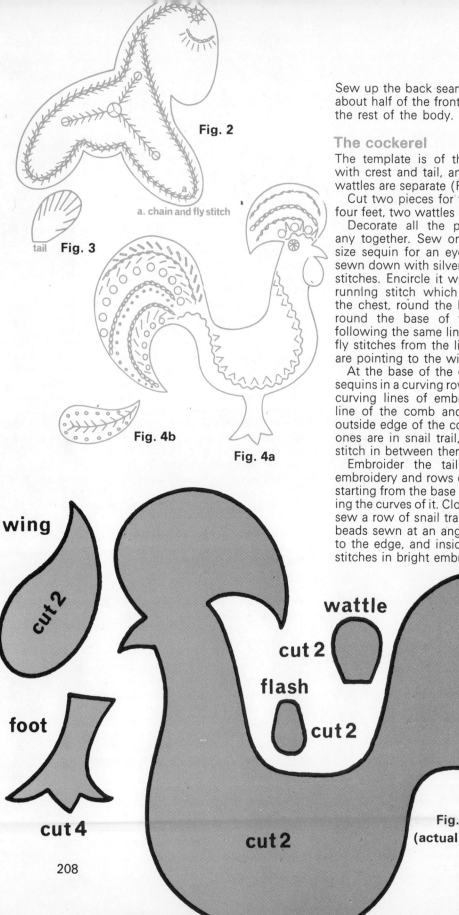

Fig. 2

a. chain and fly stitch

a.

tail   Fig. 3

Fig. 4b

Fig. 4a

Sew up the back seam of the front leg and about half of the front seam, and then stuff the rest of the body. Sew up the opening.

The cockerel

The template is of the bird in one piece with crest and tail, and the wing, feet and wattles are separate (Fig. 5).

Cut two pieces for the body, two wings, four feet, two wattles and two eye flashes.

Decorate all the pieces before sewing any together. Sew on a coloured medium size sequin for an eye, opposite the beak, sewn down with silver metal thread straight stitches. Encircle it with a line of threaded running stitch which continues across to the chest, round the lower body and curls round the base of the tail. Inside this, following the same line sew a row of single fly stitches from the line so that the points are pointing to the wing (Fig. 4a).

At the base of the comb sew three gold sequins in a curving row and from them three curving lines of embroidery following the line of the comb and curling over to the outside edge of the comb. The two outside ones are in snail trail, with a line of chain stitch in between them.

Embroider the tail with lines of soft embroidery and rows of beads and sequins, starting from the base of the tail and following the curves of it. Close to the outside edge sew a row of snail trail with a line of bugle beads sewn at an angle outside it pointing to the edge, and inside it a line of straight stitches in bright embroidery silk worked at

wing

cut 2

foot

cut 4

wattle

cut 2

flash

cut 2

cut 2

Fig. 5
(actual size)

208

the same angle. A line of sequins next, follows the same curve. Under this is a row of chain stitch with small gold beads alongside it. Next, sew a line of metal thread chain stitch with straight stitches angled from it, finished off with a row of gold sequins.

Decorate the wings with a line of fly stitch in embroidery silk, down the centre, with small bright beads all round it (Fig. 4b).

Oversew two feet pieces together for each foot, starting from the leg and stuffing each claw as it is sewn with tiny pieces of kapok, easing it in very carefully with a blunted pencil.

Pin the foot in place on one of the side pieces. Pin the two side pieces together with right sides outside, matching beaks, crests and tails.

Start sewing from under the beak, over the crest and half-way along the under seam of the crest. Stuff the tiny beak carefully, easing stuffing into the point, and stuff the head and the point of the crest. Sew the rest of the under seam, and on down the back of the neck, over the tail and a short way along the under seam of the tail. Ease stuffing gently into the point of the tail and continue sewing a little and stuffing all round the rest of the seams up to the beak. Stuff carefully and not too hard, but firmly at the two narrowest places at neck and base of tail, to prevent the head and tail drooping.

Sew a red wattle each side of the head under the beak, sewing one side of it to the head and the other hanging free.

Sew the two eye flashes (Fig. 6) under the eye just behind the wattles.

Sew a wing in place on each side with the point of it close to the back seam.

Thread a needle with a fine transparent nylon thread and thread it into their backs to find the correct suspension place for the cocks and horses. The one for the cock seems to be at the most outward curving point of the tail almost opposite the point of the comb, and for the little horses about half way along the mane. Move the thread slightly from place to place until the figure balances.

For merry-go-round frame

Cut six pieces of thick card 4 in. long and 1½ in. wide. Cut three equal scallops along one long side (Fig. 7). Use each card as a template for its two pieces of felt, reversing the template for tracing the second piece

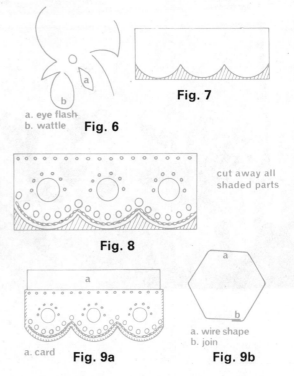

a. eye flash
b. wattle   **Fig. 6**

Fig. 7

cut away all shaded parts

Fig. 8

a. card   **Fig. 9a**

a. wire shape
b. join

Fig. 9b

and keeping the pencilled side for the wrong side. Mark each card with its corresponding felts; keeping them together will ensure a good fit, as each card can vary a little.

Embroider one piece of felt from each pair with a line of silver metal thread chain stitch near the edge with a line of sequins inside it and following the line of the scallops (Fig. 8). Sew a large sequin in the centre of the curve with small gold beads sewn round the top half of it. Sew a close row of gold beads along the top edge.

Sew the two pieces of felt together, a plain piece and an embroidered piece, on the right sides, sewing the two short sides and the scalloped edge. Insert the appropriate card and sew up the long edge (Fig. 9a). Repeat this with the other five sections.

Sew all six together in a hexagon shape by oversewing their short sides together firmly. Sew more sequins up over the joins to match those round the scallop.

On the inside, on two hexagon points, opposite to each other, sew a length of gilt cord to suspend the frame.

Take the 25 in. length of firm wire, and with pliers bend it into a hexagon shape (Fig. 9b) to fit *inside* the frame. The two ends should overlap a little. Bind or solder the

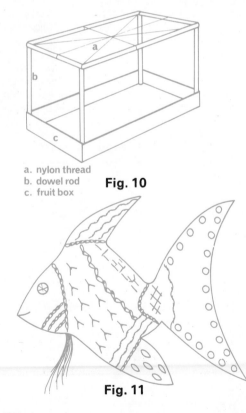

a. nylon thread
b. dowel rod
c. fruit box

Fig. 10

Fig. 11

two ends in place. Cut a 24 in. length of felt ½ in. wide and sew it round the wire to enclose it. Sew this on to the inside of the frame just below the top edge keeping the sewn side of it tucked away close to the frame. This will keep the frame in rigid shape.

Thread small bugle beads on to the nylon thread sewn on to the horses' and cocks' backs, threading twice as many on to the cocks' threads as on the horses' and this will ensure that they hang at different levels. Sew the end of each thread into the angles of the hexagon, fastening off very securely, because nylon thread tends to be slippery.

An aquarium of felt fish

Colourful, exotic-looking, imaginative fish floating around in a water-less aquarium, and all of them handmade.

You will need :
Bright many-coloured felts ;
embroidery silks ; sequins ; beads ;
fine metal threads ; an ordinary
wooden fruit box, for the
aquarium ; some ⅜ in. dowel rod ;
some green and blue Tarlatan ; two
or three sheets of cellophane ;

210

some stuffing material ; some nylon thread.

Make the aquarium first

The box should have sides about 1½ in. high. Cut four pieces of dowel rod about 9 in. high for a fruit box measuring 15 in. by 8 in. and fix them firmly with nails or glue standing upright in each corner of the box (Fig. 10). Cut four more pieces of dowel, corresponding to the measurements of the two long and two short sides of the box, and nail or glue these to the tops of the corner rods, to form a frame. The frame looks rather splendid if sprayed with gold paint.

Tie fine nylon thread across the top from corner to corner and from side to side across the middle. The fish will hang from these.

The fish

Now for the fish to go in it. These can be long and thin ; fat and stubby ; or flat ; or ordinary fishy shapes with exaggerated fins and tails and scales ; spotted ; striped ; with coloured bands which glow and flash with sequins and beads and fine metal thread.

Go to a tropical fish shop or to the aquarium in a zoo to get some ideas, then add some decorations of your own. Here are some to start you off (Fig. 17).

Some of the fish have bands of colour added to the shape and in some cases the fish template has been cut into sections and the pieces used to cut out the different colours and then sewn together to make the original shape with decorative stitching.

A black and white angel fish

A black and white and silver one is shaped rather like an angel fish with a crescent-shaped tail nearly as big as his body (Fig. 11). He is embroidered with white embroidery silk and fine silver metal thread on black felt.

Cut two shapes in felt from the template and embroider the pieces first, taking care to make them for left and right sides.

The embroidery is in stripes of zigzag chain stitch and threaded running stitch with single fly stitches to indicate scales, a sequin eye and sequins edging his tail and a fine floating fringe of white silk cord and fine silver metal thread completes him.

Sew the edges together on the right side starting at the mouth, round the top fin and all of the tail.

Stuff the tail, not too hard, and the top

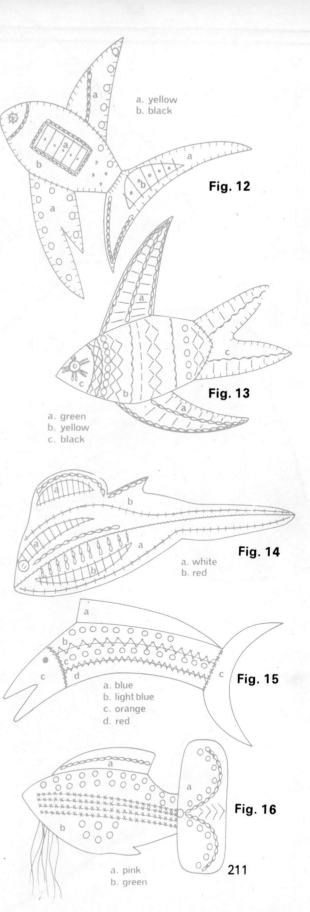

a. yellow
b. black

Fig. 12

a. green
b. yellow
c. black

Fig. 13

a. white
b. red

Fig. 14

a. blue
b. light blue
c. orange
d. red

Fig. 15

a. pink
b. green

Fig. 16

211

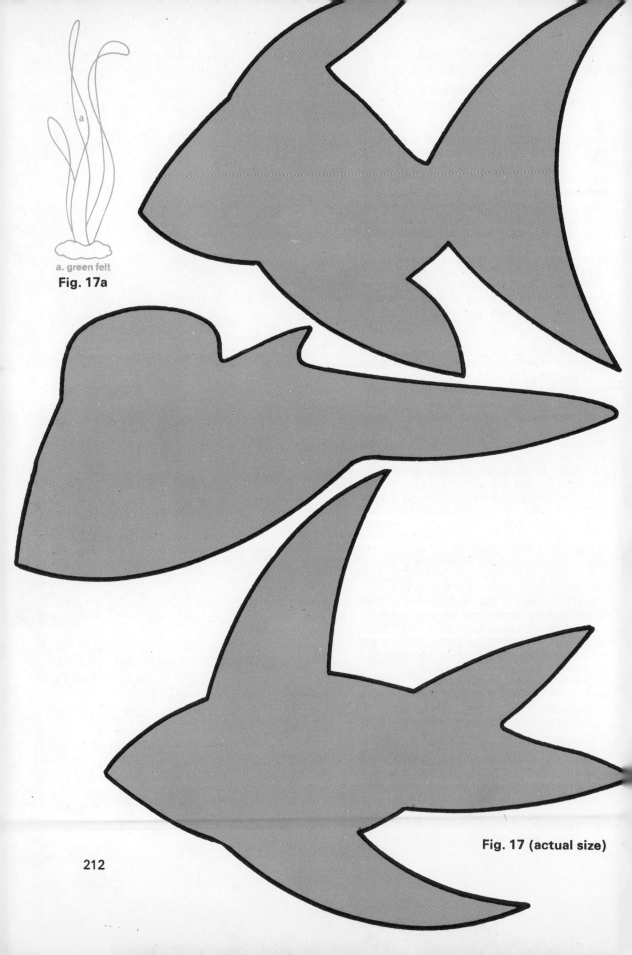

a. green felt
Fig. 17a

212

Fig. 17 (actual size)

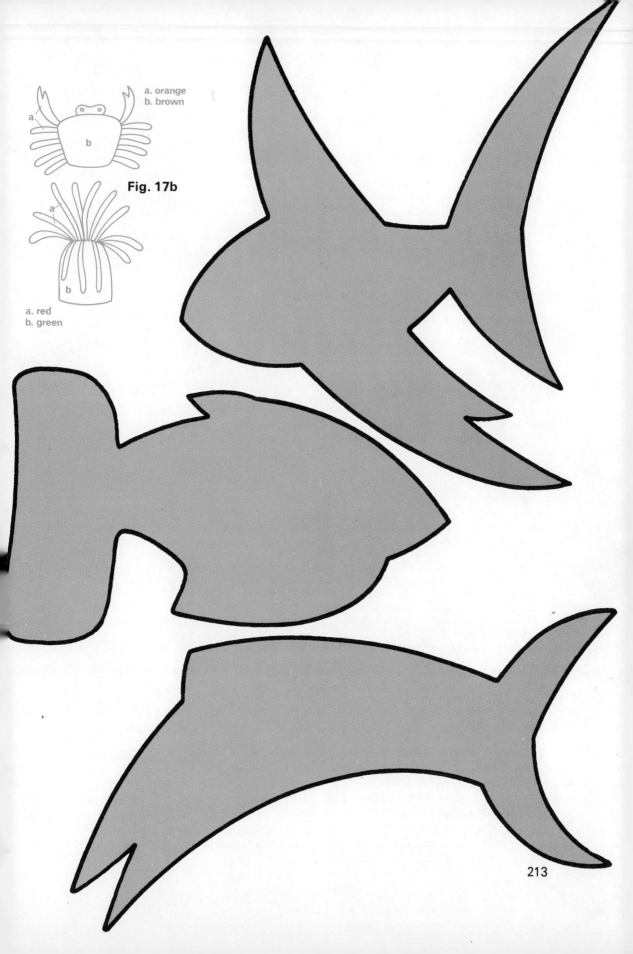

a. orange
b. brown

Fig. 17b

a. red
b. green

213

fin. Continue the sewing, stuffing as you sew. Sew a fine nylon thread in his back, testing the placing of it so that he hangs straight and not tilted.

A shark-like angel fish

Another similar angel fish shape has a more shark-like tail and a forked lower fin (Fig. 12). He is in black and yellow felt with black, orange and white embroidery. His body, fins and tail have been cut separately, the body in black felt and the fins and tail in yellow.

The body has a rectangle of yellow sewn on with long straight stitches in black, and black french knots in the spaces, and surrounded with a line of orange chain stitch.

The tail has a triangle of black in the middle of each side, sewn with white straight stitches and white french knots.

The fins are joined with black buttonhole stitch, each sewn separately and stuffed, and then joined on to the main body with straight stitches. Sequins are sewn on the fins and along the body, a sequin for an eye and a gold metal thread floating fringe from his fin.

A forked-tail angel fish

Another angel-type fish (Fig. 13) has a narrowly-forked tail; this time the body is in yellow felt; the fins and tail in bright green felt.

The head is in black felt, embroidered in a wheel design of bands of chain stitch in white and green, round a circular eye of two rings of chain stitch, in green and white.

The body is thickly embroidered with bands of double fly stitch in black, and black and orange whipped running stitch; in between them are bands of green and gold sequins and green bugle beads.

The fins are barred with black straight stitches held down by a band of orange chain stitch down the edges and the middle.

The tail is decorated with threaded running stitch, the entire edges are sewn together with black buttonhole stitch, the parts joined with black straight stitch.

A hump-backed fish

This fish (Fig. 14) has a long drooping tail, is very bright and quite grand in red and white. The template is cut in half from nose to tail, the upper half cut in red and the lower half in white felt. The two pieces are oversewn together.

The top half is decorated with curved bands of white felt held down with long straight stitches in red, with a thick white embroidery cotton couched down its length from its pearl button eye to the tail.

The lower half has a crescent-shaped piece of red felt sewn down with white stitches and above it, vertical stripes of red chain stitch along its length. Below it is a couched line of thick red embroidery cotton from mouth to tail.

The long thin graceful fish

He has a body in three bars of colour, red, orange, blue, with a long upstanding darker blue fin stretching the full length of the body, a wicked-looking beaked mouth and wide crescent-shaped tail in bright orange (Fig. 15).

The body colours are joined with black herring bone stitch, with a line of royal blue sequins on the blue band and bright pink sequins on the orange band. Head and tail are joined to the body with paler orange cross stitch.

The hammer tail

The last fish (Fig. 16) is a very gay fellow. He has a body of bright green felt with a fin and a great hammer-shaped tail of pink. He looks as though he could be related to a hammer head shark. From nose to tail his body has close bands of embroidered cross stitch and whipped running stitch in black and deep pink, with bands of green and gold sequins over it, and a semi-circle of blue and red sequins below. The pink fin has a line of green chain stitch along its length. The bold tail has two rows of green chain stitch curling out from the middle to the two ends with lines of pink sequins following them, and yellow fly stitches in between. The edges are buttonholed in green silk and the barbels under his chin are of fine golden metal thread and bright blue cord.

A crab

A crab (Fig. 71b) in light brown felt with orange-coloured legs and claws, crawls on the bottom among the anemones (Fig. 17b)

in red with waving yellow fronds and in green with red fronds.

A few embroidered pebbles among some strands of green felt seaweed (Fig. 17a), (wavy shapes of green felt sewn round lengths of wire with their ends in modelling clay). Now the aquarium inhabitants are complete.

Line the bottom of the box with a layer of blue and of green Tarlatan. Space the fish on the nylon threads across the frame and arrange the seaweed on the bottom. Cut cellophane to fit right round the frame and stick it in place with adhesive. Cover the top with a piece of blue Tarlatan, or another rectangle of Cellophane.

A merry-go-round of birds

Five little birds in bright-coloured felt, made very gay with coloured embroidery, sequins and beads, hang on a small doll-sized merry-go-round.

You will need :

Several small pieces of felt in a variety of gay colours for the birds' bodies, wings and top knots; a larger piece of yellow felt for the merry-go-round; some kapok; coloured embroidery silks; some fine metal thread in one or two colours; sequins and beads; a piece of thin cardboard; a wooden skewer; a large cotton reel or thread spool.

The bird shape for the template is quite easy to draw — a small circle for the head and an oval shape for the body. Join the two with two curved lines for the neck, add a pointed beak to the circle at one side and a larger-pointed triangle for the tail on the oval at the opposite side (Fig. 18). The templates for wing and topknot are separate and they can be varied for each bird.

Make the birds rounder in shape by sewing in a gusset under the body from beak to tail. When the body template has been drawn, measure the curve from under the beak to the tail and this will be the length of the gusset — it should be ½ to ¾ in. wide in the middle, tapering to a point at each end.

Trace round the templates on to different-coloured felts for each of the five birds.

215

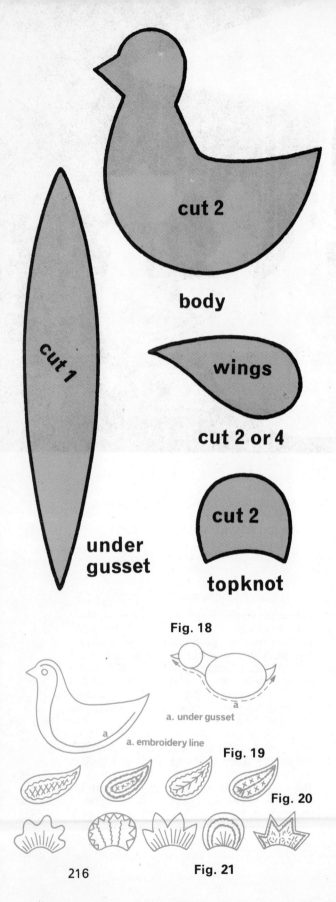

cut 2

body

cut 1

wings

cut 2 or 4

cut 2

under gusset

topknot

Fig. 18

a. under gusset

a. embroidery line

a

Fig. 19

Fig. 20

Fig. 21

Each one needs two body pieces, one gusset, four wings, and two topknots.

Embroider all the pieces before doing any sewing up. Choose a fairly simple line design for the embroidery. Using different kinds of stitches, or variations of the same stitch, and different colours on the birds will give great variety without being too elaborate.

Mark the line of embroidery wherever possible with running stitches in contrasting cotton to avoid marking the felt. Drawing on it with a pencil will result in a wide smudgy line because of the hairy felt surface and it may be difficult to cover this with embroidery. Here, a line is used encircling the eye curves down across the neck following the line of the body almost reaching the tail (Fig. 19). Embroider this in threaded running stitch with a row of slanting stitches in coloured fine metal thread along the body line.

The eye is a sequin fastened down with long straight metal thread stitches to give a starry effect.

The wings (Fig. 20) have a line of fly stitch with metal thread stitches in the spaces, and surrounded with whipped running stitch. Another has a long line of double-whipped running stitch with fine metal thread crosses above it and two lines of stem stitch on the wings following the wing shape, the inner line filled with fine metal thread herringbone stitch. Another one has single fly stitch in two colours worked along the body edge, and with straight metal thread stitches on the neck and back and with a wing outlined in buttonhole stitch with a fine metal thread cross-stitch centre. Yet another has a coloured stem stitch with a wavy metal thread line following it and a leaf vein design in metal thread worked inside a stem stitch outline on the wing.

All the topknots (Fig. 21) can be different too, with a scalloped edge worked with straight stitches in metal thread, or embroidered with metal thread round the edge and a design in straight lines in the centre, or cut in large or small points, worked in sections in a variety of colours.

Take care to embroider all the pieces in pairs for left and right sides.

When you have completed your chosen embroidery, sew the two topknot pieces together on the right side and pin it in position on one of the side pieces. Pin the two side pieces together with right sides outside and sew them together starting at the beak, over the head, stab stitching through the base of the topknot as well — it will not be stuffed — to the tail. Sew the gusset to one side piece, starting at the beak. Sew the gusset to the second side in easy stages, stuffing as you sew, first the head, pushing stuffing very carefully into the beak and into the seam along the topknot. Stuff firmly but not too hard. Complete the sewing up.

Sew a plain and an embroidered wing together and sew them on each side with invisible stitches.

Complete the making up of the other four birds in similar fashion.

To make the merry-go-round

Cut a circle about 5 in. in diameter from the card, and cut out a small segment from it (Fig. 22). Lay this shape on the yellow felt and trace round it lightly with a very fine pencil point. Overlap the two cut edges of card and stick them with adhesive tape on both sides. Fit the felt shape over it, trim off any excess turnings on it and then oversew the edges on the wrong side with matching cotton.

Cut a strip of felt long enough to fit right round the outside curved edge of the felt, and ¾ in. wide.

Draw scallops (Fig. 23) nearly ½ in. deep, round a button, and cut them out. Embroider the edge of the scallops (Fig. 24) with a threaded running stitch in bright contrasting colours of embroidery silk and sew a coloured sequin in the centre curve of each scallop. Join the two short edges and oversew the strip to the curved edge of the felt circular piece.

Cotton reel or spool base

Try to find a large size cotton reel or thread spool for the base because it will balance well. Cut a strip of felt long enough to go right round it and wide enough to fit from edge to edge. Cut two circles of felt to fit top and bottom. Join the side seams and sew a circle of felt to one end of it (Fig. 25). Seal the hole in one end of the spool with layers of adhesive tape, and drop it, sealed end down, into the felt case, and sew on the second circle. Cut a very small cross in the top over the hole in the spool.

Make a sharp smooth point at one end of the skewer and make a ridge about ¼ to ½ in. from the point, by binding a thick thread firmly all round it several times.

Fig. 22

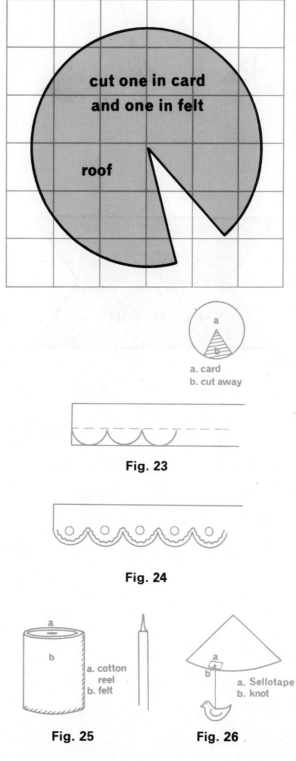

cut one in card and one in felt

roof

a. card
b. cut away

Fig. 23

Fig. 24

a. cotton reel
b. felt

a. Sellotape
b. knot

Fig. 25

Fig. 26

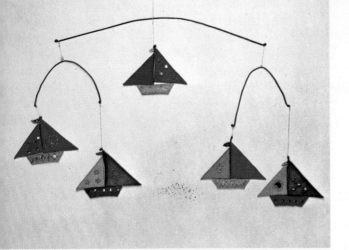

Paint it with a thin adhesive or gum to keep it in place. Pinch round it to accentuate the ridge.

Make a small hole in the point at the top of the cone-shaped card so that the skewer point fits in and the card rests on the ridge. Mark five equi-distant points round the edge of the circle and ½ to ¾ in. from the edge. With nylon thread take a stitch in the birds' backs near the base of the neck and test for balance. If the head tilts forward, move the thread forward, and vice versa, until it hangs straight. Take the end of the thread through a hole at one of the marked spots, and knot it on top of the card. Seal it down with adhesive tape (Fig. 26). Test the heights of the other four birds from this first one and when all are in position fit the felt canopy on top of the card one and your merry-go-round is ready.

Sailing ship mobile

This mobile of sailing ships is gay with many-coloured felts and sparkling with fine metal thread and sequins. The sails are squares folded in half diagonally, after embroidering, and mounted on the small boats. You can use different colours for each sail and each boat, and for this quite small pieces of felt can be used.

You will need :
Small pieces of different-coloured felt; sequins; metal threads; beads; matching cotton; a small quantity of kapok; 4½ feet of plastic-covered wire; some thin tinsel cord (the kind sold for Christmas wrappings).

Cut five squares (this is for the five ships) of felt measuring 2¼ in. and five measuring 1¾ in. and five boat shapes from the template shown here. The boat will be folded along the dotted line which is the base (Fig. 27).

Cut five pieces of wire 4¼ in. long for the masts. Twist each end of wire into a small ring and bend nearly ½ in. at right angles at one end of each (Fig. 28a).

Embroider each boat each side of the base line, in a very simple design (Fig. 27a).

Place a mast with the short side 'a' along the base of the boat so that the 'mast' is in the centre, and sew it in place (Fig. 28b).

Fold the boat in half with the right sides outside and sew from the base, up one side

boat

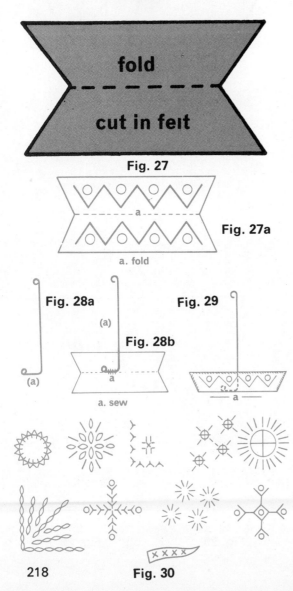

fold

cut in felt

Fig. 27

Fig. 27a

a. fold

Fig. 28a   (a)   **Fig. 29**

(a)   **Fig. 28b**

(a)   a

a. sew

a

218   **Fig. 30**

and along the top as far as the mast. Stuff this half very lightly with small pieces of kapok, keeping it smooth. Continue sewing and stuffing along the top. Sew up the side (Fig. 29). Mark the diagonal line on a square of felt with running stitches and embroider a motif on each side of the line (Fig. 31). The designs used are shown in Fig. 30. They combine the use of sequins with various coloured fine metal thread.

Fold each square along the diagonal with right sides outside, and oversew the edges (Fig. 31). Attach it to the mast at top and bottom with a few stitches taken round the wire, and also catch it down to the end of the boat. Put one large and one smaller sail on each boat (Fig. 32).

Cut five small pennants, embroider and sew them on at the mast head.

To make the mobile frame

Cut three pieces of wire, one piece 14 in. long and two pieces 8½ in. long. The two short wires will be suspended from each end of the long wire. Cut about 20 in. length of tinsel cord and split it, using a single strand. Make a small notch with a nail file in the middle of the long wire and tie the cord round it so that there is a short length to tie on the boat and a longer piece for suspending the mobile. Use a clove hitch knot for this (Fig. 33). Tie shorter lengths of cord like this to the middles of the other two wires.

Bend each end of each wire into a small loop. Tie a small loop in the short cord on the long wire, about 1 in. from the wire and slip it over the wire loop in the ship's mast. Cut two lengths of cord about 12 in. long, split them and make a loop in one end of each piece. Slip them over the wire loops in the other ships' masts (Fig. 34). Lay out the wires in hanging position and decide on the position for each ship. To be really effective they should hang at different levels. Tie small loops in the cord at the required level and slip over the wire loops on the frame. A last loop tied in the hanging cord and the mobile is ready. The ships should be able to swing freely without touching one another.

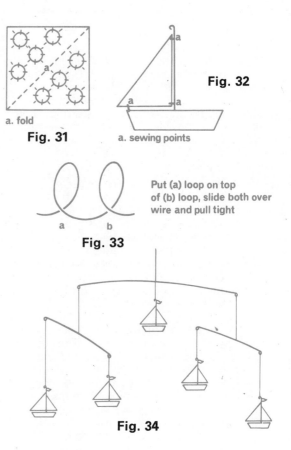

a. fold

Fig. 31

Fig. 32

a. sewing points

Put (a) loop on top of (b) loop, slide both over wire and pull tight

a   b

Fig. 33

Fig. 34

A royal elephant

A royal elephant, richly decorated and embroidered, carries his prince on his back in a howdah, with a young attendant mahout to guide him. He stands nearly 9 in. tall and is made of grey felt which shows up his gay colouring. Over his back, under the howdah, is an embroidered brocade saddle cloth.

You will need :

A piece of grey felt 20 in. square ; a small piece of black felt for the soles of the feet and for his eyes ; some white felt for his tusks ; a length of wire for the tusks, trunk and legs ; a piece of brocade 8 in. by 6 in. ; some fringe ; kapok or similar for stuffing ; beads ; sequins ; embroidery silks ; grey cotton.

The template is cut from a silhouette including the trunk (Fig. 35). The under gusset for the legs to make him stand up is cut from the same silhouette of the legs, from a curved line following the under body shape and stretching from near the end of the inner trunk at the mouth, to the tail (Fig. 36).

The head gusset stretches from a point near the end of the trunk, over the head and back, to the tail. It is pointed at each end, is narrow at the trunk, broadening very gradually to its widest part at the top of the head and near the shoulders.

Draw round the templates on to the grey felt, reversing the template when drawing each second piece.

Cut two side pieces, two under gussets, one back gusset, and four ear pieces from the grey felt ; four oval soles and two small eye circles from the black felt ; and four strips in white felt, pointed at one end for the tusks

Embroider the legs of the side pieces, the sides of the trunk, and two of the ear pieces, pairing them all for left and right sides. Sew the black felt eyes in position near the top of the head and embroider a circle round them, add sequins and beads to the coloured embroidery for a rich effect.

Sew in the back gusset, matching the joining points on the two sides. Oversew the curved seam of the under gusset on the wrong side. Pin it on to one of the side pieces, starting at the front edge of the foot,

up the leg and down the trunk. Sew this piece, sewing from the trunk and down the front seam of the front leg. Fasten off here.

Sew up an inch or so of the back seam of the front leg, and leave the thread hanging while you sew a sole piece to the leg, the long side of the oval stretching from the front seam to the back seam. Oversew the edges.

Cut a piece of wire 14 in. long and mark the centre of it. Twist each end into a small flat loop and bend them at right angles to the main wire. Pad the loop with a little stuffing. Place the wire loop flat on the sole and pad all round loop and wire keeping the wire in the middle of the leg. Sew the back seam an inch at a time, and stuff firmly, completely enclosing the wire (Fig. 37).

Sew the under body and down the front seam of the back leg. Fasten off at the foot. Sew the back leg in the same way as the front leg, inserting a second length of wire and sewing and stuffing the leg about an inch at a time. Sew the seam round the end of the trunk between the ends of the two gussets.

Cut a piece of wire about 9 in. long, and twist one end up to cover the sharp end of the wire. Pad with a little kapok and push the end into the trunk, padding all round it with small pieces of stuffing, keeping it firm but not hard. Twist the other end of the wire round the marked centre of the front leg wire.

Pin the under gusset to the second side starting again from the front foot to the trunk and carefully matching the pinning with the side already sewn. Start sewing from the trunk, about an inch at a time, and padding as you sew, all round the trunk wire, keeping it away from the edges. Stuff the head firmly and smoothly keeping it a good shape.

Continue sewing down the front seam of the front leg, fastening off at the foot. Pad the loop of the other end of the front leg wire and finish off in the same way, fastening off at the top of the leg.

Stuff the front part of the body, packing stuffing firmly round all the wires, particularly at the tops of the legs. Finish off the back leg in the same way as the others, leaving the under body seam between the legs, open for stuffing. Complete the stuffing and sew up the opening.

Make a short cord in black wool, fringe the ends and sew on for a tail.

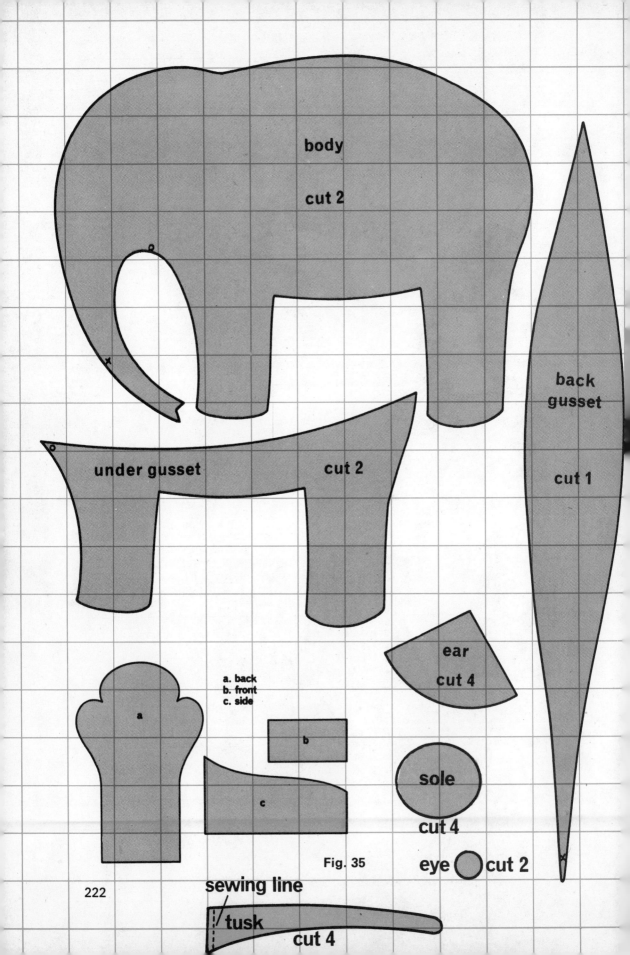

body

cut 2

back
gusset

cut 1

under gusset   cut 2

a. back
b. front
c. side

a

b

c

ear
cut 4

sole

cut 4

eye ⬤ cut 2

Fig. 35

222

sewing line

tusk
cut 4

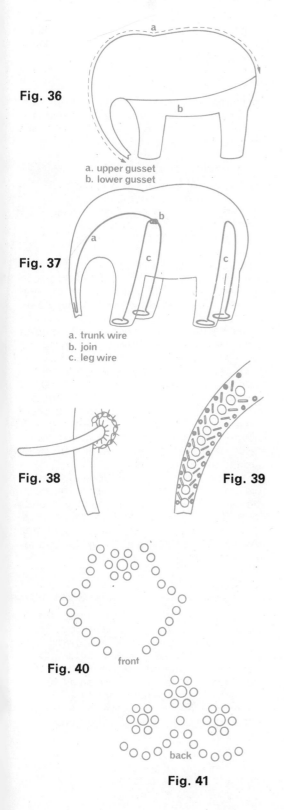

Fig. 36

a. upper gusset
b. lower gusset

Fig. 37

a. trunk wire
b. join
c. leg wire

Fig. 38

Fig. 39

Fig. 40   front

back

Fig. 41

Join together two pieces for each ear, one embroidered and one plain, pairing them for left and right sides. Sew in place just behind the eyes, pointing to the back.

For the tusks, cut two pieces of wire 2 in. longer than the felt. Join two pieces of the felt along one seam and about ½ in. along the second seam. Turn back one end of the wire, pad it thinly with kapok, or a strip of thin material, and insert in the tusk, pushing it gently down to the point. Continue sewing the seam pushing in kapok round the wire as you sew. About 1¾ in. of wire should be left at the end of the tusk. Make a very small hole beside the top of the trunk and push in the bare wire. Sew the open end of the tusk on to the body, and work a ring of embroidery around the join (Fig. 38). Make up the second tusk in the same way.

Sew a line of bright red sequins down the front of the trunk with bugle beads and small beads in between them and along the side (Fig. 39). Couch down a thick bright silk thread over the joins of trunk and gusset.

Make a narrow hem on each of the edges of brocade, decorate the long sides with embroidery and sequins and sew fringe along the short sides. Sew it in place on the back.

The howdah

This is made from four shaped pieces of thick card, each covered with embroidered felt and then joined together to form a hollow box. The back is high and throne-like, the sides curving down to a narrow front (Fig. 35).

In thick card, cut one back, two sides and one front piece. Trace round the card shapes on to the felt, cutting two backs, two fronts and four sides, all slightly larger than the card to allow for its thickness.

Embroider both pieces for the back, one piece for the front and one for each side, left and right (Figs. 40 and 41).

Join the two back pieces together with right sides outside, halfway to the top of the back curve, insert the card shape and continue sewing enclosing the card. Join three sides of the front pieces, insert the card and sew the fourth side. Join the curved edges and the short side of the side pieces, insert the cards and sew up the remaining side. Join all the pieces together with right sides outside.

Sew it in place on the elephant's back

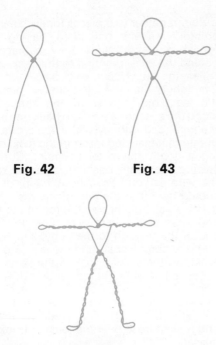

Fig. 42   **Fig. 43**

Fig. 44

Fig. 45   **Fig. 46**

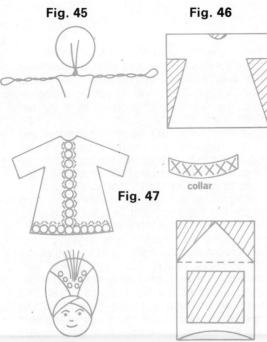

Fig. 47

collar

Fig. 48

Fig. 49

cut away all shaded parts

on top of the brocade, taking stitches through the actual <u>back</u> if possible to keep it firmly in place.

The little prince

He is made from soft wire covered with strips of dark nylon stocking; his head is a polystyrene ball or could be a loop of wire padded. He is nearly 6 in. tall.

> *You will need:*
> A piece of wire about 30 in. long;
> a 1-inch polystyrene ball; some
> dark nylon stocking; some pieces
> of gay silks to dress him; some
> sequins and beads.

Make the frame for his body from the piece of wire. Fold it in half, insert one finger in the fold, and twist, making a small loop (Fig. 42). Bend back each wire about 2½ in. from the twist, and twist these wires together for the arms, leaving a small loop at each end for the hands (Fig. 43). Bring the two ends of wire together and twist together at the waist forming a triangle for the body. Bend back the remaining ends of wire and twist round the waist, forming the loops so formed into legs, making them and leaving small loops for the feet (Fig. 44).

Twist a strip of bias cut material round the limbs and body and cover all with strips of dark coloured nylon.

Cut the loop of wire at the head to make two ends. Make a small hole in the polystyrene ball and push in the two ends firmly (Fig. 45). Cover the ball with the dark nylon, keeping the front smooth and free from wrinkles for the face. Draw the features with felt-tip pens.

Trousers

Make his full trousers, gathered round the ankles, in bright fine blue metal thread material, two rectangles 3 in. by 2½ in.

Fold each piece in half lengthwise and seam them together for half the length for the legs, then join both legs together with a back and front seam. Make a small turning at the legs and gather them to fit closely round the ankles. The waist is likewise gathered up and sewn to the figure.

Tunic

Over these he wears a tunic top in white satin, cut from a rectangle 5 in. by 3½ in.

Fold it in half and cut out the sides (Fig. 46).

Sew the side and arm seams. Turn under small hems at sleeves, neck and bottom and sew the front and bottom edge closely with red and blue sequins and fine metal thread crosses in green and gold (Fig. 47). A neckband embroidered with fine metal thread crosses encircles the neck closely.

A turban in material matching the trousers is folded round the head, envelope fashion, the folds coming in the front and fastened with red sequins with a plume of fine gold metal thread (Fig. 48). He will, sit proudly in the howdah.

His elephant's mahout

You will need:
About twelve black pipe cleaners and some scraps of white cambric for his turban and loincloth.

Fold a pipe cleaner in half, forming a small loop as foundation for the head. Twist two more for the arms, leaving very small loops for the hands. Twist together the ends of head and arms. Twist on to them two more pipe cleaners for the body and two more for each leg, to the bottom of the body, and twist all the ends firmly. Bind two more cleaners round the top of the body to give it some shape — it will be bare — and bind some round the head loop to shape the head. Do not make the head too large.

Cut a crossway strip of cambric and bind it round the head in three or four folds for a turban, and sew the end at the back. Cut a second, wider crossway strip and fold it round legs and waist for a loincloth, sewing the ends underneath out of sight.

Bend the legs outward and down to make knees and you will find that he sits quite well on the elephant's neck, above the ears. A pipe cleaner sewn on one hand could be his goad.

Another howdah

A different type of howdah with closed sides and roof can also be made from thick card covered with felt.

You will need:
Four rectangles of card measuring 2½ in. by 4 in. (the 4 in. to be the height).

Cut out all the shaded parts (Fig. 49) and score across the dotted line for the roof. The two end pieces will need a slight curve cut out from the bottom to enable the howdah to fit over the elephant's back.

Trace round the cut out card shape on to some coloured felt and cut out eight shapes, remembering to cut them slightly larger than the cards.

Embroider four of the pieces with sequins and fine metal thread and sew together an embroidered piece and a plain piece, sewing round three edges and leaving the roof open.

Score the dotted line on the card and bend the roof triangle away from the cut. This scored side will be the outside so that it bends in towards the centre.

Insert a card and complete the oversewing of the roof and the window.

Repeat this for the other three sides and then sew them all together, first the sides and then the roof. Sew it on to the elephant's back like the other.

A decorated camel

He is a fine fellow and obviously knows he is a very superior animal. Gaily decorated he is made in purple felt, has a fine silky mane and tail laced with silver. His coat sparkles with fine metal thread and sequins and he has a very fine saddle cloth for his master or mistress to sit on.

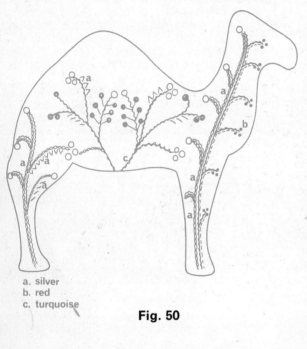

a. silver
b. red
c. turquoise

Fig. 50

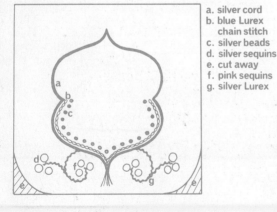

a. silver cord
b. blue Lurex
   chain stitch
c. silver beads
d. silver sequins
e. cut away
f. pink sequins
g. silver Lurex

Fig. 51

You will need :

A piece of purple felt 16 in. by 24 in. ; some soft white nylon silky wool ; a 4 in. square of bright pink felt for a saddle cloth ; embroidery silks ; fine metal thread ; coloured sequins ; beads ; silver cord ; little pearls or gold beads ; kapok or similar for stuffing ; purple cotton.

The templates are similar to those for the giraffe in Chapter Seven, with sides, under gussets, and top gusset. The under gusset is curved to follow the line of his curved chest and stretches up to reach just under his chin and then round to his tail, following the curve of the under body (Fig. 52).

Trace round the templates on to the felt with a very sharp white pencil, and cut out two sides, two under gussets, one top gusset, two ears, and four soles in purple felt.

Trace each side of the camel on to thin tracing or tissue paper and draw the embroidery design. Pin the paper on to the felt side piece and sew the design through the paper and felt with tiny running stitches in cotton. When finished tear away the paper and embroider on top of the running stitches. It is a branching design from a central stem on each leg (Fig. 50). The one on the front leg starts near the foot and stretches to the face with little branches decorated with beads and sequins on each side. It is worked in threaded and whipped running stitch with fine silver metal chain stitch on one side of it. That on the hind leg is similar but shorter. In between them on the broad space of body near the hump it is more intricate, but following the same style and using the same stitches. Embroider both sides pairing them for left and right.

For an eye, embroider a crescent in fine silver metal thread in chain stitch with straight stitches radiating from it for eye-lashes.

Sew the head gusset to the two sides. Join the two under gussets, oversewing the curved seam on the wrong side. Pin it to one of the side pieces, with right sides outside. Sew, starting from the neck, down the front seam of the front leg and fasten off. Leave the base of the foot unsewn. Sew for 1 in. along the inner seam of the leg. Leave the thread hanging, and sew a sole piece on to the foot, the length of it stretching from back to front between the two seams.

A

back
gusset

cut 1

B

Stuff this foot very carefully and very firmly with small pieces of stuffing. Carry on sewing and stuffing, sewing about an inch at a time. Repeat this for the back leg.

Make a short cord for a tail with long fringed ends. Interweave the cord with fine silver metal thread and bind the fringed end with silver. Tie a knot in the other end and pin it in place under the point of the upper gusset.

Sew up the seam under the chin and down to the beginning of the under gusset. Stuff the head softly but firmly, pushing stuffing well into the muzzle and the seams to keep a good shape.

Pin the second side to the under gusset, starting at the neck. Follow the directions for sewing the front leg. Now stuff the neck, pushing the stuffing well up into the head, stuffing it to keep it smooth and with no weak places. Leave the under body seam open. Sew the inner seam of the back leg and fasten off. Sew up 1 in. of the outer seam and then sew on the sole. Stuff the foot. Continue sewing and stuffing about 1 in. at a time. Sew up the remainder of the seam, sewing in the tail as well. Stuff the rest of the body and sew up the under seam.

Fold the corners of the straight edges of the ears to the centre, and sew in place on the head near the top and pointing back-wards.

Embroider nostrils with a single chain stitch and a mouth curve in chain stitch in black embroidery silk.

Sew loops of the white nylon wool across the chest from under the chin to just under the bulge in the chest. Cut the loops and fluff out the wool.

Embroider a scalloped edged design (Fig. 51) on the pink felt square. Draw the design on thin paper and transfer it to the felt in the same way as for the camel. Embroider it with a row of silver cord couched down following the shape, and inside this, a row of fine blue metal thread chain stitch and inside this a row of silver beads. Two scrolls each side of the point in fine silver metal thread chain stitch with three sequins sewn at each scroll end.

Sew the saddle cloth in place on the hump with invisible stitches.

Sew a small string of tiny seed pearls or gold beads as a diadem on the head with a pearl drop on the forehead.

A silver cord bridle completes him.

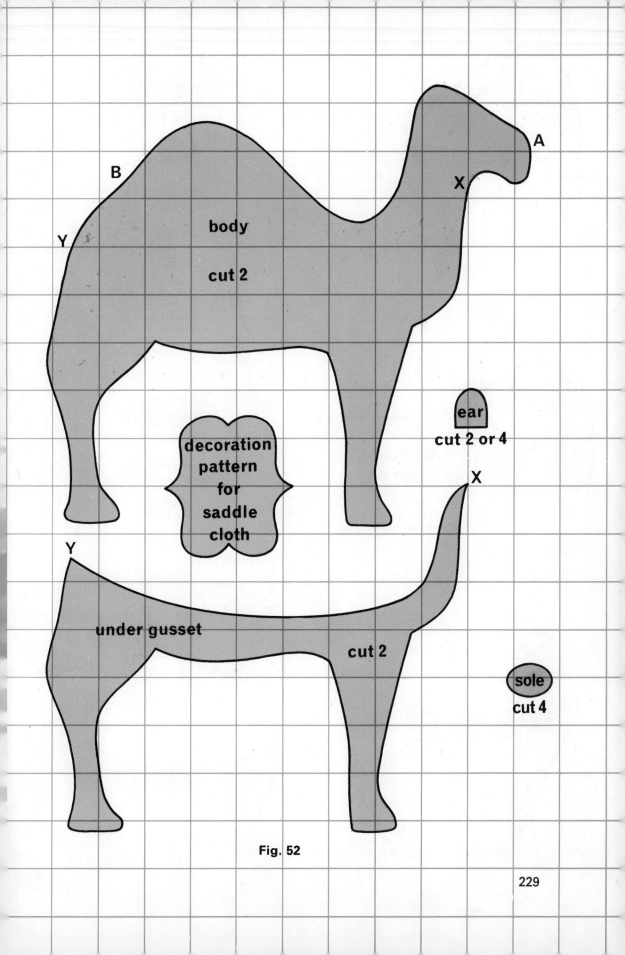

B

Y

A

X

body

cut 2

ear
cut 2 or 4

decoration
pattern
for
saddle
cloth

X

Y

under gusset

cut 2

sole
cut 4

Fig. 52

229

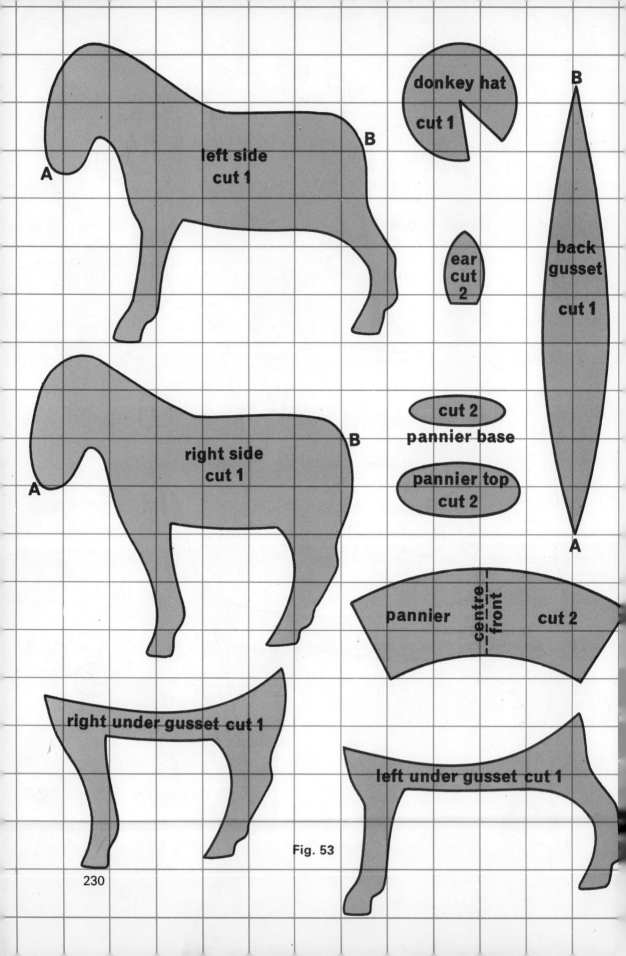

donkey hat
cut 1

left side
cut 1

A

B

ear
cut
2

back
gusset
cut 1

B

right side
cut 1

A

B

cut 2
pannier base

pannier top
cut 2

A

pannier   centre front   cut 2

right under gusset cut 1

left under gusset cut 1

Fig. 53

230

An Italian flower donkey

This little grey donkey is walking and not just standing or sitting or lying as the other toy animals have been.

To make him you will need:

Grey felt; a small piece of orange felt for a hat; some red felt for the panniers; some embroidery silks; sequins; beads; fine metal thread; black wool for a tail; kapok for stuffing; some grey cotton.

Because the donkey is walking you will have to make a more complicated template, because the two sides are different and so are the two under gusset pieces. If you are drawing your own silhouette to make templates, you must draw a right and a left side, with the front and back legs in the correct position for walking (Fig. 53).

Make a template for each. Draw a curved line on each of them from chest to tail, and each side will then have its own under gusset. Check that the under gusset curves stretch between identical points on both chests and tails. The head and back gusset are in one, stretching from under the nose, over the head and back, to the tail. The ears are large and leaf shaped.

Cut two sides, two under and one top gusset, two ears.

Make up the donkey in the same way as the tiger in Chapter Seven, taking care with the pairing of pieces for left and right sides. Sew in the top gusset to both side pieces starting under the nose each time, and now continue as for the tiger.

Hat

For the hat, cut a circle of felt on a 3 in. diameter, and cut out a segment of it, leaving about ¾ of the circle (Fig. 54). Join the two straight sides to make a shallow cone. Embroider the edge with loops of coloured silks. Mark the two places for the ears on the head and cut two small slits in the hat to correspond with these (Fig. 55). Push the bottoms of the ears into the slits and sew them in place. Sew the ears to the head, keeping them upright (Fig. 56). Sew the hat on to the head with invisible stitches.

Cut two panniers from the template and two tops and two bases.

Embroider the middle section of each pannier — this will be its front. At the top overlay a line of orange chain stitch with fine silver metal thread fly stitch (Fig. 57). Sew three lines of green fly stitch spraying out from the bottom edge. Sew blue and silver sequins down each side of the fly stitch. Join the two straight edges and sew the base piece on to the bottom edge of the pannier.

Pack some kapok into the pannier.

Thread two strands of purple silk into a large-eyed needle and sew loops all over the oval for the top of the pannier (Fig. 58). Sew scattered loops of yellow among them and finish with loops of fine green metal thread between them. Cut the metal thread loops. Sew this oval on to the top of the pannier enclosing the stuffing.

Cut a rectangle of orange felt 4 in. by 2 in. to fit over the donkey's back.

Embroider the centre parts of the two long sides with fine silver metal thread herring-bone stitch.

Sew the panniers on each side, fit it on to the donkey's back and fasten it in place with a band of felt sewn underneath the body.

Embroider two almond-shaped eyes in black stem stitch with straight stitches above for lashes and an orange centre.

Tie a thread round the neck as a guide and embroider a wreath of flowers with sequin centres and red bead petals and fine green metal thread leaves round the neck (Fig. 59).

An open chain stitch each side of the nose for nostrils and a curved line of stem stitch for a mouth complete the little donkey.

Fig. 54

a. slits for ears   **Fig. 55**

Fig. 56

Fig. 57

Fig. 58   **Fig. 59**

a. sequins
b. beads
c. Lurex thread

231

CHAPTER ELEVEN

Gifts to make

A carry-cot or bassinet and baby doll

A shoe box was used as the basis for the carry-cot, and the doll baby in it is made from woven material from an old T-shirt. The inside of the box has been padded and lined and the outside covered. The one in the picture has white lining with a blue overcheck pattern, whilst the outside reverses this and is blue checked with white. It has a pillow and mattress, sheets, blankets and padded cover, with two handles for easy carrying.

You will need :

The shoe box, which measures 10 in. by 7 in.; two pieces of material for covering it — the outside piece measuring 16 in. by 21½ in. and the inside piece 16 in. by 19 in.; for the mattress and pillow a piece 15 in. square; two pieces for sheets 15 in. by 9 in. each; two pieces of flannel 7½ in. by 11 in.; a pretty piece of nylon 10 in. by 11 in. for a cover; a piece 7 in. by 11 in. for a padded quilt; some narrow lace for edging; wadding or thick interlining; sewing cotton; two or three strands of embroidery silks.

The cot

Cover the outside of the box first. Cut off a strip from the larger piece of material measuring 2½ in. by 16 in. to make the handles, leaving a piece 19 in. by 16 in. From each corner of this cut off a square of 4½ in. leaving a cross-shaped piece (Fig. 1).

Use this shape as a pattern, placing it on the wadding and cutting a similar shape from it, the base measuring 10 in. by 9 in. but the sides measuring 4 in. instead of 4½ in. because it needs to reach only to the top of the box, with no turnings.

Fit the wadding inside the box and fix the top edge in place with masking tape, or stick it with a clear adhesive. Fit the box on to the rectangle in the middle of the cross on the material and turn up the shorter pieces at the ends of the box and pin one side firmly to the wadding on the inside edge. Gently pull the material taut from the other side so that it is firm and pin that side too. Do not pull it too tightly or it will tear the wadding. The sides of material should lap over on the long edges (Fig. 2). Stick them in place with adhesive pulling them taut.

Make a single turning on the edges of the long sides and pin it up the corners on to the stuck down pieces. Lap the material over the top edge of the box and fix it in the same way as the short sides. Sew up the corner seams neatly and catch down the top edges to the wadding, to help in holding it in place.

Cut the 16 in. length of material in half, for handles fold each piece in half lengthwise with the right sides inside and seam them. Turn them inside out and press the seams flat. Pin them in position on the inside of the long edges of the box, with the ends at an angle pointing to the bottom corners of the box. Catch down the edges to the wadding and the covering material.

Sew together the edges of the lining material on the wrong side, so that the base measures 10 in. by 7 in. (turnings of ½ in. have been allowed for in the pattern). Press the seams flat. Fit the lining into the box, wrong side down, and pin into the corners to keep it in place. Make a turning all round the top edge to come just inside the box, and sew it neatly all round the top, sewing in the handles as well.

If the stitches at the top show, or are not neat enough, couch down a cord or several strands of embroidery silk round the top to cover them. Lay the cord along the join and sew over it through the top edge of the material.

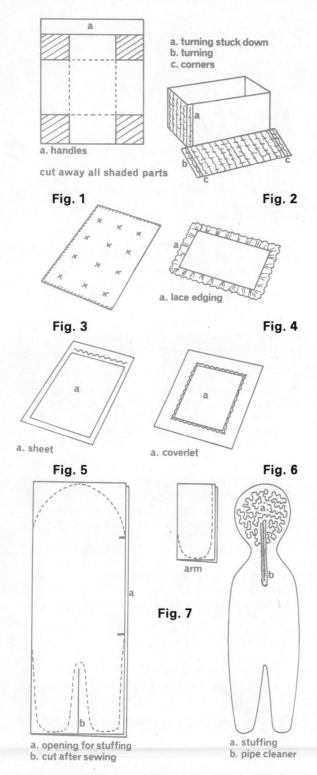

a. turning stuck down
b. turning
c. corners

a. handles

cut away all shaded parts

Fig. 1

Fig. 2

Fig. 3

a. lace edging

Fig. 4

a. sheet

Fig. 5

a. coverlet

Fig. 6

arm

Fig. 7

a. opening for stuffing
b. cut after sewing

a. stuffing
b. pipe cleaner

Fig. 8

The mattress

Cut a double thickness of wadding to fit the bottom of the box — about 6¼ in. by 9¼ in. From the material for pillow and mattress cut a piece 10¼ in. wide for the mattress. Fold it in half with right sides inside and seam it together leaving one side open. Turn inside out. Insert the pad of wadding and sew up the opening.

Sew cross stitches in about twelve places all over the mattress through all the thicknesses to hold the wadding in place (Fig. 3).

The pillow

Fold the remaining piece of material in half for the pillow, and seam it on the wrong side leaving one short side open. Turn inside out. Fill it with kapok, and sew up the opening. Sew the lace gathered into a frill all round the edge (Fig. 4).

The sheets

For the sheets, sew small hems round three sides of the material making a bigger hem on one of the short sides, and embroidering this with threaded or whipped coloured running stitch (Fig. 5).

The blankets

Make small hems similarly on all sides of the flannel pieces for the blankets, sewing a row of coloured blanket stitch along the edge of one of the short sides.

The nylon coverlet

This has inch wide hems on all the sides, sewn down with a decorative running stitch or other embroidery. When finished it should measure about 6½ in. by 7½ in. (Fig. 6).

The padded quilt

Make a single turning all round the piece of material so that it measures 6¼ in. by 12½ in. Cut a square of wadding in double thickness to measure 6 in. Place it on one half of the material and fold the other half over it. Tack round the edges including the wadding edges. Gather up the lace on one edge until it measures 25 in. Pin it evenly all round the edges of the quilt and sew edges and lace together.

The baby doll

You will need :

A piece of cotton knit measuring
10½ in. by 6 in. and two pieces
2½ in. by 3 in. for arms; (if the
material is from a used garment,
make sure that no thin, worn parts
are included or the doll will not
wear well) ; some kapok or other soft
stuffing ; a strand each of red, blue,
black embroidery silk ; some wool
for hair ; a piece of soft material
for a nightgown.

Fold the knitted fabric in half with the right
side inside, lengthwise, and backstitch the
shape (Fig. 7). Machine stitching is not
very successful because the material
stretches out of shape very easily.

Legs

Cut up between the legs after they have
been sewn. Turn it inside out and press out
the seams. Stuff the legs and backstitch
across the hips to give some movement and
so that the doll can sit. Stuff the head firmly
but not hard enough to stretch the fabric
and so pull the head out of shape.

Neck

To strengthen the neck and prevent the head
drooping, fold a pipe cleaner in half, twist it
together and push it into position so that it
is in the middle of the neck, half in the
head and half in the body (Fig. 8). Be careful
to pack stuffing all round it to keep it central.
Tie a thread tightly round the neck.

Body

Stuff the body firmly, not quite so firm as
the head, pushing stuffing well up into the
neck. Sew up the opening.

Arms

Fold the arms pieces in half lengthwise on
the wrong side and sew the seam, rounding
off the corners for the hands. Turn it inside
out and stuff softly, and sew them in place
across the shoulders.

Features

Embroider a mouth in red silk, two blue
spots for eyes surrounded with black backstitch, a few straight stitches for eyelashes
and crescents of eyebrows (Fig. 9). Sew
on wool loops for hair, or lay strands of
wool across the head and sew down the
middle for a parting, tying it with bows at
the sides of the face (Fig. 10).

Clothes

Her nightdress is cut from flannelette type
material with a small floral pattern, gathered
in at the neck, with a lace frill round the
neck and hem. Cut it from a length of material
10½ in. by 7 in. Fold it in half and cut out
(Fig. 11). Make a narrow hem on the
sleeves, neck and bottom. Sew on the lace
frills. Run a gathering thread round the
neck, draw it up and tie in a bow.

Pop the doll into her cot, cosily between
the sheets, and she is ready to go for an
outing.

Fig. 9

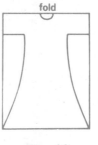

Fig. 10

Fig. 11

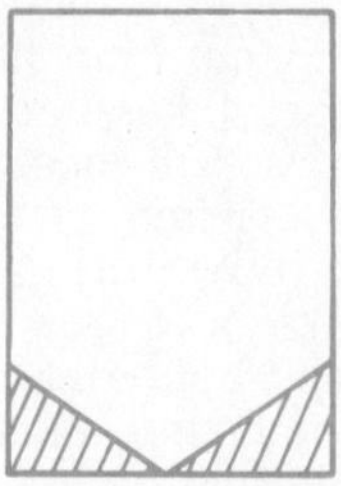

cut away all shaded parts

Fig. 12

(a) ⋀⋀⋀⋀⋀⋀⋀

(b)

Fig. 13

An easy flat money purse

Shaped like an envelope with a triangular flap, the purse is fastened with a looped button, or could have a press stud.

You will need :
A piece of felt 8½ in. by 4½ in.; a piece of lining material 9½ in. by 5½ in.; some embroidery silks; matching sewing cotton.

Mark 1½ in. up each side at one end of the felt, and mark the middle ½ in. of the short side of the same end. Cut off these corners to form the front flap (Fig. 12). The front of the purse under the flap is 3 in. deep, the back is 3½ in. deep and the flap at its widest part in the middle is 2 in.

Embroider the felt before putting in the lining.

The front of this one is embroidered ½ in. inside the edge with pointed buttonhole stitch. This is done by putting the needle *in* the same hole three times, but bringing it out each time a little to the right of the last stitch (Fig. 13a).

The flap has a centre heart-shaped design in whipped running stitch, the centre filled with leaves of long single chain stitch and yellow backstitch (Fig. 13b).

Each side of it is a curlicue in double whipped running stitch.

The button is made of two small circles of felt sewn together, the top circle embroidered in double buttonhole stitch.

A loop for it is made by sewing a double loop on the end of the flap, long enough to encircle the button and these loops then button-hole stitched.

Cut the corners from one end of the piece of lining, make ½ in. turnings all round it, and sew it on to the wrong side of the felt. Fold the purse, sew up the side seams and button the flap.

A folding needlecase

You will need :
Two pieces of contrasting coloured felt; a strand each of red, blue, white thick embroidery cotton; red and white embroidery silk; a piece of flannel.

This shape can quite easily be adapted to use as a purse or a needlecase. The one in the picture is a needlecase made of dark blue felt, and is lined with white felt. The fasten-

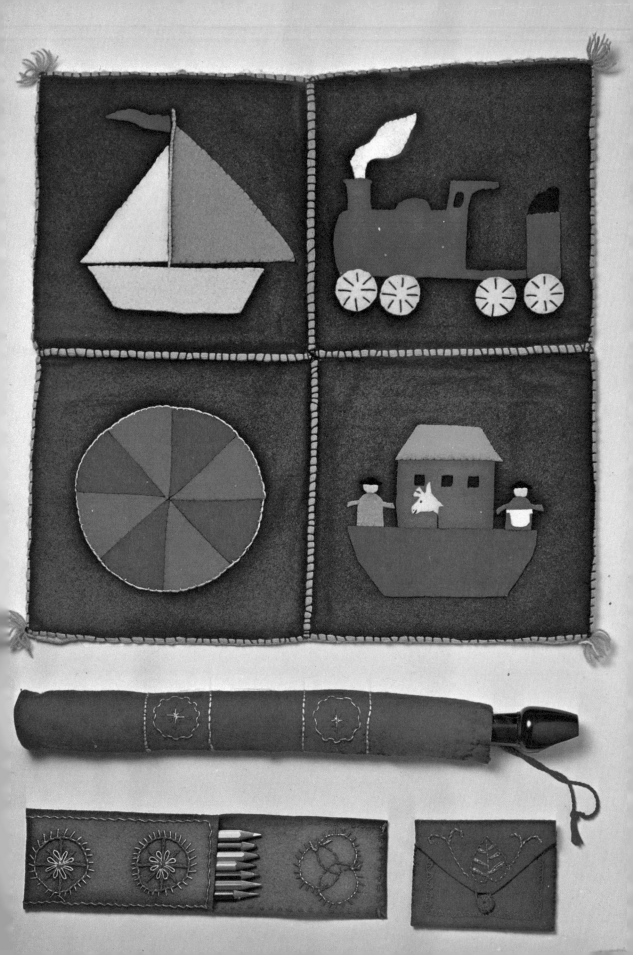

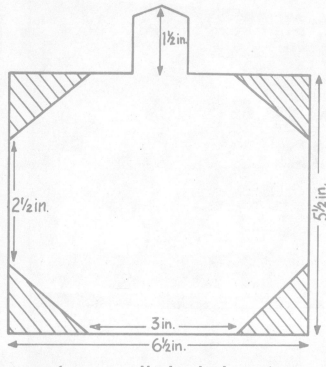

cut away all shaded parts

Fig. 14

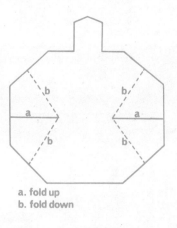

a. fold up
b. fold down

Fig. 15

ing flap is cut in one with the case (Fig. 14).

Trace once round the template on each piece of felt, and cut round the pencil lines with pinking shears to give a serrated edge. Two lines of couching are the only decoration on the outside and one line on the inner side.

Couch a line of thick red embroidery cotton close to the edge with white embroidery silk, and inside that a line of thick white cotton couched down with a red thread. Similarly, on the white lining felt couch down a line of blue thick cotton with white thread.

Sew three small rectangles of serrated edged flannel to the middle of the white felt, the short side nearest to the flap. Place the two felt shapes together with right sides outside and sew them together with invisible stitches, hidden by the couching. Fig. 15 will help you in making the folds on each side — the middle ones fold *up* towards the centre and those each side fold down from the centre. When folded correctly, the corners of the serrated edge should be together. Fasten with a stud.

An embroidered pencil case
This is an easy envelope shape.

You will need :
A single strip of felt measuring 17 in. by 3 in. ; another strip of different-coloured felt for lining to make it stronger also 17 in. by 3 in. ; or a piece of closely-woven material 18 in. by 4 in. to allow ½ in. turnings all round ; red and yellow embroidery silks.

The front is 6 in. deep and the flap 5 in. A line of whipped running stitch is sewn ¼ in. in from the edge and all round it.

On the flap, three interlaced circles are outlined in yellow chain stitch, whipped with red on the inner arcs and blanket stitch worked over it on the outer arcs (Fig. 16a).

On the front are embroidered two separate circles. The edges are blanket stitched in yellow which is whipped with red. A cross of red chain stitch from edge to edge of the circle has shorter diagonal lines of chain stitch in between. In their spaces, are single chain (or lazy daisy) stitches in yellow (Fig. 16b).

Make ½ in. turnings on the lining and sew it on to the wrong side of the felt. Turn the front of the case up 6 in. and oversew the edges. If felt is used for lining, then oversew the two pieces together all round and then sew the side seams.

A case for your recorder

It is a tube of felt, with a circle of felt-covered card at one end and a drawstring at the other.

> *You will need :*
> A piece of felt as long as your recorder plus 1 in. and about 5 in. wide ; a piece of lining 1 in. longer and 1 in. wider than the felt ; a circle of felt 1⅛ in. in diameter and the lining 2 in. in diameter ; a circle of card slightly less than 1⅛ in. in diameter.

This case is embroidered in two panels running round the case. Two circles of threaded running stitch have an eight-pointed star of straight stitch in the centre, each stitch tipped with a single chain stitch (Fig. 17). Two lines of couched thick embroidery cotton each side of the circles complete each panel.

Sew the lining side seams (½ in. turnings are allowed). Make ½ in. turnings at the top and bottom, press the seam flat and lay the lining tube on the wrong side of the felt.

Pin the top and bottom edges of the felt to the lining. Pin the side seam of the felt taking care to match the embroidery. Oversew the felt seam and sew the lining in place at top and bottom.

Snip nearly ½ in. cuts round the lining circle, turn it in to the centre and place it on the felt circle (Fig. 18). Oversew the circles together half way round, slide in the card circle and complete the oversewing. Oversew this circle to one end of the felt tube.

Sew a row of running stitches with embroidery silk ½ in. from the top edge and a second row ½ in. below it. On the lining cut a small slit between the two rows of running stitches. Oversew all round the slit to make an eyelet hole. Run a cord or ribbon through the two rows of running stitch and draw up the top.

A housewife

This seems a very strange name for a little case which holds pins, needles, and cotton, a useful travelling case on holiday when you need to do some quick repairs.

This one is made of dark red felt em-

Fig. 16

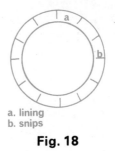

Fig. 17

a. lining
b. snips

Fig. 18

broidered in black, yellow and turquoise and is lined with white felt. A cord running through the centre holds the spools of cotton in place.

You will need:
Two pieces of felt 8½ in. by 3½ in.; two circles of felt in each colour 1½ in. diameter; a piece of flannel; yellow, turquoise and black embroidery silks; two small circles of card.

Embroider the outside felt first. Quarter the length of the felt and mark the places with three 1 in. crosses in contrasting cotton (Fig. 19). On these crosses, starting from the outside of each line, embroider fly stitches to the centre in black embroidery silk. In each angle put three single chain stitches in turquoise with a small straight stitch in yellow between each chain stitch and four small yellow straight stitches forming a cross in the centre (Fig. 20). At each end, and in between these embroidered motifs, work a line of yellow chain stitch starting and finishing ½ in. from the edge, with a row of black running stitches each side of it. Whip the running stitches with turquoise silk.

Sew a rectangle of flannel at one end of the white felt. Place both pieces of felt together with right sides outside and sew together with stab stitch in black silk. (Stab stitch is done by inserting the needle at right angles from back to front and then from front to back).

In the centre of the card and felt circles punch a small hole (Fig. 21). Work a ¾ in. larger circle of yellow chain stitch round it with a small yellow straight stitch from the centre of each chain towards the edge. Oversew a red and a white circle together with a card circle in between, turn the circle over and do a second row of oversewing to cross over the first row.

Make a cord 15 in. long from black and yellow embroidery silk. To do this, take four lengths of each colour 30 in. long, and tie the ends. Put one end over a hook, put a pencil through the other end and twist. Or get someone to help you, twist your pencils in opposite directions and you will make your cord twice as quickly. When the twist is fairly taut, put both ends together, hold the middle and let it twist into a cord. Tie the two ends tightly about 1 in. from the end, tie a second time just below the first one and make a tassel.

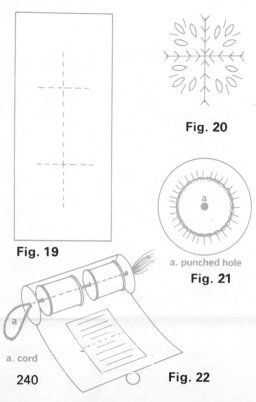

Fig. 20

Fig. 19

a. punched hole
Fig. 21

a. cord

240

Fig. 22

Thread the double end of cord through one circle from the red side, thread it through the two spools of cotton, and then through the second circle keeping the red side outside (Fig. 22). Oversew the rectangle to the circles for about ¾ of the circumference.

In the middle of the opposite end work a buttonhole loop in black silk and sew a yellow button on the case to fasten it.

A drawstring bag in felt

Made in red felt lined with red and white checked gingham, on a circular base, this bag is embroidered round the lower part with a design based on a circle and a square. It measures 11½ in. on a 6 in. base. Made in a smaller size, in a pastel shade and embroidered with sequins and pearls, it would make a lovely party or theatre bag.

For one this size you will need:

A piece of felt measuring 17½ in. square, a piece of gingham 19½ in. by 18½ in., a 6 in. circle of thick card; embroidery silks (here they are black, white, green, yellow); red silk for a cord; some red sewing cotton.

Cut a rectangle of felt 17½ in. by 11½ in. and one of gingham 18½ in. by 12½ in., this for the main bag.

Mark the 17½ in. width of felt into three equal spaces with lines of tacking stitches. Mark this width on thin paper and in this space draw the design of square and circle. The square measures 1½ in. and the circle 2 in.

Pin the paper in one of the spaces and transfer the design to the felt with running stitches in contrasting cotton taken through the paper and the felt. Your embroidery will cover the running stitches.

The square has a line of yellow chain stitch double threaded with black silk, three yellow chain stitches in a line from each corner with five black single chain (lazy daisy) stitches round them (Fig. 23a).

The circle has a ring of green chain stitch whipped with white silk, with single white stitches raying out from the edge (Fig. 23b). The centre of the circle is filled with five rows each way of long green chain stitch, forming squares, couched down at each join with white silk. Repeat this design in the other two spaces.

Fig. 23a

Fig. 23b

Make ½ in. turnings on both long sides of the gingham and join the side seams on the wrong side. Oversew the side seams of the red felt, matching up the line of embroidery. Sew the lining into the felt tube at top and bottom edges, keeping seam to seam.

With red embroidery silk sew two lines of running stitches 1¾ in. and 2¼ in. from the top edge.

Make a small slit in the lining between these lines and oversew all round the slit to make an eyelet hole.

Make a cord from the red embroidery silk and thread it through the hem, tying the ends and fringing them into a tassel.

Trace round the card base on the wrong sides of the remaining pieces of felt and gingham, and cut them out, allowing a little extra on the felt for the thickness of the card and an extra ½ in. all round the gingham for turnings. Snip round the gingham circle and turn down on the pencil line. Pin it on to the wrong side of the felt and oversew about half way round. Slide in the card circle and complete the oversewing. Pin the base of the bag round the circle and oversew the two together.

Fig. 25

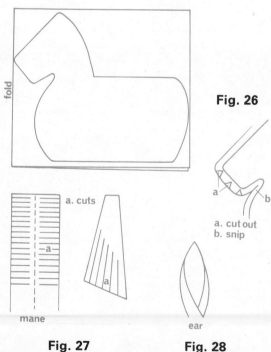

a. cuts

mane

Fig. 27

a. cut out
b. snip

ear

Fig. 28

Cushions for children

A horse cushion

He is soft and cuddly to hug, is just as soft to lean against, or rest your head on, and can be made very bright and gay in almost any kind of firm material, gingham, linen weave or wool. Here, he is made in white cotton material spotted with green spots and little black stars. His mane and tail and features are in black felt, or could be in Vilene.

You will need :

A piece of material 15 in. by 28 in.; black and white felt or bonded interlining ; some kapok or other soft stuffing ; sewing cotton.

Fold the material in half to measure 15 in. by 14 in. with the right sides inside. Trace round the template (Fig. 24) on to one side of the folded material (Fig. 25).

Tack round the outside edge of the shape, and machine carefully, or sew in backstitch all round the pencil line, leaving some of the bottom edge open for stuffing.

Trim off the edges close to the stitching, snip 'v's in all rounded edges and snip into any corners, at the neck particularly (Fig. 26). Turn it inside out and press the seams flat.

Stuff it with kapok or chosen stuffing, softly and evenly.

Make small turnings on the bottom open edge and sew it up either with ladder stitch or with oversewing (which is not so neat).

Cut two 1 in. long ovals in white with a circle of black (drawn round a button) placed off centre on them, and sew on each side of the face near to the top of the head and pointing to the chin.

Sew on an oblong of black for a nose.

For the mane, cut a strip of felt 12 in. by 3 in. and cut a fringe on each long side (Fig. 27). Fold it in half and sew it on to the back seam, starting on the forehead opposite the eyes, and finishing at the bottom of the neck.

The tail is a triangular-shaped piece 4 in. long and 3 in. wide tapering to 1 in. Cut it in a fringe from the wide end to the narrow end and sew it in place.

The ears are triangles, 3 in. by 2 in., the 2 in. being the base. Fold the two corners to lap over in the middle of the base (Fig. 28) and sew on near the top of the head,

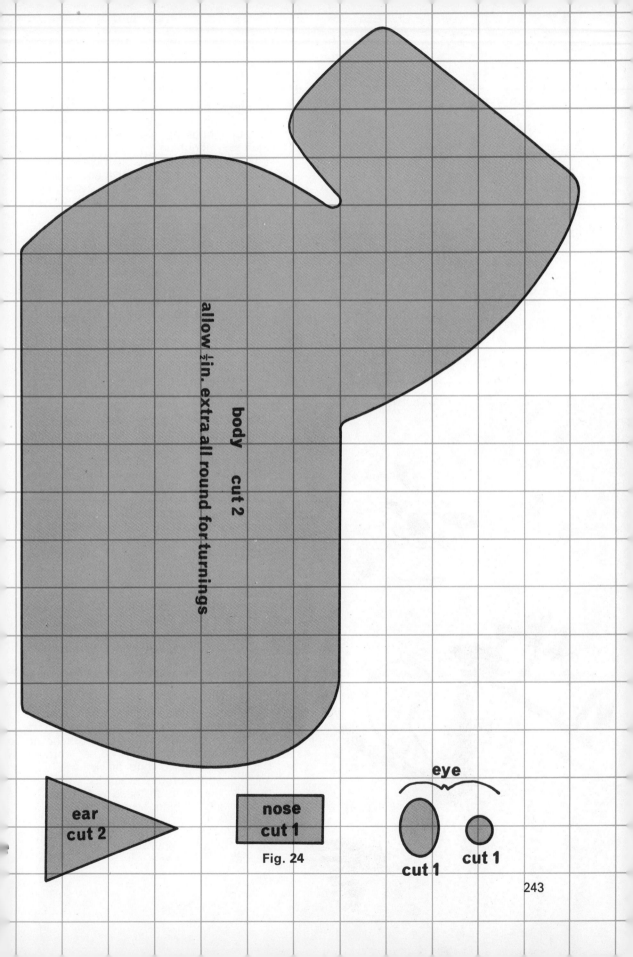

body   cut 2
allow ½in. extra all round for turnings

ear
cut 2

nose
cut 1

Fig. 24

eye

cut 1   cut 1

243

Fig. 30

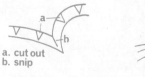

a. cut out
b. snip

Fig. 31   **Fig. 32**

pointing upwards, again using ladder stitch and sewing them on both sides. Keep the ears upright as you sew them and they will then stay upright.

Bridle and reins of felt can be added if it is going to be a toy rather than a cushion.

A cat cushion

Fat and comfortable-looking, with a happy grin on her face, she is a cuddly cat to play with and also very nice to lean against.

> *You will need:*
> ½ yard of 36 in. wide red and white plaid gingham, but any bright cotton-type material would be suitable; black felt or interlining for features; kapok or other soft stuffing material; black silk for whiskers; sewing cotton.

Fold the material in half with the right side inside, and trace round the template (Fig. 29) of the cat; the tail template will fit in the space over the back (Fig. 30).

Tack the shape together outside the pencil line, and machine or backstitch round the pencil lines on each shape, leaving open the narrow end of the tail and some of the bottom edge of the cat. Trim off edges close to the stitching, snip 'v's out of all curves and snip into any corners close up to the stitching (Fig. 31). Turn it inside out. Press all the seams flat, carefully pushing out the corners of the ears.

Stuff the body smoothly and softly, and sew up the opening with ladder stitch. Stuff the tail with small pieces of kapok to keep it smooth and flat rather than round. Sew it on at the back, curling it round to the side and fastening it in place with invisible stitches.

Cut a shield shape in black and sew it in the middle of the face with two lines of black chain stitch curling from the bottom of it for her smiling mouth. Long stitches in black from each curve will be her whiskers (Fig. 32). Cut two long black ovals with pointed ends for the eyes, with a green circle in the centre fastened with a vertical bar of black stitching. Sew the eyes on at an angle, slanting in towards the nose.

A bright-coloured ribbon tied round her neck with a big bow will make her look a real pet.

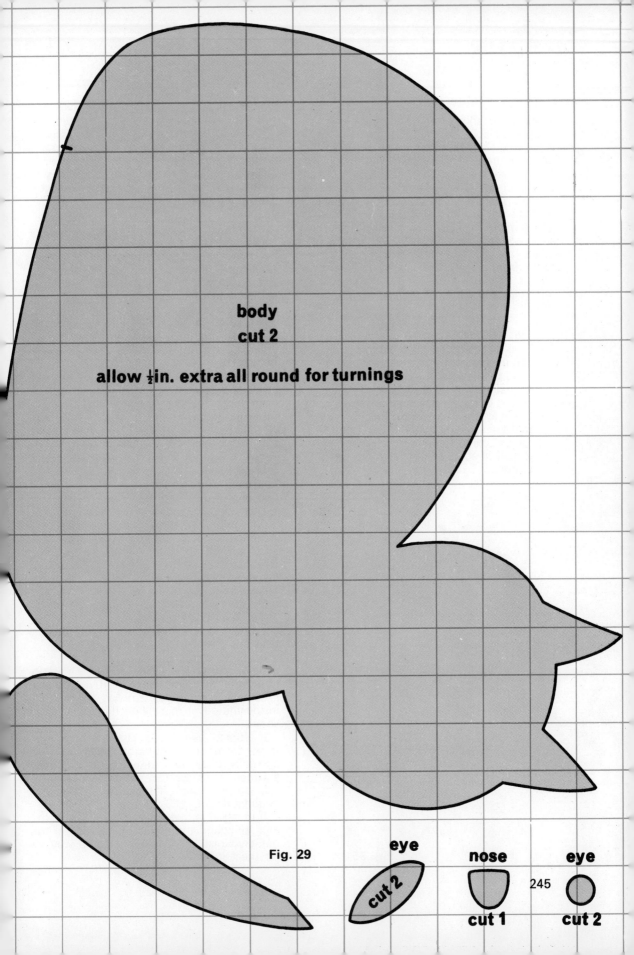

body
cut 2

allow ½ in. extra all round for turnings

Fig. 29

eye
cut 2

nose
cut 1

245

eye
cut 2

A lion cushion

A special cushion for a special person, a lovable amiable lion like the one in *The Wizard of Oz*. Make him in gay colours in felt, or cotton or velvet, patterned or plain. The actual cushion base is made of two square pieces of felt. The lion face can be worked straight on to one of these pieces for the front of the cushion, if the colour of it is suitable, and the back need not be the same colour. Or, you can make the face on a separate piece of material and sew it on to the front piece of the cushion. The lion's face is an oval shape, slightly wider at the top than the bottom, rather like an egg in fact.

You will need :

Two pieces of felt 15 in. square ; (16 in. square if other material is used to allow for turnings) ; scraps of material for features ; two pieces of tawny-coloured felt or fabric for the mane, each piece measuring 24 in. by 4½ in. ; a little kapok ; some embroidery silks ; a length of cord ; some matching cotton.

nose

a. leave open

Fig. 33

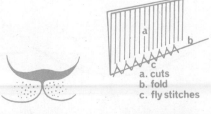

a. cuts
b. fold
c. fly stitches

Fig. 34   **Fig. 35**

Nose

Cut out a long thin oval (Fig. 33), broader at the base, for the nose, and sew it in the middle of the face, leaving about 2 in. open at the top, thin end. Through this opening gently push in a little kapok or other soft stuffing, to pad out the nose — it should be flat rather than rounded. Sew down the opening.

Eyes

For the eyes cut two thin ovals, pointed at each end, in white felt and two similarly-shaped smaller ovals in orange felt to fit in the centre of these for the eyes. Sew them together with an upright bar of whipped chain stitch in black silk. Sew the eyes in position slanting in towards the nose.

Nostrils

Cut the shaped piece for the nostrils in black and sew on at the lower end of the nose (Fig. 34). Sew two curved lines for the mouth in whipped chain stitch or whipped stem stitch. Work some little seed stitches in each curve of the mouth.

Mane

Fold each long piece of felt in half lengthwise and tack it all along the fold. Cut the two edges along the entire length into a narrow fringe (Fig. 35). Pin it on round the face with the fringe spreading outwards, starting from the chin and overlapping on the forehead, the front piece of the overlap lower to give added thickness to the top mane. Sew down the length of the fold with single fly stitches, taking each stitch about ¼ in. up into the fold.

Work in a few whiskery straight stitches over the eyes.

If the cushion is made up as a 15 in. square, you will have the corners showing round the face. Trim these off if you do not like them, but the cushion pad which goes inside the cover must then have this same shape.

If felt has been used, tack the back and front together with right sides outside and join them together with crossed oversewing in contrasting colour embroidery silk, or lay a cord along over the join and couch it down.

If material is used, then make ½ in. turnings all round the edge and tack them together. Finish this off in the same way as for the felt lion.

A nursery cushion of felt pictures

These little felt pictures could easily be framed and hung up on the wall in a frieze, but here they have been sewn on to a linen cushion and would give much pleasure to a small child.

You will need :

1 yard of 36 in. wide crash or linen ; an 18 in. square of felt ; some pieces of felt in various sizes and colours for the actual pictures. The engine picture needs red, yellow, black, blue, white felt, the ark needs, in addition, pale blue, flesh, green felt and the sailing ship needs fawn felt as well ; matching sewing cottons ; yellow wool or cord for couching.

If you are making pictures to hang up, cut the big piece of felt into four equal squares, but for the cushion, mark it into four equal squares with contrasting tacking.

The engine has been split up into separate templates (Fig. 36) for body, tender, coal, wheels and smoke — this is an old-fashioned steam engine.

Trace round the templates on to the wrong side of the felt with a very sharp pencil, using red felt for the engine, blue felt for the tender, black felt for coal, white felt for smoke and yellow felt for wheels. Place all the pieces in position before sewing, so that the finished whole will be in the centre of its square.

Sew the engine first, then the tender, coal, wheels and smoke, sewing with very small stitches in the same colour as the felt being sewn. Spokes for the wheels are straight stitches in black silk.

The template for the boat is cut from a 4 in. square. Use Fig. 37 as a guide for cutting. The two corner pieces are the sails and the middle part the boat.

Trace the pieces on to their felts — the boat is fawn felt, the sails pale blue felt and yellow felt, and the pennant red felt. Again place all the pieces in position before sewing. Sew on the boat first.

The mast is several strands of orange embroidery silk couched down with contrasting silk. Place a sail each side of it and the pennant flying from the top of the mast.

The ball is a 6 in.-diameter circle cut into eight equal pieces and these used as templates to cut four royal blue felt and four pink felt segments (Figs. 38a and 38b).

Before cutting up the circle place it in the centre of the background square and mark round its edge with running stitch in contrasting cotton. This will be a useful guide for placing the segments so that they fit together exactly. Sew them in place in alternate colours, checking each one so that it only takes up its own space and no more, otherwise the last segment to be placed may have to overlap and that would spoil the effect.

When all are sewn, couch down round the edge some strands of matching pink embroidery silk.

The ark with Mr. and Mrs. Noah is again cut in sections to make the templates. Boat, ark and roof are separate and the figures are cut into body, face and hat, plus apron for Mrs. Noah (Fig. 39). Trace them on to the wrong side of the felt and place the pieces in position when cut.

Sew the red ark first, having cut a doorway and three windows in it. Then sew the boat and roof, the boat royal blue and the roof green.

Mr. and Mrs. Noah stand on each side of the ark, with one of the animals (it need not be a giraffe ; it can be your own favourite animal) poking its head out of the door, probably hoping it is dinner time !

Sew all the pieces with matching cotton. Transparent nylon thread would be very useful for sewing this many-coloured kind of picture.

To make up the cushion, fold the linen in half and machine stitch together the two sides leaving open the two selvedge sides. Turn it inside out and press open the seams. Place the felt square on to it and pin it all round the edge, keeping it flat and trimming off any surplus felt. Tack it in place with small matching stitches.

Couch down yellow cord or strands of yellow wool across the middle from side to side each way, forming a cross to divide the pictures.

Finish it off by couching cord or wool all round the outside edge of the cushion to cover the tacking stitches, and taking the couching stitches (oversewing) through the cushion edge and the felt. Finish off the corners with loops of cord or small tassels of fringed wool.

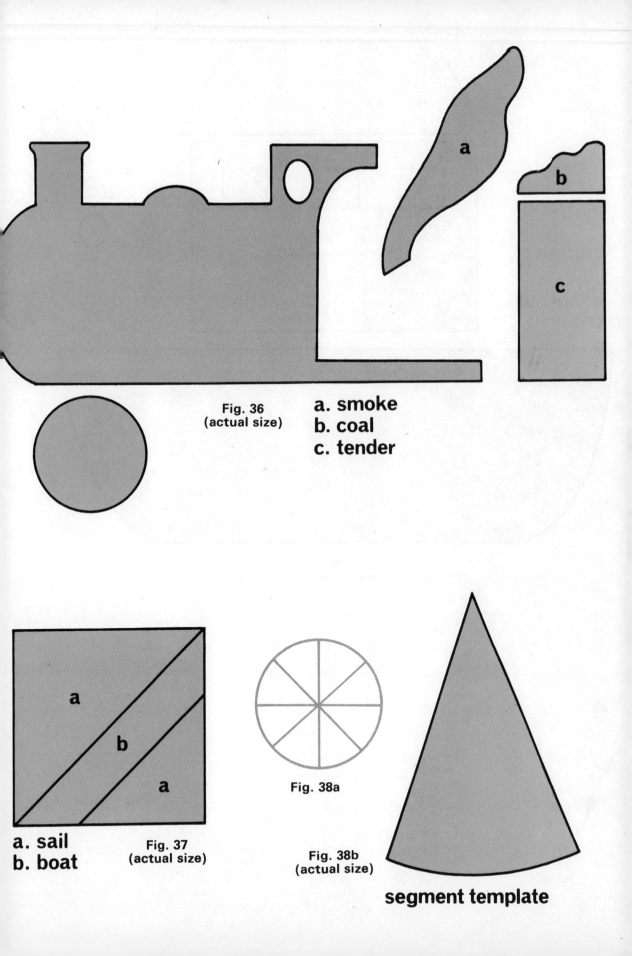

Fig. 36
(actual size)

a. smoke
b. coal
c. tender

a. sail
b. boat

Fig. 37
(actual size)

Fig. 38a

Fig. 38b
(actual size)

segment template

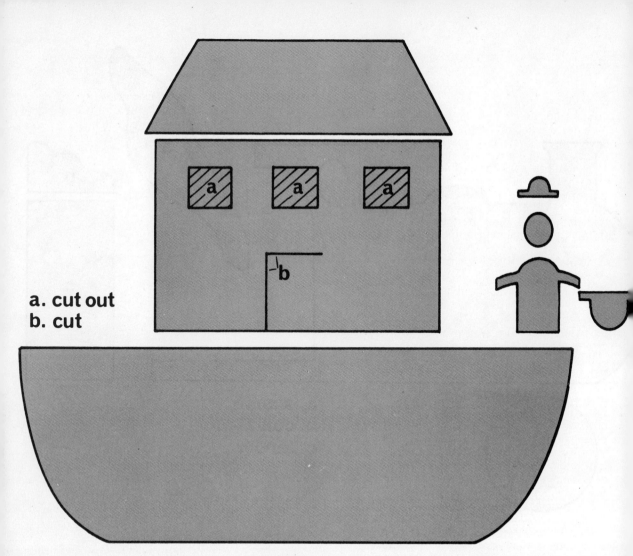

a. cut out
b. cut

Fig. 39
(actual size)

A Bonzo hound

He can be made from almost any kind of material, if it is fairly firm in weave, and can even be a patchwork of several pieces, if they are all the same thickness.

This Bonzo has the body in one pattern, head and tail in another, and the under-gusset of a quite different pattern and colour (Fig. 40). His ears are in plain material or felt, and he measures 24 in. from nose to tail and stands 10 in. high.

You will need :
Material for making ; kapok for stuffing ; cotton for sewing.

Draw the pattern on to thin card and use it as a template. Do all the tracing on the wrong side.

If your material is big enough you can cut head, body and tail in one piece for each side. If you are cutting each side in three parts, then place head, tail and side body templates on the folded material and cut out two of each. The under gusset is of the legs from a curved line stretching from under the chin to under the tail. Cut two under gussets, four ears, two ovals for eyes, and a circle of 2 in. diameter for his nose.

Machine or backstitch all pieces together on the pencil lines on the wrong side. Stitch a tail piece on to each side piece, and a head piece on to the neck of the side pieces. Trim some of the surplus material and press the seams flat.

Place the two bodies together with right sides inside, matching neck and tail seams and sew the head and back seam, starting at the front of the neck, round the head and down the back, along both sides of the tail and finishing there. Trim and press open the seams.

Sew the curved seam of the under gusset on the wrong side. Pin it to the side pieces with the right sides together, starting at the feet. Sew round all the legs leaving the under body seams open on each side. Press open the seams. Turn it inside out.

Stuffing is done through the under body openings and care must be taken not to split the seams as the openings are not very big. Stuff the head, pushing the stuffing well into the seams and corners of nose and mouth and packing it as firmly as possible without pulling the stitches. Stuff the tail with small pieces, pushing it well into the

pointed end. Fill the legs and then the body, packing stuffing well into the root of the tail and the tops of the legs to keep them firm. Sew up the openings with ladder stitch.

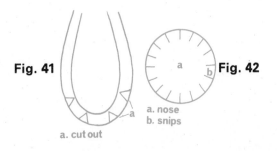

Fig. 41

a. cut out

Fig. 42

a. nose
b. snips

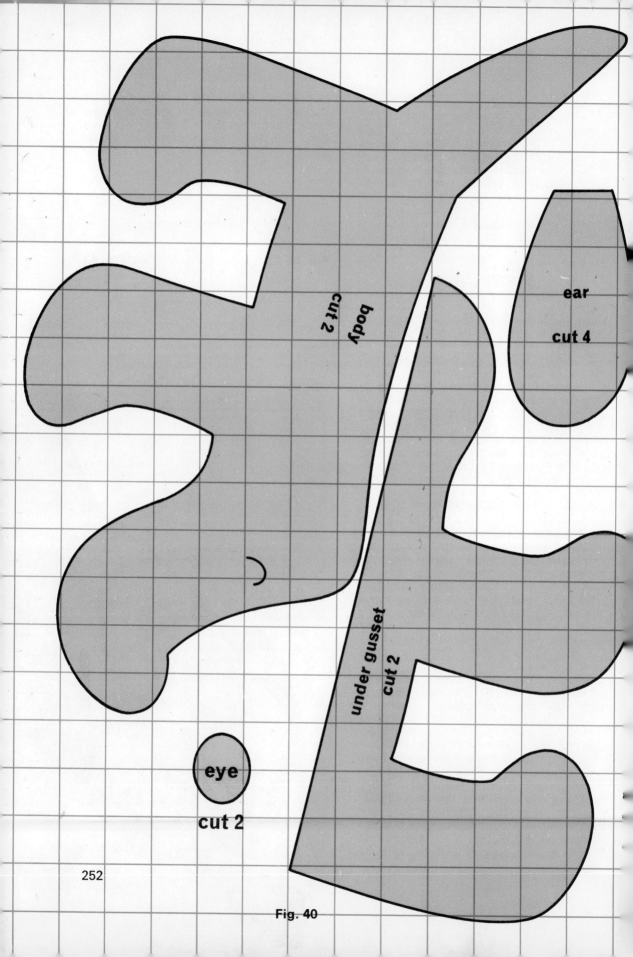

body
cut 2

ear
cut 4

under gusset
cut 2

eye

cut 2

Fig. 40

Machine stitch together two ear pieces for each ear, trim off surplus turnings, snip out 'v's on the curves and turn it inside out. Stuff them sparingly, to give only a slight padded effect, turn in the raw edges at the top and sew on to the head near the top and slanting slightly to the back (Fig. 41). Sew on the two eye ovals.

Snip the edges of the circle for the nose, gather up the snipped edges, put a ball of stuffing in the centre and sew it on the point of the nose with ladder stitch (Fig. 42).

There he is, patiently waiting for a walk, or his dinner, or both.

A little girl's needlework box

This embroidered box, worked with some of the aids to needlework, would make a lovely present for a little girl who likes to sew — all her cottons, embroidery silks, scissors, needles, and pins, fitting into a colourful box and ready for her to use. It is made from rectangles of thick card covered with felt, the outside of royal blue and lined with pale blue.

You will need:

Two pieces of card measuring 8½ in. by 5 in. for top and base; two pieces 8½ in. by 2 in. for the long sides; two pieces 5 in. by 2 in. for the short sides; a piece of royal blue felt 14½ in. by 10¾ in.; a piece of pale blue felt 14½ in. by 10¾ in.; four short lengths of coloured embroidery silks; some silver fine metal thread; 24 very small hooks, size 00; 12 very small-shaped eyes; 16 size 00 press studs; 16 small silver beads; dark blue sewing cotton.

Cut both pieces of felt as shown in Fig. 43. Each of the pieces will be ⅛ in. larger than the corresponding card shapes, this to allow for the thickness of the card.

Embroider one of the large pieces of dark blue for the top of the box. Mark the diagonals from corner to corner on it (Fig. 44), and across the middle from side to side, with tacking stitches in contrasting cotton, on the right side. Sew a ½ in. pearl button in the centre and around it a ring of 'eyes' with the loops of them nearest to the button (Fig. 45). Mark a 2½ in. diameter circle with contrasting running stitches, on the right side, and from its edge sew

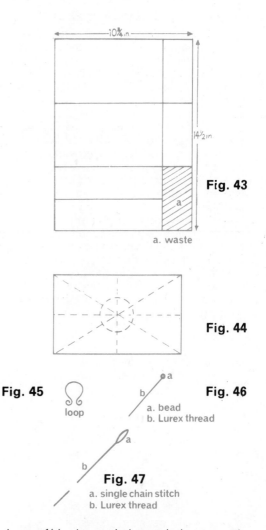

Fig. 43

a. waste

Fig. 44

Fig. 45
loop

Fig. 46
a. bead
b. Lurex thread

Fig. 47
a. single chain stitch
b. Lurex thread

sixteen ½ in. long stitches pointing towards the centre, in fine silver metal thread, and sew a silver bead on the circle at the end of each one to simulate pins (Fig. 46).

Place the template of the scissors at the sides of the box shape between the diagonals, with the points towards the centre. Outline the template in tiny running stitches in contrast cotton. The shapes are filled with close herring-bone stitch in silver fine metal thread, and the finger rings in silver chain stitch.

At each corner sew the press studs, each in two pieces, six along the long side and two along the short side.

Sew a ring of six small hooks in each of the four spaces between the press studs and the ring of 'pins'. Sew them on with the hooks pointing outwards.

On the long sides in the centre space sew a long and a short stitch in line, in silver thread, diagonally, and a second lot of two stitches crossing it, with a single chain stitch at the outer end of each long stitch to simulate needles (Fig. 47). In coloured embroidery silk work a trailing line of stem stitch from each 'eye' of the 'needle'. This completes the embroidery. (See Fig. 48).

Place a piece of pale blue felt behind the embroidered dark blue piece, with right side outside, and oversew three of the sides. Insert the appropriate card and oversew the remaining edge. Sew each of the other dark blue pieces to its lining, inserting the cards and sewing up the fourth sides. Oversew the four side pieces to the base, on the right side and make into a box by sewing up the short sides on the corners. Oversew one long edge of the lid to the box.

Sew a pearl button in the middle of the front edge of the box, and make a buttonhole loop on the lid to fasten over it.

Fig. 48

An embroidered trinket or jewel box

A very attractive effect can be obtained if the box is lined with a paler shade of the outside covering, which in a rich jewel colour sets off the glitter of sequin and fine metal thread embroidery. The box in the picture is covered with purple felt and lined with pale mauve. It measures 6 in. by 3 in. and is 2 in. deep. It is richly embroidered on lid and sides with beads, sequins and pearls and fine metal thread.

You will need :

Felt in two colours ; beads ; sequins ; pearls ; fine metal thread in one or two colours ; embroidery silks ; matching cotton ; a length of fine silver or gilt cord ; some thick card.

The six pieces comprising the box are made up separately and then all joined together.

Cut six pieces of thick card as follows —

Two pieces 6 in. by 3 in. for top and base,
Two pieces 6 in. by 2 in. for the long sides,
Two pieces 3 in. by 2 in. for the short sides.

The corresponding pieces of felt must be cut slightly larger to allow for the thickness of the card. Allow an extra ⅛ in. on each piece for this.

Cut a second corresponding set of pieces from the lining felt.

Now embroider all the outside pieces except the piece for the base and embroider one lining piece for inside the lid.

For the top (Fig. 49), on the wrong side of the piece of felt draw diagonal lines from corner to corner. Use a white pencil on dark colours. Tack along these lines in contrasting cotton taking long stitches through to the right side.

The design is composed of concentric circles of embroidery with diagonal lines of embroidery stretching to the corners. Start in the centre with a big red sequin fastened down with silver thread. Outside this is a ring of twelve single chain (lazy daisy) stitches in bright turquoise silk with a bright blue bead between them touching the centre sequin. At the tip of each chain stitch sew a bright gold sequin

with a small gold bead in between. A ring of bright pink chain stitch whipped with green fine metal thread round them, and outside this a ring of emerald green shiny beads sewn closely together. A row of gold-coloured fly stitches with a pearl sewn at the tip of each point completes the circle which should measure between 2¼ in. and 2½ in. from side to side.

On each diagonal work 1¼ in. of green stem stitch with a fly stitch at the end and five slanting stitches down each side. Sew a bright red sequin in the fly stitch and at the end of alternate side stitches.

The long front side

On the wrong side draw a line lengthwise down the middle. Mark the middle of it and mark 1 in. from each end, and draw cross lines. Tack along these lines, again taking long stitches through to the right side.

In the centre piece sew a medium-size gold sequin with red fine metal thread, and round it a row of ten bright pink single chain stitches. In between them sew emerald green bugle beads, and at the tip of them a bright blue sequin. At the tip of each sequin and each bugle bead sew a turquoise bead and sew straight stitches of silver fine metal thread spraying out all the way round. (See Fig. 50).

Fig. 49

Fig. 50

The motif each side of the centre one has a silver sequin centre with eight silver metal thread stitches round it. At the end of each stitch is sewn a small yellow bead with a turquoise bead in between the stitches.

The long strip for the back has three similar motifs on it. The middle one has a red sequin centre with eight silver fine metal thread stitches round it, a turquoise bead at the end of each stitch and an emerald green one in between. The end ones differ in that they have gold sequin centres and silver beads in between the stitches.

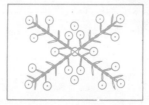

Fig. 51

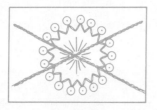

Fig. 52

The two sides

Mark the diagonals as on the other pieces. Sew a bright green sequin in the centre. From the centre sew each diagonal in mauve stem stitch for an inch with a single fly stitch at the end and three slanting stitches each side. Sew gold sequins in each fly stitch and at the ends of alternate slanting stitches. Sew a red sequin between the two gold ones which come together in the wide angle (Fig. 51).

On the mauve lining for the lid, embroider a flat design in silks and sequins. Mark the diagonals and embroider 3 in. on each in pink chain stitch whipped with emerald green fine metal thread. From the centre, embroider straight stitches in red fine metal thread in a sunburst design. In a circle ¾ in. radius from the centre embroider turquoise fly stitches and sew red and gold sequins alternately on each point (Fig. 52).

Pair all the pieces with their lining pieces with right sides outside and oversew three sides on each, insert the appropriate cards and sew up the fourth side.

Make up the box in the same way as the work box.

Sew a fine silver cord all round the top edge of the box, beginning at the centre of the back. Use an oversewing stitch, but put the needle *through* the strands of cord and not over the top of it, so that the effect of the cord will not be spoilt by the stitches. Overlap the cord slightly at the back and finish off securely.

In the same way, sew cord round the edge of the lid starting about ½ in. round the corner of the back edge, continuing round the side to the middle of the front edge. Here make a small loop for lifting the lid. Continue sewing, finishing off firmly about ½ in. round the back corner, and not sewing any cord along the back.

Sew the lid to the box with fishbone stitch, putting the needle each time between the strands of the cord and bringing it out first through the lid and then through the back of the box.

All decoration on a box of this kind must be done before any sewing together is attempted.

In working out designs for the embroidery first make a plan of each piece and square it off and mark the diagonals. Using coloured pencils or felt-tip pens, to denote sequins, beads and threads in the design, will help to give some idea of the effect of the colour scheme.